Critical Digital Humanities

TOPICS IN THE DIGITAL HUMANITIES

Humanities computing is redefining basic principles about research and publication. An influx of new, vibrant, and diverse communities of practitioners recognizes that computer applications are subject to continual innovation and reappraisal. This series publishes books that demonstrate the new questions, methods, and results arising in the digital humanities.

Series Editors
Susan Schreibman
Raymond G. Siemens

Critical Digital Humanities

The Search for a Methodology

JAMES E. DOBSON

UNIVERSITY OF ILLINOIS PRESS
Urbana, Chicago, and Springfield

Publication of this book was supported by funding from
Dartmouth College.

Library of Congress Cataloging-in-Publication Data
Names: Dobson, James E., author.
Title: Critical digital humanities : the search for a methodology /
    James E. Dobson.
Description: [Urbana, Illinois] : University of Illinois Press, [2019] |
    Series: Topics in the digital humanities | Includes bibliographical
    references and index.
Identifiers: LCCN 2018030226 | ISBN 9780252042270 (hardcover : alk.
    paper) | ISBN 9780252084041 (paperback : alk. paper)
Subjects: LCSH: Digital humanities—Research—Methodology.
Classification: LCC AZ105 .D59 2019 | DDC 025.06/0013072—dc23
    LC record available at https://lccn.loc.gov/2018030226

E-book ISBN 978-0-252-05111-1

Contents

Preface   vii

Acknowledgments   xiii

1   Protocols, Methods, and Workflows:
    Digital Ways of Reading   1

2   Can an Algorithm Be Disturbed? Machine Learning,
    Intrinsic Criticism, and the Digital Humanities   32

3   Digital Historicism and the Historicity
    of Digital Texts   66

4   The Cultural Significance of k-NN   101

    Conclusion   131

    Notes   141

    Works Cited   161

    Index   173

Preface

Hail, Screen, on which screen-theory may be thrown
While we sit back reflecting! As it grows,
Reflect indeed; for is this our reflection?
What lends it what authority? Who knows
If not this casement opening on—Its Own?

—I. A. Richards, "The Screens"

[T]he science of literature is an always infinite discourse,
an always open enunciation of a *search* for the laws of the practice
known as literature. The *objective* of this search is
to make *manifest* the very *procedure* through which this "science,"
its "object" and the relationship are brought about, rather than to
apply empirically such and such a technique
to an indifferent object.

—Julia Kristeva, *Desire in Language: A Semiotic Approach
to Literature and Art* (italics in original)

What follows is a critique of existing and potential computational methods
for the analysis and interpretation of text and data within the humanities.
Quantitative formalism, distant reading, algorithmic criticism, macroanalysis,
computer-aided text mining: whatever we call and however we conceptualize

these methods, they all add, in one way or another, forms of computation to our understanding of the interpretative act.[1] The data-based and algorithmically powered methods introduced and examined in the following pages present both new opportunities and new complications for humanists. Neither the complications nor the opportunities necessitate outright rejection or unreflective acceptance. This book takes as its founding assumption that the exploration and investigation of humanities texts and data with sophisticated computational tools can serve the interpretative goals of humanists.[2] At the same time, it assumes that these approaches cannot and will not make obsolete other existing interpretive frameworks. The discourse of the humanities, as Julia Kristeva reminds us, is an infinite discourse. Neither the methods nor the objects within such a framing are capable of settling into inertia or abruptly coming to a breaking halt. It is the infinite search for a method that prevents the humanities from staying fixed long enough for anyone to say that the objects or the methods have finally given it their all and spoken all there is to say. Take, for example, the multitude of ways in which the most canonical collection of texts, Shakespeare's plays or the works of Homer, have been reimagined and rethought by every generation using the approaches and tools of almost every school of criticism and theory.

There are those who argue that a wholesale reinvention underpinned by the algorithmic manipulation of texts and other objects is the only way to recover an assumed loss of disciplinary prestige and an interest in the humanities from our students. Drawing on what appears to be a successful model in the sciences, advocates of a "big data" experimental and lab-based quantitative humanities take the obsolete nature of critical inquiry as a given.[3] These advocates propose as a replacement an empirical model organized around falsifiable quantitative experiments that sample social evidence from mostly textual sources. This model of research depends on a certain mode of inquiry and a philosophical orientation that is already existing within some humanities fields. This orientation or mode of research is compatible with the goals of many humanists, but it does not come close to exhausting the range of inquiry found within literary studies. The major assumptions animating this experimental model of the humanities are that the artifacts and objects of inquiry within the humanities function only to provide evidence and that they can reliably serve as a source of "information" about culture. After collection or some form of extraction from authorized cultural sources, this evidence, as the argument goes, can then be used as the basis for larger claims about the culture in which these objects reside. This founding assumption has served some scholars well, especially those working within the interdisciplinary field of cultural studies, but it has also been subject to numerous critiques for broad generalizations, overreaching, and inadequate understandings of the lived experience of people within a culture.

The objects of culture that seem at present to be of the most interest to humanists making use of these computational methods are creative and imaginative texts—fiction, and especially the nineteenth-century English language novel with its more standardized formatting and spelling, remains the dominant object of analysis. While these objects might refer to extra-textual events and people and certainly make use of a range of language that can index cultural formations and dominant ideologies, novels are incredibly unreliable sources of information about culture. Narrative fiction, for example, could be understood as a rhetorical strategy that negotiates the difference between showing or telling and in the process "[calling] attention to the author's selecting presence" or perhaps it might be understood as providing an "imaginary resolution of a real contradiction."[4] No matter our view of fiction, it cannot be used naively and uncritically in an experiment that desires to "extract information from and about texts as indicators of larger cultural issues."[5] Nor can the computational literary critic assume that the collection of fiction produced and reproduced by university libraries can adequately represent culture—now or at any time in the past.

This book takes seriously the arguments that quantitative and computational methods have already enabled humanists to produce new insights and that these methods will increasingly lead humanists to develop fascinating new arguments. But at the same time, it reminds scholars that possibilities for reading and interpretation exist other than the documentary realist treatment of digital or digitized sources. The extraction of "information" about culture from texts, in short, does not fully capture the methodological variety of humanistic practices, nor does this type of evidence or even the category of information trump other categories of evidence or strategies of reading, digital or otherwise.

The following four chapters seek to outline core problems with many of the assumptions found in the basic building blocks of any text-based computational analysis used in the humanities. The examples of text mining and other computational methods invoked will tend toward describing these procedures as abstractions of classes of activity—potential and projective forms of computational criticism—rather than concrete steps in any single researcher's workflow.[6] Classes of activity examined in the following pages include segmentation, normalization, classification, clustering, and modeling. The computational methods used in the humanities are undergoing rapid change—many of these methods are still in their infancy—and this book offers a critical account of these developing procedures and methods. These procedures and methods extend the horizon of interpretive possibilities, in the Husserlian sense, but this horizon is not unlimited, despite the potentially vast quantities of an object's qualities that are brought into aspect. This book examines the conditions of what might be called the seen and unseen of the interpretive scene in computational criticism.

Yet, as we proceed down through the "stack" of computational methodology from datasets to algorithms, as we slowly work our way through the multiple vectors and layers of critique, we will need some example data that are freely accessible, understandable, and ready for analysis. I borrow the term *stack* from systems engineering to describe the interlinked and dependent layers of tools and abstractions that make up any contemporary computational application or procedure. The presence of these obscured layers plays an important role in the major claim of this book, that computational criticism is a situated rather than an empirical and objective activity. This critical situation, as it were, can be better made visible through the friction generated by the application of method to data. Almost all of the data or texts used as examples in the following chapters are found within the North American Slave Narrative archive of the University of North Carolina's Documenting the American South digital library.[7] This archive, assembled over a decade and edited by William L. Andrews, was initially created to expand the restrictive and reductive canon—an important goal shared by this book's centering of slave narratives. It is an exemplary archive for digital humanities research, exemplary not because of its archival completeness or its thorough description and structured organizational schema, but precisely the opposite—this digital archive demonstrates, through its disorganization, its partial and almost haphazard construction, important truths of all archival projects.

The archive claims to contain a collection of slave narratives, those "narratives by fugitive slaves before the Civil War and by former slaves in the postbellum era."[8] In collecting texts published in what scholars have long designated as two distinct professional fields and literary periods, the antebellum and postbellum period, the archive enables scholars to bridge gaps and included a wider range of texts. Andrews explains the rationale for including texts published into the early years of the twentieth century: "One reason to create a complete collection of post–Civil War ex-slave narratives is to give voice to the many former slaves who shared neither [Booker T.] Washington's comparatively benign assessment of slavery and segregation nor his rosy view of the future of African Americans in the South. Another reason to extend the slave narrative collection well into the twentieth century is to give black women's slave narratives, the preponderance of which were published after 1865, full representation as contributions to the tradition." The year of publication of the texts included in the archive range from 1734 to 1980. The clear majority of these texts were published before the end of the Civil War (149 of the included texts are antebellum or earlier, 70 belong to the postbellum period, and 47 were published in the twentieth century). If this archive can be seen as crossing traditional field boundaries, it should also be recognized as disregarding all major genre distinctions, for despite Andrews's emphasis on "narratives by fugitive slaves," it includes many nonautobiographical and prose texts, including fiction, biographies, diaries, and even poetry. The archive also includes a number of texts whose authors were not formerly enslaved, including white people. For the purpose of evaluating and critiquing computational methods used in various text and data mining in the humanities, these inconsistencies and irregularities add rather than detract from its appropriateness as an object of critical analysis. The presence of such textual variety, within an archive that remains organized around a topic, provides opportunities for testing various data "extraction" and classification procedures that would otherwise be impossible to conduct on other freely available humanities datasets.

The descriptive document, the "readme.txt" file, included within the digital distribution of the archive outlines the goals and potential use of the dataset:

> Documenting the American South is one of the longest running digital publishing initiatives at the University of North Carolina. It was designed to give researchers digital access to some of the library's unique collections in the form of high quality page scans as well as structured, corrected and machine readable text. . . . Doc South Data is an extension of this original goal and has been designed for researchers who want to use emerging technology to look for patterns across entire texts or compare patterns found in multiple texts. We have made it easy to use tools such as Voyant (http://voyant-tools.org/) to conduct simple word counts and frequency visualizations (such as word clouds) or to use other tools to perform more

complex processes such as topic modeling, named-entity recognition or sentiment analysis.

This "Doc South Data" edition of the North American Slave Narrative archive is available as a single compressed Zip file from the University of North Carolina Libraries website. It contains 294 ASCII- and TEI/XML-encoded slave narratives. The archive provides fairly rich descriptions of the collected texts and descriptive and nearly complete basic metadata (formatted as a comma-separated value listing in "toc.csv") in an easy-to-read format and all the texts are included in plain (UTF-8/ASCII) text as well as in TEI/XML formatting, with additional metadata.

The following pages seek to document and illuminate a collection of concepts and computational methods through spirited critique. All of the commented code and data necessary to reproduce, evaluate, and modify any of the results and approaches shown in the following pages can be found in my GitHub repository: https://github.com/jeddobson/cdh.

Acknowledgments

There were two crucial sites that provided me with the opportunity to think through the core of this book's argument. The first was the multiday and multinational "Critical Digital Humanities" symposium that was conceived and planned by Aden Evens and Kaja Marczewska. Aden and Kaja graciously invited me to participate as an organizer after all the hard work was done. The participants of the symposium, Janneke Adema, Caroline Bassett, David Berry, John Cayley, Michael Dieter, Duncan Forbes, Alexander Galloway, Fred Gibbs, Alison Hearn, Lauren Klein, Tara McPherson, Marisa Parham, Miriam Posner, Jentery Sayers, Barbara Herrnstein Smith, Patrik Svensson, and Jacqueline Wernimont, energized my thinking at a decisive point in the assembly of my manuscript. The University of Westminster supported the symposium in London and the one at Dartmouth College was supported by the Leslie Center for the Humanities. I owe a special thank-you to Graziella Parati, director of the Leslie Center, and Barbara Will, associate dean for the humanities, for their support of the humanities and the digital humanities at Dartmouth. The second site, The Futures of American Studies Institute, has long been my intellectual home. Innumerable debts are owed to the institute director, my friend Donald E. Pease. Thank you to fellow plenary speakers who participated in important sessions dedicated to interrogating the methods of the digital humanities: Russ Castronovo, Elizabeth Maddock Dillon, David

Golumbia, and Ivy Schweitzer. Duncan Faherty, without a doubt the most generous and supportive figure in American studies, provided me with key criticisms of several sections of the manuscript. Futures Institute codirectors and regulars, including Eric Lott, Cindi Katz, Hortense Spillers, Colleen Boggs, Eng-Beng Lim, Donatella Izzo, Soyica Diggs Colbert, and Winfried Fluck, have all contributed in numerous ways to my thinking about American studies and theoretical criticism.

I owe many thanks to my colleagues at Dartmouth College. In English, especially, Colleen Boggs, Michael A. Chaney, George Edmondson, Aden Evens, Andrew McCann, Donald E. Pease, and Melissa F. Zeiger. Louis A. Renza has been a constant friend and an authority on all matters theoretical and critical. Thank you to my many colleagues in psychological and brain sciences, especially George Wolford, Terry Sackett, Yaroslav Halchenko, and Chandana Kodiweera. Scott M. Sanders offered constructive and much appreciated readings. Thank you to the many undergraduate students who have explored text mining with me and to the graduate students in my digital humanities seminars in the Masters of Arts in Liberal Studies program, especially Alexis Liston and Margaryta Kremneva.

Thank you to Susan Schreibman and Raymond G. Siemens, for the support of this book from early stages; Geof Garvey, for the excellent copyediting; and the University of Illinois Press team, especially to Dawn Durante, Alison Syring, and Tad Ringo.

A section of the second chapter was first published in *College Literature* 42, no. 4 (2015), 543–64. Copyright © Johns Hopkins University Press. Reprinted with permission by Johns Hopkins University Press.

Finally, I need to give my most important acknowledgement to the labors, love, and friendship of Rena J. Mosteirin, my first and best reader and my most important interlocutor on every subject.

Critical Digital Humanities

CHAPTER 1

Protocols, Methods, and Workflows

Digital Ways of Reading

One of the dreams of positivism in the human sciences is the
distinction, even the opposition, between interpretation—
subjective, vulnerable, ultimately arbitrary—and description,
a certain and definitive activity.

—Tzvetan Todorov, *Introduction to Poetics*

The phrase "digital humanities" first appeared in the early years of the twenty-first century. Digital humanities emerged after the fact as an institutional and organizational label for a set of disconnected approaches, objects, and strategies for addressing the growing awareness that the digital transformation of everyday life and the methods used in academic work in the past few decades have altered the protocols of humanities research. The history of the digital humanities, brief as this history is at present, has several times already been reconstructed and articulated alongside various definitions that give to each descriptive effort a slightly different trajectory and focus.[1] This book is primarily concerned with what I will argue is the intellectual core of any understanding of the digital humanities: the use of computational methods in humanities research and scholarship; more specifically, the use of sophisticated quantitative methods for text and data mining.[2] While some scholars and practitioners consider computational approaches a minor area or a subfield of the digital humanities, this book offers a vital and, more important, a critical digital humanities that emerges from the specific affordances and limitations of computation and computational thinking. In its effort to critically deploy and frame these affordances, this book will show both the promises and the perils of using advanced computational techniques as part of the research, discovery, and interpretive process within humanities fields committed to text-based scholarship.[3]

So why do theoretically informed critical questions relating to the use of complicated computational methods matter to print-oriented humanists, those who might be more comfortable with the matter and material of archives and the abstractions of theory? And why do questions proposed by critical theory, including questions of historiography, subjectivity, and governmentality, matter to researchers developing and deploying computational tools, those who understand themselves to work primarily within the digital humanities and with digital tools and artifacts? The answer to both these questions is that approaching computational methods at the ontological level enables humanists to reexamine many of the unquestioned assumptions about existing hermeneutical methods and that by bringing the resources of critical theory to bear on computational methods, we can construct an array of compelling and possible humanistic interpretations from multiple dimensions including the ideological biases informing many commonly used algorithms, the complications of a historicist text mining practice, the examination of feature selection for sentiment analysis, and the critique of the fantasies of human-subject-less analysis activated by machine learning and artificial intelligence. These methods belong to the strain of digital humanities approaches that are variously labeled distant reading, macroanalysis, computer-aided criticism, and cultural analytics. They include a range of computational methods that are heavily used in the biological and social sciences, including the humanities-adjacent fields of linguistics and sociology, and are the favorite approaches used by the new class of knowledge workers known as data scientists, who are increasingly employed by many large and medium-sized corporations and universities.

Once a critical mass of existing books and other textual objects were digitized and enough new "born digital" texts became available in easy-to-read and even easier to database, count, and query digital formats, it seemed rather obvious that literary scholars would want to begin some minimal amount of mining of these texts. Why thumb through your paper copy—even if you intend on using this same printed and bound text for just plain reading and for close readings, to search for the appearance of some keyword or phrase you recall or think might be important to some research inquiry? Certainly, if you had easy access to a list of frequently repeated phrases or words or perhaps automatically generated clusters of possible topics and words, you could imagine wanting to glance at them before or while reading. It is certain that computational methods can change how we read and how we interact with a text. Despite their limited access and functions, the basic tools provided by Amazon and Google Books have already brought a version of "datafied" computational analysis to a wide, nontechnical audience. Just as everyday habits, such as checking the weather, locating directions, or filling a gap of empty time during the day by scrolling through the latest news, have been changed by the use of smartphones, easy access to even the simplest computational tools and digital texts have altered reading habits. All this has caused many critics to wonder whether the turn to the digital in the humanities is not just the latest turn of the humanities, but its future.

The critical digital humanities unfolded, explained, and interrogated in the following pages calls into question the renewed positivist dream that has been activated by the computational turn at present taking place within the humanities. David M. Berry has proposed that the notion of *computationality* might form the proper subject of the digital humanities. For Berry, computationality is an ontotheological concept that has brought into a being "a new ontological 'epoch' as a new historical constellation of intelligibility."[4] A focus on computationality would thus form what he conceives of as a possible third wave of the digital humanities. Berry builds on the notion of digital humanities waves established by Jeffrey Schnapp and Todd Presner in their "Digital Humanities Manifesto" to argue that these earlier phases are distinct moments in the institutionalization of the field; these included as the first wave the digitization of existing cultural artifacts and then, in the second wave, a shift to study "new media" and other so-called "born digital" objects that do not require conversion. Berry gives, in his argument for this proposed third wave of digital humanities, particular attention to the software and to the computer platforms that make computation of the products of the first wave and the digital objects of the second wave possible, but the practices of software studies that he advocates as part of the critique of computationality are just one tool in the critical digital humanist's toolbox. In order understand the operation and results of computational methods, to use and think about these tools critically within the humanities context, an analytical framework needs to be in place that can critique computation as such in addition to bringing into the question the presentation of computation as an ontological displacement.

Throughout this book, I use the terms *critique* and *criticism* to include both the aspect associated with the classical understanding of critique as a form of comprehension, the careful procedures of examination that attempt to come to grips with the significance of a phenomenon, and the stronger sense of critique, as used in common cultural studies formulations such as ideology critique. Critique is a tool for examining an object or concept and for locating what remains unthought and undertheorized in the imaginative and material construction, the explication and framing, and the use of this object, tool, or concept. Because of the complex, multilayered, and abstracted nature of computational tools and methods, humanists must not withdraw into positivism or outsource understanding to computer and informational scientists but revitalize the concept of critique. Comprehension of computational tools and the digital environment or ecosystem by humanists will take some considerable effort, for some algorithms, especially those using machine learning approaches, remain opaque even to their authors and developers, yet such understanding is essential, whether we choose to use these tools in our own work or not.[5]

The computational methods described, used, and critiqued throughout this book originated, for the most part, within other fields and were discovered, either by the original developers or by humanist researchers observing the results of these methods, to be useful for examining the type of digital objects traditionally studied by literary scholars: novels, poetry, and nonfictional texts. These computational methods, because of the speed and sophistication of the algorithms and the large-scale digital archives that serve as data for these tools, appear to ask for a shift in thinking that exceeds the other transformations associated with any so-called digital revolution. The potential insights gained from these new tools are exciting, yet the existing critical and theoretical approaches found within the humanities have something valuable to say about these methods.

The appropriation and incorporation of computational methods into humanities fields follows the transformation of other fields of academic research: biology, psychology, anthropology, and linguistics, for example. All these disciplines are "sciences" that are more or less committed to a rigorous description of the methods used within their respective fields; what differences and complications might be found in the integration of these approaches into humanities and those fields of research and study in which multiple methods and an endless number of interpretations always have been possible? There has been much debate over the question of whether the use of computational methods in the humanities should require scholars using these tools to follow the conventions, the questions, procedures, and protocols, of those disciplines or whether digital humanists should work within the existing norms of the humanities. When a group of leading field scholars propose that "Digital Humanities is born of the encounter between traditional humanities and computational methods," do they mean to suggest that computational methods can be simply substituted for the methods of the traditional humanities while the research questions and interpretive strategies remain the same?[6]

In her review of recently established digital humanities programs and centers, N. Katherine Hayles outlines the two main strategies that she sees as operative within this burgeoning field: assimilation and distinction. Hayles describes the philosophical difference between these two modes of practice as such: "Assimilation extends existing scholarship into the digital realm; it offers more affordances than print for access, queries, and dissemination; it often adopts an attitude of reassurance rather than confrontation. Distinction, by contrast, emphasizes new methodologies, new kinds of research questions, and the emergence of entirely new fields."[7] Distinction, for Hayles, involves making the digital humanities less like the humanities by appropriating the methods and questions of other fields. Assimilation, she argues, involves only the incremental adoption of digital tools and platforms—here essentially reduced to electronic publication. Distinction leaves the critical past behind by confronting and then obsoleting the methods and questions of existing scholarship. Divisions of digital humanities work into "assimilation" and "distinction" is ultimately neither useful nor helpful. What is needed for humanities scholars to use sophisticated computational tools is not a disruptive break with the past in favor of any particular "distinctive" approach but instead a *critical digital humanities*—a vocabulary and framework constructed around a set of contested concepts and methodologies rather than a tacit agreement in terms of approach and objects.

Theory and methodology, within many academic disciplines, are all too often opposed to each other. Methodology, for many, suggests praxis, a concrete set of easily comprehensible and reproducible steps that signify the existence of a shared and professionalized discourse with readily accepted component piece parts. Theory belongs to the world of abstraction and generalization. Within the digital humanities the labels "hack" and "yack" have been used as shorthand to schematize scholarship focused on building, making, or "hacking" software and hardware and the "yack" work that is understood to be dedicated to conceptualizing and thinking through the implications, assumptions, and

5

complications of digital approaches.[8] The critical digital humanities articulated by this book attends to both the practice and the theory of computation and the computational humanities. In deploying a recursive reading of computational transformations and text, digital humanists do not have to opt for either theory or method; in turning the entire scholarly apparatus into an open-ended set of interrogatable positions, protocols of reading are directed toward both execution and interpretation. This is to say that while computationalism and the use of digital methods in humanities work *can* render the study of culture scientific and structural, only a critical digital humanities can foreground cultural and epistemological questions about computationalism.

The alluring promises of the use of large-scale computational methods for the humanities have enabled many literary critics to assert that it is now possible to deploy entirely new ways of reading and that these approaches have obsoleted the slow interpretive and critical work associated with most humanities scholarship. These computational tools, however, are not transparent nor are they value-free; computational methods bring with them an entire set of assumptions and concepts derived from the empirical sciences that may or may not be antithetical to the goals of humanities research, including—just to name a few—falsifiability, sampling, statistical significance, and the notion of semantic meaning embedded in many of these tools. The incorporation of digital methods into humanities research requires more methodological awareness and self-critique. When searching for an answer to what made the human sciences distinct from the natural sciences in the midtwentieth-century era of growing rationalization and scientific administration, Hans-Georg Gadamer could take as a founding assumption that "methodological self-consciousness," if nothing else, was a characteristic of the human sciences.[9] In importing computational methods of evidence gathering, analysis, and interpretation into humanities research, one should attempt to fully understand the stakes of all choices made and procedures followed and allow for the possibility of critique to enter into all stages of the research project. These problems were not solved during this earlier collision between humanistic fields and the methods of the sciences. It is the argument of this book that not only are these conflicts still not resolved, but they remain fundamentally unresolvable.

If the humanities can be said to be methodologically self-aware, humanities scholars are also especially aware of the historicity of their methods. Humanists understand that every potential concept or object is produced by culture and that there is what could be thought of as a cultural residue residing within every object, even digital objects. Just as humanists have cri-tiqued the appearance and popularity of certain modes of cultural criticism during particular historical moments, so too should humanists question the assumptions that inform the imagination of the researcher who conceives of a particular set of objects as data or the assumptions that produce the mechanical or mathematical logic at work within any particular algorithm. The assumptions, for example, held by programmers, digital humanists, and program managers might be those of the dominant culture or perhaps even oppositional. They might be inherited from prior formulations and remain otherwise unarticulated but still reside in the choices, distinctions, and logic that collectively frame what is considered possible and thinkable. Within the humanities research context, everything touching computational methods, from the lowest level of computational logic to the output of algorithmically derived data, is subject to one form or another of critique.[10]

The following chapters, in many ways, reconstruct and rehearse the critiques applied to structuralist and formalist readings in the wake of the deconstruc-tive turn that occurred during the last quarter of the twentieth century. This is because, as I will argue, many digital humanities scholars in the postpoststruc-turalist and "posttheory" present are either naively repeating the mistakes made by those in the past or explicitly attempting to resurrect structuralist methodologies. The stakes of understanding digitally transformed interpre-tive work in the humanities are increasingly high. Whereas humanists once imagined the work of theoretical and practical criticism as the application of concepts and ideas from outside the field and the use of these within an already existing interpretive framework that included an ongoing and shared sense of what counted as a text, the use of digital methods transforms the target and even the entire project of criticism. For example, computational methods almost universally require some standardization of the input that serves as the object for any particular computational process. This involves, among other potentially problematic moves, the conversion of the text into data. Data must be comparable in order to categorize, to transform, and to serve as a potential source for the extraction of information.

Humanities research is a self-critical enterprise and as such must be opposed to the notion that there are areas in which interpretive questions cannot be asked. At the project level, we can see the problem by thinking through the implications of what could be called the Fordist model of academic research. Collaborative research projects with well-defined and instrumentalized roles for each participant—such projects are certainly rather rare outside the digital humanities within the humanities at large—partition knowledge in such a way as to enable an environment in which scrutiny cannot be equally applied to all components of the project. In the scope of an individual "investigation" of a digital text with computational tools, we might find an example of this same problem with an application, or an algorithm embedded within an application. These partitioned, obfuscated, or simply highly abstracted spaces function as what is frequently called a black box, a component in which data flows in and out without the operator or researcher having any understanding of what happened during the transformation. These components or atomized steps in a research method are black boxes because of the complexity of the algorithm or because we cannot fully account for why the algorithm made certain decisions. Despite the possibility of this uncertainty, questions about the assumptions and operation of such black boxes remain pressing and answerable.

All this is to say that any computational method used in the humanities cannot be imagined as containing components not subject to humanistic modes of questioning.[11] This means that, on one level, there are no algorithms or codes that are free from subjectivity. At a higher level, in the case of machine learning algorithms, any decisions or distinctions produced by an algorithm from prior decisions cannot be isolated from critique. Humanists must be opposed to bracketing *any* questions applied to the operations and procedures used within these methods.

Workflow is an important concept in this book (see figure 1.1). The term *workflow*, in the sciences, is used to describe the formalization of the experimental process as a set of discrete components. A formal methodological description is a prerequisite for any computational process. Those fields that consider themselves data-intensive are especially invested in formalization as workflows typically take the output of other scientists and researchers as their input. Even those fields constructed as nonexperimental sciences, for example, social geography, are deeply embedded in the concept of workflow insofar as they name their interpretive objects data and they apply algorithmic transformations to these objects. A workflow is a descriptive and discursive object, it is a normative narrative—by normative, I mean that workflows are "written" or constructed in terms understandable and contestable by others within a field—of the application of computational methodology to a problem. Any analysis that makes use of computational tools requires some formalization of the methodology. Data need to be carefully prepared to meet

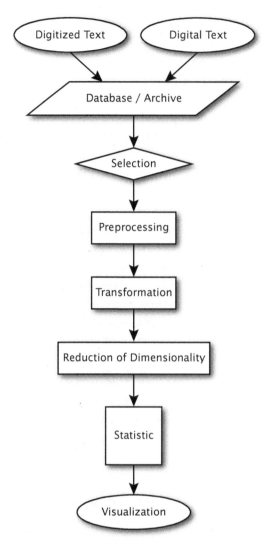

FIGURE 1.1   Generic computational workflow
for the Humanities

the requirements of the program or code and its algorithm in order to be computable. The flow of data through a variety of processing, analyzing, and visualizing components becomes, after the fact, the selected methodology. To some degree, all methodologies can be formalized and described in terms of workflow; when methodologies are computational, workflows are necessary in order to construct and share descriptions of each component of the digital methodology. Such processes are well suited to the organization and orchestration of computational processes since the term *digital*, after all, is used to describe all such discrete systems, as opposed to analog systems constructed with scales and gradations of values. Discrete components also afford a certain amount of flexibility; with well-defined interfaces for each individual step within a computational workflow, elements can be examined and executed piecemeal and swapped for alternative and potentially improved, or perhaps just different, approaches.

Given that a computational digital humanities makes heavy use of procedures, algorithms, and concepts from the types of data and text mining found in computational linguistics and other fields, one might wonder what makes digital humanities work different from the quantitative and qualitative social sciences. If, in the process of studying some particular phenomena, a digital humanist makes use of the exact same methods and data as a computational sociologist, what distinguishes the interpretive procedures of the digital humanities scholar from those of the social scientist? Do disciplinary boundaries matter to digital methodologies? What lines of distinction can we draw between the use of computational methods in scientific fields and humanities disciplines like literary and cultural studies? Is the difference just a matter of how one interprets the data? Is there a distinctive methodological difference or do we distinguish a humanities approach in the way in which the data and results are interpreted? Why even invoke the humanities when studying culture with computational methods? These are the questions that motivate this book.

Methodological Arguments

There is, at present, a sense of exhaustion with familiar arguments and the typical framing of these arguments equal to a thrill of discovery at the variety of new methods entering humanities work. This conjuncture of exhaustion and discovery is heavily loaded with the anxieties and questions that are, at their core, existential questions for the humanities. This climate of disciplinary uncertainty makes it possible to return, with renewed enthusiasm, to a series of important debates concerning the protocols of reading and the task of interpretation. Some of this shifting ground is the result of departmental closures, the collapsing of some fields, radical defunding—especially at the state level in the United States—and other causes or correlates, including racing after new sources of funding, industry partnerships, and pressure from administrators to engage in experimental and cross-disciplinary research and pedagogy. Other sources of this shifting originate in the present scholarly generation's desire to break with what has come before. In spite or because of this unsettling, there is once again serious engagement and thinking about the goals and methods of humanities work. Recent discussions of surface reading, distant reading, the new formalisms, the turn to aesthetics, various forms of pleasure, other forms of postcritique, and even the new materialisms have all invoked different approaches to the study of cultural objects.[12]

Rather than providing evidence of the outmodedness of humanities approaches in an era dominated by social scientific and computational methods, the debates concerning methodology within the humanities demonstrate the vitality of the discipline and a very much alive and active cross-field dialogue. Rita Felski's *The Limits of Critique* (2015) outlines the range of interpretive positions offered to critics at present: "Should we be close readers or distant readers? Dive in or draw back? Thanks to a recent surge of interest in method, spatial metaphors are now front and center in literary debates. Critics stew over the implications of proximity versus distance and brood over the merits of surface and depth."[13] Surface and depth, distance and closeness mark out oppositional pairings that frame the debates over humanities methods. Felski's invocation of "distant readers" in her description of these debates demonstrates the extent to which quantitative and digital approaches have now emerged as serious contenders for inclusion in the critical toolbox. In order to move beyond the stewing and brooding identified by Felski, humanists need even greater methodological awareness; greater awareness of the stakes of the various positions, evidence, and the types of arguments that can be made. New or recently imported computational methods are crucial for this discussion because these tools, the components that make up the workflow of the digital researcher, can both expand what we do and raise important questions that proposed alternative methods might not.

Debates about methodology emerge at exceptional times in the humanities—generational division points, the creation of new subfields, institutional shifts, and moments of disruption produced by game-changing theories and techniques.[14] Reading and the practices of interpretation required a more formalized sense of method at the inception of midcentury literary criticism. In his 1948 metacritical account, *The Armed Vision*, Stanley Edgar Hyman gives a working definition of the modern criticism, by which he means to group the new criticism, an explicitly scientific criticism, and what he calls working or "practical" criticism.[15] Hyman glosses the modern criticism as "the organized use of non-literary techniques and bodies of knowledge to obtain insights into literature" (3). He continues with an account of these new forms of criticism that is remarkably compatible with our present concern, computational methods: "The tools are these methods or 'techniques' and the nuggets are 'insights,' the occupation is mining, digging, or just plain grubbing" (3). Well before the arrival and institutionalization of the digital humanities and computer-aided text mining, literary critics had an understanding of methodology as the adoption of a tool or technique that generates or locates evidence, what Hyman refers to as "nuggets." It is clear, despite Hyman's attacks on these diverse schools, that he believes that a range of methods can successfully coexist. At least from this important moment in the institutionalization of literary criticism, humanists have depended, in part, on importing nonliterary techniques into the methodological toolbox.

Alexander Galloway's essay "The Cybernetic Hypothesis"—it was collected in a special issue of *differences* titled "In Shadows of the Digital Humanities," dedicated to examining the various genealogies and existing field formations of the digital humanities—suggests that the turn to methodology and the authorization of numerous approaches in our present digital moment are the sign of a major shift but part of the "liberal hue" (111) of theory in the humanities that has as its origins midtwentieth century cybernetic thinking.[16] While we might disagree that the digital humanities are the culmination, the "final period at the end of a very long sentence," of what Galloway conceives of as the "natural evolution stemming from several decades of historical momentum" (125), it seems likely that he is right in arguing the critical environment of figures like Stanley Hyman might be complicit, or at least compatible, with liberal imperatives. "In order to be successful today," Galloway writes, "a student or scholar must internalize the many options and enact them appropriately given the task at hand; this method of that problem, followed by a new method for the next." And thus, for Galloway, "the very question of method refers to that moment in history when knowledge becomes production, when knowledge loses its absolute claims to immanent efficacy, when knowledge ceases being intuitive and must be legitimized via recourse to some kind of metadiscourse" (108).

Yet the question of methodology was present even earlier than the arguments captured and neatly partitioned in 1948 by Stanley Hyman. A number of the critical works he examines—and his range of reference is, for its time, rather wide—were published years and even decades before *The Armed Vision* appeared. Questions of how humanists put together the part-objects of a scholarly apparatus were present when the study of literature was becoming institutionalized—they were, in fact, *the question*. Scholarly communities were very new and many were just getting off the ground and protocols of reading were required to share scholarship and research. Contra Galloway's cybernetic history of literary criticism, the question of how to read and the multiplicity of possible readings motivated critics as early as I. A. Richards. *Practical Criticism* (1929) is organized around student-supplied commentary on poems distributed by Richards to his students "at Cambridge and elsewhere."[17] Richards calls these student responses "protocols." His experiment to solicit these protocols began, during each week of the term, with the distribution of four printed poems to a group of around one hundred students. All identifying information about the poems has been removed; the poems are not labeled with the author or title. He gives his students one week to formulate a response to the poems based on their multiple readings of the poem. He defines a reading as "a number of perusals made at one session were to be counted together as one 'reading' provided that they aroused and sustained one single growing response to the poem, or alternatively led to no response at all and left the reader with nothing but the bare words before him on the paper" (4). Multiple readings were inscribed on the reverse side of the printed poems and returned to Richards. He collected the responses and used them, in part, to inform his lectures to these very same one hundred students in the following week. Of course, Richards did not use his protocols to demonstrate the validity of variant readings; rather, he used these readings as a tool for producing a norm. Poems, for Richards, were purely instrumental. They enabled him to construe the various receptions of the communicative act of the poem as deviations from his ideal reader.[18] Richard's *Practical Criticism* demonstrates an early concern with formalizing and critiquing the protocols and methods of reading. His book also predates the foundational theories of information and computation established by Claude Shannon and Alan Turing.[19]

In the larger debates over the use of computational methods within the digital humanities there has been marked concern about a loss of the political awareness and critical commitments that have informed so many of the humanist approaches used throughout the past several decades. A polemical essay appearing in the *LA Review of Books* in May 2016 takes much work in the digital humanities to task for its failure to attend to some of the field's methodological assumptions. "Traditional"—in other words, noncomputational—humanities work has been, since at least the 1970s, characterized by a deep concern with examining the assumptions that inform the selection of objects for analysis and the political implications of particular choices in how one approaches these objects.[20] In "Neoliberal Tools (and Archives): A Political History of Digital Humanities," Daniel Allington, Sarah Brouillette, and David Golumbia trace a genealogy of the digital humanities that they see as providing the foundations for a field without critical consciousness.[21] The genealogy traced by Allington and his coauthors is but one of several origin stories for the digital humanities but it is one that flows through several of the major figures within the field. The authors note that digital humanities has appeared at exactly the right time in the history of the neoliberal entity we call the corporate university and appears to support some of the goals and desires of administrators that are not exactly friendly to humanist scholarship. Their essay was quick to find support from suspicious humanists while also generating a cacophony of tweets and defensive responses on blogs from numerous digital humanists.[22]

A major point of contention shared among these respondents was the specific genealogy and field history offered by Allington et al. This historicopolitical reading of the digital humanities foregrounds what the authors see as the institutional effects of the digital humanities and the neat alignment between these effects and those desired by a group of conservative textual scholars known as the "New Bibliographers," the origin point for the explicated genealogy: "What Digital Humanities is *not* about, despite its explicit claims, is the use of digital or quantitative methodologies to answer research questions in the humanities. It is, instead, about the promotion of project-based learning and lab-based research over reading and writing, the rebranding of insecure campus employment as an empowering 'alt-ac' career choice, and the redefinition of technical expertise as a form (indeed, the superior form) of humanist knowledge."

While they acknowledge that there is some diversity in the plural digital humanities, the *Los Angeles Review of Books* critics focus on this specific genealogy because, in their words, "*this* is the Digital Humanities that has proved itself so useful to university administrators and to funding bodies." The textual scholarship wing of the digital humanities focuses almost entirely on building tools, on the construction of methods, rather than the application of these tools. The *Los Angeles Review of Books* critics write, "digital humanities has often tended to be anti-interpretive, especially when interpretation is understood as a political activity. Digital Humanities instead aims to archive materials, produce data, and develop software, while bracketing off the work of interpretation to a later moment or leaving it to other scholars—or abandoning it altogether for those who argue that we ought to become 'postcritical.'"

This is a strong critique, and much of it makes sense: the majority of the work that has thus attracted external funding and that has been held up as a model for humanities scholars is not offering anything recognizable as interpretation. Almost all three major activities just mentioned—in particular archiving and developing software—properly belong to other parts of the university and are primarily the responsibility of technical and research staff. The *Los Angeles Review of Books* critics point out that humanists should not replace interpretive work with tool building as the criterion by which departments grant degrees or assess progress toward tenure—this, as they correctly point out, would not pass muster in computer science nor in any field that makes heavy use of computation. There is, however, an overly rapid dismissal in the *Los Angeles Review of Books* essay of computational methods that depends on understanding these tools as just a simple appropriation of the methods of another field. The *Los Angeles Review of Books* critics describe Google's popular Ngram Viewer as "exactly the kind of 'success' that drives [the digital humanities] public relations: a technique is appropriated from an academic field not associated with humanist scholarship (here, linguistics), shorn of the theoretical checks that once regulated its use, and given the appearance of revolution through application to a data set that appears capable of silencing all criticism through sheer size." Modern criticism consists almost entirely of such an operation, minus, of course, the excessive size. What Stanley Hyman calls the "organized use of non-literary techniques and bodies of knowledge" is part and parcel of close reading and much of the critical tradition that the *Los Angeles Review of Books* critics want to defend. From legal and biblical hermeneutics to psychoanalysis to Saussurean linguistics, so much of the "traditional" criticism engages with extraliterary thought and extrinsic concepts. Despite the existence of some readings "shorn of theoretical checks," there is already a regular disciplinary injunction to apply a critical gaze backward, throughout the entire scholarly workflow, to the ways in which scholars find, collect, or produce evidence, to the ways in which this evidence is framed, the protocols by which it is interpreted, and the arguments finally presented to readers. What is needed is an effort to bring both the capabilities and the critical perspective fostered within the humanities to bear on computational methods.

Big Data and Transforming the Text into Data

The computational turn presents numerous complications to the reading and interpretation of texts. The question of how we read now, or to put it another way, how humanists should read under what N. Katherine Hayles calls "the regime of computation" has become increasingly pressing as computational tools proliferate alongside newly digitized and "born digital" texts.[23] Many humanists have accepted the conversion of the text into data, and discussions of reading and interpreting data have started to saturate academic discourse, even within fields centering critique and boasting a nuanced understanding of textuality. In an interview with Judith Butler—most certainly by now a traditional humanist—that appears in the journal *Sexualities*, Butler's interviewer, Sara Ahmed, opens with a question concerning the legacy of Butler's *Gender Trouble*. In response to Ahmed's observation that there has been a "changing context of reception" for her paradigm-changing book, Butler says the following: "[I] never reread my work, so it is not really possible to check the text. Anyway, the idea of checking the text is strange, since one can certainly go back to see whether there is textual evidence for an interpretation, but textual evidence is not exactly data. And we end up interpreting it again."[24] The interesting question here is not how it is possible that Butler does not recall her own argument or why she claims not to reread her own texts, but rather why Judith Butler distinguishes between textual evidence and data. Recognizing the difference among data, information, and textual evidence is crucial for an understanding of the stakes of the various reading methodologies used and proposed for work within the digital humanities.

The phrase "big data" started to appear early in the twenty-first century, right around the same time as the phrase "digital humanities" was coined. Big data, an increasingly common phrase, names the collecting, databasing, and indexing of large archives and repositories of data and information. Big data animates the excitement and possibilities that many imagine for a more hopeful and modern version of the humanities that would participate in the shared norms of the scientific culture that dominates the research university at present, including funding opportunities and more widely shared research methodologies. The phrase "big data" was introduced along with an accompanying shift in explanatory logics from the interrogation of causation to a dependency on correlation that we might call the ideology of correlationism. Correlationism is a defensive attitude that resists skeptical efforts to backtrack through decisions and data by methodological obfuscation and figurations of large data sets that draw on imagery of the mathematical sublime. Viktor Mayer-Schönberger and Kenneth Cukier's analysis of the early days of the big data phenomenon seems almost humorous now in retrospect.[25] The book opens with the anecdote of Google's investigation of influenza trends as a research project that was published in the highly respected scientific journal *Nature*. Fast-forward a few years later and we find this same project the prime example of what one critic has called "big data hubris."[26] Big data, the field and promise, was poised to change so much in those early years of the twenty-first century. The promises of big data and correlations did not pan out exactly as these early evangelists predicted. Big data, according to Mayer-Schönberger and Cukier, would enable people to find their own versions or editions of the news, making human journalists and editors obsolete. In the wake of the 2016 US presidential election, many were surprised to learn the extent to which algorithmically produced news stories and social media streams did not reflect the world as it was, but the world as viewers and observers of these algorithms wished it to be.[27]

In an important chapter of their book, Mayer-Schönberger and Cukier describe what they understand to be the difference between text and data, but their concept of digitization does not exhaust the numerous differences between text and data.[28] Computable data, big or small, involves different ways of thinking about the input and transformations or algorithms applied to the objects and files. Mayer-Schönberger and Cukier introduce the term *datafication* and the difference between it and digitization via recourse to the transformation of text, "when words become data" (83), in their terms. For the authors, datafication names a process that comes after digitization, in the case of texts produced and printed prior to the digital transformation of printing, and the treatment of texts born digital (those texts published or "printed" in already computer-readable formats). Datafication is not just digitization because it names the process of converting text into strings that can be indexed and searched, objects that permit "an endless stream of textual analysis" (84). To render text as data means more than conversion and standardization, it also means to make text available for large-scale algorithmic analysis. Datafication, if the term is to have any use whatsoever, would also apply to numbers, for datafication cannot be just the use of quantitative methods but the treatment of input as computable. Datafied texts, for Mayer-Schönberger and Cukier, are always already data. These texts have been imagined as data before they have even been loaded and read by any computational method. They have been imagined as sources for the algorithmic readings that draw out unimagined correlations. Mayer-Schönberger and Cukier describe, for example, how the new method of random sampling worked to make it possible to examine large populations and to make predictions based on smaller, random selections of groups that could be analyzed and then generalized to the complete data set. This leads them to claim that randomly sampled data has "transformed a big part of what we used to call the humanities into the social *sciences*" (23, emphasis in original).

As N. Katherine Hayles notes, one way of resolving the problems introduced by the return of scientific methods to the posttheory, postcanon humanities would be to split the digital humanities from other modes of analysis. Lev Manovich proposes exactly this in his creation of what he calls "cultural analytics." Cultural analytics, Manovich argues, should be tasked with the study of everyday culture. Objects deemed to possess some sort of literary or artistic merit should be the province of the digital humanities. Cultural analytics, he claims, is what the digital humanities looks like at a larger scale.[29] This reorients, in the case of those primarily textual fields of study, humanists back to the study of "literary" discourse, while other disciplines and fields would be tasked with everyday people and the ways in which they interact with culture— a distinction between "high" and popular culture that has long been contested by humanists.

But this divide splits the resources and attention of the critical humanities and risks enabling a mode of cultural analysis without an understanding of the complexity of culture while reifying a questionable notion of the literary. "Quantitative Analysis of Culture Using Millions of Digitized Books," a study published in 2011 in the journal *Science* and written by Jean-Baptiste Michel et al., is an early argument for a big-data approach to analyzing the digitized textual archive of the nineteenth and twentieth centuries. The authors of this essay argue that their approach, what they call culturomics, will extend "the boundaries of rigorous quantitative inquiry to a wide array of new phenomena spanning the social sciences and the humanities" (176). Culturomics ignores and replaces critical accounts of culture with computational thinking.

Michel and his colleagues make the common critique that humanities scholars have been limited to small objects and to what they consider to be small data sets and therefore humanist approaches cannot address the truth of culture: "Reading small collections of carefully chosen works enables scholars to make powerful inferences about trends in human thought. However, this approach rarely enables precise measurement of the underlying phenomena. Attempts to introduce quantitative methods in the study of culture have been hampered by the lack of suitable data" (176). While Michel assumes that the goal of humanist scholarship is to discover "trends in human thought" and computational approaches can produce "precise measurements" of the phenomena that make up "human thought," what the critical digital humanities provide is a way for humanists to participate in using these methods but with a nuanced understanding of the intricacies of culture, measurement, and data.

If there is no real consistency to the notion of a digital method, there is also no single category of digital object. Richard Rogers, a sociologist who researches networked digital objects, notes that there are important differences between digitized and digital content and that this difference might structure the grounds of possibility for digital methodologies: "an ontological distinction may be made between the natively digital and the digitized, that is, between the objects, content, devices, and environments that are 'born' in the new medium and those that have 'migrated' to it. Such a distinction opens up the question of method for Internet-related research. Should the current methods of study change, slightly or wholesale, given a focus on objects as well as the contents that are 'of the medium'?"[30] For Rogers, the digital researcher needs to ground claims in the affordances and conditions found in the digital or online—although one should note that digital and online are not synonyms—medium, through what he calls "online groundedness." While digital humanists can, and indeed must, recognize the importance of context for their critical work, what N. Katherine Hayles calls "media-specific analysis" in reference to the study of digital texts, there are hermeneutical questions that can be directed at both types of digital objects offered by Rogers as well as to his framing of the difference as a question of ontology.[31] An example of this type of questioning can be found in David Golumbia's emphasis on "new media" not as an object for analysis, the digital products produced with the assistance of digital devices, but rather as a particular type of discourse, founded on the notion of infinite newness, that he sees as shared by new media critics, artists, and corporations and otherwise uninterrogated.[32] Following Golumbia, a

19

humanistic question, a critical question, would be to ask about the discourse of the computational. Humanists need to do so because the appearance of sophisticated and complicated computational methods constitutes the greatest potential benefit and threat to business as usual within the humanities. While the *Los Angeles Review of Books* critics, who include Golumbia, ignore much of the work found in this area in their essay, it too is subject to their institutional critique, and many of its proponents hold an express desire to separate method from interpretation.

We might be familiar with text mining and machine learning algorithms from our everyday online lives. Amazon's recommendation engine, Netflix, Google's AdWords, your e-mail provider's spam filters, Facebook's various privacy-challenged tools—these are all locations in which we see complicated algorithms categorize, label, and distort textual data. Such computational methods have been applied with different degrees of success to more complicated textual sources, including those objects we once called literature. These tools have been suggested by some as an alternative to the critical tradition— the critical tradition generally refers to the schools and practices of criticism emerging from perspective of what Paul Ricoeur terms "the hermeneutics of suspicion" and the approaches others refer to as symptomatic reading—because their proponents believe that these tools can remain free of the taint of subjectivity and that they enable their users to break free from dominant modes of reading.[33] This is decidedly not true, for, as this book demonstrates, every step in any research activity remains subject to the influence of human subjectivity. But that does not mean these tools are not interesting or that their intrusion into the garden of literary study should be treated with outright hostility.

In their introduction to their co-edited volume, *Research Methods for Reading Digital Data in the Digital Humanities* (2016), Gabriele Griffin and Matt Hayler make the provocative claim that the digital humanities are methodologically distinct from other fields: "digital humanities are understood . . . as distinct methodological practices developed in conjunction with and in response to new digital tools, with all that this implies for the related construction of knowledge."[34] For Griffin and Hayler, what makes the digital humanities distinct is not the type of arguments deployed or objects studied, but the computational tools that are located somewhere between objects and claims of the digital humanities workflow. Yet it is not at all clear that these tools are, in fact, particular to the digital humanities. Indeed, all the methods described in the essays found in Griffin and Hayler's collection appropriate already existing methods from other fields. Many of the authors of the individual essays do not even appear to be humanists or even particularly well versed in humanistic approaches—they are much more likely to make their arguments in conversation with sociologists and computational linguists than humanists. Griffin and Hayler, like many others, see the digital humanities as split between the production of digital texts and the computational analysis of the digital or digitized text, the text transformed into data: "Two broad developments in the use of digital research methods in the Humanities might be discerned: one is the creation and curating of digital data to which we devote another volume . . . the other is the development of new reading methods, often for new kinds of texts, including the 'framing' or analysis of existing digital data, a practice increasingly common among Humanities researchers exploring the new forms of textualisation and visual display that digital media afford" (1). Humanists can never assume that the products of computational analysis were simply produced by objective procedures for the interpretation of the researcher deploying the tool. Instead, they must continue to ask a series of probing questions that should be recognized as digital variants on long-existing procedural inquiries asked of any object analyzed within the humanities: where the output came from, what computational transformations were executed to produce them and why these, what influenced the possible uses and processes afforded by these transformations, what the input data for these transformations were, and where they came from. These questions are the critical digital humanist questions.

In posing the questions, it should be acknowledged that there are many sites from which we can launch our critical analysis and numerous targets. While most of the critical digital and information scholars at present have given attention to the phenomenological experience of algorithms, what we see displayed on our screens and devices, the histories and implementation of these algorithms, remains relatively unexamined, for two main reasons. First, scholars give their primary attention to our experience with algorithms at a distance because so many more people have remote and abstracted experiences of computational tools. A minority of users download software packages in source form and explore the implementation of algorithms at a level in which parameters can be examined, noted, and altered—for example, a topic modeling package written in the Python programming language using several popular open-source libraries or a Web browser plug-in or add-on developed in JavaScript. The second roadblock for algorithmic analysis of many common interactions with digital tools, computational methods or not, rests in the fact that the majority of these everyday interactions depend on proprietary and opaque algorithms. While, for example, some published details about Google's PageRank search algorithm are available, its exact operation remains a corporate trade secret. Despite these problems, digital humanists should give critical attention to both the black box or opaque algorithms that are presented in easy-to-use interfaces as well as the open-source components that make up the toolbox of most academic researchers using computational methods. While the latter, because of the ubiquity and vetted quality of open-source tools, are the primary focus of this book, humanistic critique should be applied to all varieties of computation.

But in the existing accounts of computational tools used within digital humanities work there has been little critical analysis of the approaches, tools, and algorithms selected and deployed. In an essay in the Griffin and Hayler collection, for example, Dawn Archer examines a range of what she calls representative text-mining methods—she selects "lexical/statistical frequency profiling, concordancing, collocations, ngrams—used in the humanities and in the social sciences.[35] Archer's essay rapidly moves from one approach to another in order to give a sense of how these tools can be deployed in a variety of research projects. The data-mining, or more properly text-mining, tools she mentions almost entirely originate in computational linguistics, the source for many of the tools most used and desired by digital humanists. Her essay ends with a self-citation that evidences the continual separation of interpretive from evidence-gathering methods: "The best means of ensuring that the kinds of CL [corpus linguistics] techniques discussed here help—rather than hinder—the research, in the final instance, is to take seriously Archer's (2009) suggestion that such techniques provide a way of *mining* the data only. For, ultimately, it must always be the researcher who decides what is (and is not) meaningful, based on all available data" (88, emphasis in original). Mining is not meaning, in Archer's formulation, but to say so is to ignore the theories of meaning in the form of models embedded in all these algorithms and tools.

The concept of collocations, words frequently appearing near each other in a source text, for example, involves potentially normative understandings of what counts as meaningful to linguists. These same understandings of the meaning or significance of words and language are shared with other text-mining methods popular with humanists. The theory of meaning embedded within the concept of collocation is a contextual theory of meaning that draws on ideas from British linguistics—in particular, the work of John Rupert Firth, coiner of the famous aphorism: "you shall know a word by the company it keeps."[36] The collocation algorithm, in the implementation used in the following examples, attempts to locate word pairs or phrases within a small contextual window within the stream of words in a document. The software documentation provided by one popular implementation of a collocation tool, the collocations() function from the Python programming language package called the Natural Language Toolkit, or NLTK, gives some examples of the default values and possible parameters that can be used to find collocated terms:

collocations(self, num=20, window_size=2)
Print collocations derived from the text, ignoring stopwords.

:seealso: find_collocations
:param num: The maximum number of collocations to print.
:type num: int
:param window_size: The number of tokens spanned by a collocation
    (default=2)
:type window_size: int[37]

We find, within these default values, at least two objects of critical importance. The first, found within the description of the collocations function, informs us that this function will drop a number of words, what are called stopwords, before searching for collocated word pairings. This means that words connected by articles such as "a" or "the" along with other words deemed lacking of semantic content will now be located closer together. The second default value, the one labeled "window_size," determines how closely located together these terms must be to appear in the collocation list. The default value of 2 might be appropriate for certain kinds of texts and not at all appropriate for others. The following shows these defaults used to extract the default number of collocated terms, using the default window size, from both the plain text of Amanda Smith's *An Autobiography: The Story of the Lord's Dealings with Mrs. Amanda Smith the Colored Evangelist* (1893), as found in the DocSouth North American Slave Narrative archive, and a version that has been preprocessed.

Collocated terms:
n't know; New York; Cape Palmas; Methodist Church; shall forget; Amanda Smith; Bishop Taylor; Holy Ghost; never forget; Sierra Leone; camp meeting; Praise Lord; said "Lord; shall never; Mrs. Smith; God bless; Sister Smith; Sabbath School; could get; Lord helped

Preprocessed collocated terms:
cape palmas; amanda smith; new york; camp meeting; shall forget; praise
lord; methodist church; sierra leone; bishop taylor; holy ghost; sister smith;
never forget; god bless; shall never; mrs. smith; lord help; lord helped; two
weeks; thank god; miss drake

This reading of the documentation and execution of NLTK's collocations()
function demonstrates just one of the ways in which text mining registers
and encapsulates aspects of an already existing theory of meaning. I examine
the preprocessing routines used to produce the results displayed above in the
second chapter. All this is to say that these embedded approaches to meaning
making that are found within software must be taken seriously as a site of
critical analysis if one is to make use of these tools, and that meaning cannot
be attached solely to the output of the tool.

These problems are also present in Matthew L. Jockers's explanation of
the use of computational methods in evidence gathering in his *Macroanalysis*,
which was one of the first major books to offer an argument to humanists with
a rationale for using text mining, computer-aided searching and categorization, and other forms of computational criticism. While much of his work
in the book is a derivative of computational stylistics, in his introduction he
calls *Macroanalysis* "a book about evidence gathering."[38] Jockers believes that
computer-aided approaches are especially well suited to locating materials
with which a humanist might make a strong argument. This is because, as he
writes, "massive digital corpora offer us unprecedented access to the literary
record and invite, even demand, a new type of evidence gathering and meaning
making" (8). Big data and big data computational techniques, as invoked earlier
in this chapter, have produced much excitement that has almost always been
coupled with calls to obsolete old interpretive methods. Jockers thus spends
many of the early pages of *Macroanalysis* engaged in a critique of close reading
of a single text or, what he has termed through a backformation, microanalysis.
"The literary scholar of the twenty-first century," he writes, "can no longer be
content with anecdotal evidence, with random 'things' gathered from a few,
even 'representative' texts" (8). Jockers's casting of the various reading practices that supposedly have been obsoleted by big data and computational criticism as tainted by unscientific methods and therefore mere nostalgic leftovers
depends on an association with randomness and the anecdotal. It also requires
him to posit that work in the humanities has always separated method from
interpretation, an assertion not supported by the long history of critical and

theoretical interpretive methods. Jockers describes his understanding of this separation as "back in the 1990s . . . gathering literary evidence meant reading books, noting 'things' (a phallic symbol here, a biblical reference there, a stylistic flourish, an allusion, and so on) and then interpreting: making sense and arguments out of those observations" (8).

A year after the appearance of *Macroanalysis*, Jockers published a hands-on explorative guide to using computational methods to analyze text using the R statistical package. Springer published this book, *Text Analysis with R for Students of Literature*, in 2014 in a series titled "Quantitative Methods in the Humanities and Social Sciences." In what is a familiar introductory formula used in the teaching methods within other fields and professional practice, Jockers guides his students of literature through computational analyses that increase in complexity as they acquire familiarity with the explained R commands and functions. Here is how Jockers explains one such procedure, the "microanalytical" measurement of lexical variety within a single text:

> *Moby Dick* [sic] is a complicated book with a complex vocabulary. Readers of the book inevitably remember Chapter Thirty-Two. This is the cetology chapter in which Melville offers a zoological and pseudo-scholarly, pseudo-comical account of whale history and physiology. Students frequently complain that this section of the novel is more complex or *difficult*. One way to measure the complexity of language is to calculate a measure of vocabulary richness. Such measure can be represented as a mean word frequency or a relationship between the number of unique words used (i.e., the working lexicon) and a count of the number of word tokens in the document.[39]

While this book was intended to provide readers with some quick payoff for working through the carefully charted and scaffolded lessons, it troublingly, especially for a text intended for students of literature, leaves almost all humanist considerations to the side. Jockers does not primarily work on American literature, and *Text Analysis with R for Students of Literature* is not a work of literary criticism, but his use of one of the best known literary works from the canon to explain computational methods lacks any awareness of how humanists have treated this text. After introducing a method of calculating lexical frequency, Jockers explains that, as it turns out, Herman Melville's language in "Cetology" is no richer or more complex than his other chapters. He writes, "the cetology chapter, which readers so often remember as being one of denser, richer vocabulary, is not exceptional at all. Words in the cetology chapter are repeated fairly often. In fact, each unique word type is used an average of 3.5 times" (63). This is evidence gathering entirely cut off from the humanities. If this type of analysis was used to produce arguments about *Moby-Dick* or other texts, one might wonder what possible worth there is to the humanities and why one would need humanists at all. This analysis does not tell humanists, especially literary scholars working within American literature, anything that they did not already know; no scholar familiar with *Moby-Dick* would argue that "Cetology" is a difficult chapter for students because of the chapter's diction, the choice of words in this particular first-person narrated chapter. It is true that the cetology chapter is different from the preceding chapters, but the question is much more one of a sudden switch of form and genre—specifically, the humorous and obviously pseudo-scientific content of this "encyclopedic" chapter that is a send-up of nineteenth-century scientism and classification—than Ishmael's diction as he explains the library science of whales.

A final example of the need for a critical digital humanities comes from another recent entry into the emergent field of computer-aided criticism, Geoffrey Rockwell and Stéfan Sinclair's *Hermeneutica: Computer-Assisted Interpretation in the Humanities* (2016). Rockwell and Sinclair's book is something rather remarkable for the humanities—it is both a printed text, published by MIT Press, and a companion website with excerpted chapters and small, single-purpose "Voyant" computational tools that enable the interactive analysis of small textual data sets. *Hermeneutica* breaks some important ground in the digital humanities with its theoretical awareness of some of the more difficult problems in interpretation raised by what they judiciously call computer-assisted interpretation.[40]

Rockwell and Sinclair make some effort to move beyond the complications involved in the computational methods used in the digital humanities identified above, but there are still some significant limitations in how far they are willing to commit to the hermeneutical project. In theorizing that small algorithmic tools, the individual components of a larger computational workflow, could be considered "things" that generate data for human interpretation, Rockwell and Sinclair link these tools to scientific instruments. They do so, however, not to examine computational tools as imagined and socially constructed things in themselves, but in order to deemphasize certain questions that one might ask about the tools and their algorithms. Rockwell and Sinclair want us to think of the algorithmic procedures located on their own website as generating experimental results for the humanities researcher. They call these tools hermeneutica, and despite being virtual—or a combination of the virtual (software) and physical (hardware)—they claim that these tools have a "material" existence. They ask, "what if we could read the things (toys, websites, tools such as Voyant, and so on) and their uses as discursive practices? How would we do that? How might our interpretation then be different? Is it possible to think through interpretive things?" (151). Throughout *Hermeneutica*, Rockwell and Sinclair display what could be called a nostalgia for an older mode of scientific method, one dependent on physical instruments, that they troublingly couple with technological evangelicalism without taking seriously the complicated nature of their own algorithmic investigations.

There is a moment in which the authors of *Hermeneutica* take Stanley Fish to task for his critique of the digital humanities without, according to them, engaging with computational tools: "Fish doesn't actually look at, interact with, or ask about any of the artifacts made in the Digital Humanities. He ignores the digital stuff of DH because he wants it to be another theoretical fad that can be read" (151). This argument turns out to be weak at best and disingenuous at worst. As tool developers, they are eager to have digital humanists use their instruments, their modular hermeneutica, as long as they do not put too much pressure on the ways in which their tools selectively and subjectively read and produce evidence. And even more worrisome is the opaque nature of Rockwell and Sinclair's tools and the way in which they want researchers to interact with these tools. Stating that the tools have a material existence enables them to hide and obscure the underlying code and algorithms. If one is going to engage with the artifacts of the digital humanities, then the artifacts themselves need to be open and available for researchers to examine and understand. A critical digital humanities takes as its proper object the entire workflow used in computational analysis. No areas of inquiry, from the origins of the text and data to the history and ideology of the algorithms used, can remain closed to the gaze of the critic.

The Exorbitant Question of (Digital) Method

In order to correct for some of the problems introduced through the use of computational tools in the collection or production of evidence, N. Katherine Hayles asks us to combine what she sees as different modes of reading. But in her proposal to combine reading methodologies, Hayles still holds onto the assumption that the hermeneutical questions involved in close reading are somehow isolated from the tools, from the machine or computational reading. She wants digital humanists to produce what she calls, with an unfortunately imported term from late-twentieth-century businessspeak, a "synergy" (*How We Think*, 75) between modalities of reading. Hayles argues that there are "productive interactions between close, hyper, and machine reading" (78). By connecting scale to context, she wants critics to select the appropriate approach for what she thinks is the appropriate object. Hyperreading is skimming, what you do on the Web or with most academic essays—it is the middle ground with a multilocal context between machine reading, in which, as she argues, "the context may be limited to a few words or eliminated altogether, as in a word-frequency list" (74). Close reading provides what Hayles calls a monolocal context. She describes the interaction thus: "Relatively context poor, machine reading is enriched by context-rich close reading when close reading provides guidance for the construction of algorithms; Margaret Cohen points to this synergy when she observes that for computer programs to be designed, 'the patterns still need to be observed [by close reading].' On the other hand, machine reading may reveal patterns overlooked in close reading" (74). To state my main claim of this chapter once more, computational methods and machine readings are not immune to critique and close readings of their operation. Following Lisa Gitelman and Virginia Jackson, we might say that there is no such thing as raw data, or perhaps we might hold to the division between "capta" and "data" made by Johanna Drucker.[41] The historicist asks about the contingencies of the present registered in the writing, borrowing, or buying of code, assembling the packages, algorithms, libraries, the encoding schemes, and even the symbolic logic. The feminist asks about the epistemological assumptions that privilege certain questions and modes of inquiry. The gender theorist draws our attention to our desire to draw distinctions, to our categorical imperatives.

Barbara Herrnstein Smith places the methodological and interpretive changes proposed by some digital humanities scholars in relation to her historical account of the methods used in literary studies. Her essay, "What Was 'Close Reading?,'" provides the best account of what is at stake in the current framing of the methodological difference between computational criticism and close reading. Smith's essay takes us from John Crowe Ransom's "Criticism, Inc." through the corporate-friendly pseudo-digital humanities methods of Google, Inc. In approaching her conclusion on this long history, Smith argues that in their direct opposition of the humanities method, digital humanists like Matthew Jockers have essentially moved themselves outside the humanities:

> More use of big data or computer algorithms by literary scholars will not solve the methodology problems that Jockers sees in literary studies. The problems, if that is what they are, are built into standard scholarly practice in the field, the legacy of classical humanistic practices reinforced by various contemporary approaches. The only way to end the embarrassment at what literary critics and historians do would be to persuade them to do something else instead, something more like social-science research. That seems, in fact, to be what Moretti proposes in the name of "distant reading" and what Wilkens, Jockers and others are promoting in the name of "digital humanities."[42]

Smith is absolutely correct that much so-called digital humanities work is not actually engaging with the methods and practices of the humanities. Some humanists have embraced certain approaches because they seek the dubious authority of the social sciences, while some social scientists are eagerly pursuing digital humanities funding sources.[43] Smith's use of "embarrassment" is provocative here—the material condition of research today requires the moonshot and then, rather quickly, a tidy resolution confirming already predicted and planned outcomes. Problems, within the humanities, are never fully solved.

There are those who use computational methods to analyze the products of human culture and elect to or claim to be able to separate method from interpretation from analysis. This division recapitulates some of the gravest interpretive mistakes of past humanities work. In upholding this division, some digital humanists repeat the structuralist era methods but with a difference—with a marked desire to bypass the post-structuralist critique. Humanists bring to the digital the ability to apply the hermeneutics of suspicion to digital methods. Take, as an example, the process of self-critique proposed again and again by Dominick LaCapra. LaCapra asks historians to undergo an examination of their investments in the past and the ways in which they might be participating in the logics of transference that blind them to their own misreadings of the archives.[44] The digital humanities need the hermeneutics of suspicion, *especially* as it applies to methodological choices and interpretations.

The methods of the digital humanities require a constant rereading. The stakes of this act of rereading are visible in an important scene within the history of critical theory. This scene appeared in an interview that took the form of an exchange in which Gerald Graff posed a set of written questions to Jacques Derrida. The questions and answers are included as a supplement to the essays and responses that make up the text of Derrida's *Limited Inc*. Graff asks Derrida about a certain chapter, a subsection, really, in *Of Grammatology* and what he means by his use of "doubling commentary" in "The Exorbitant Question of Method." Derrida responds thus: "I have just finished rereading *Of Grammatology* . . . from which the proposition you cite, 'on the moment of doubling commentary,' is drawn. To economize on what would otherwise be an overly long answer, I proposed that the interested reader also reread the chapter."[45] It is a humorously exorbitant moment that puts the concept of the doubling commentary into action. Derrida responds that there is no such thing as a simple paraphrastic reading, a gloss of the text, because this gloss, the first reading, the first commentary, is itself an interpretive act. This claim is foundational to his famous statement, appearing just lines later, that there is no outside to the text.

Readings, for Derrida, traverse a certain path within and through a text. This "certain path" may be contingent, maybe idiosyncratic, maybe historically determined. It may be just one of many paths. "But are other paths not possible?" Derrida asks. "And as long as the totality of paths is not effectively exhausted, how shall we justify this one?"[46] It is an important question and the center of the humanities. For if there is a humanities method, it is a metamethod that enables the endless asking of this exact question: "how shall we justify this one?" What sustains the possibility of any critical method is the limit of the coherency of that particular method. That very same coherency is addressed, acknowledged, and limited by the heterogeneity of methodology. What is most interesting and distinctive of work in the humanities is the acceptance of a ceaseless variety of methods. Humanists have an openness to other accounts, histories, and practices—it is a catholicism that cannot abide the technological evangelism found in other disciplines that renders past methods moot while moving along a near-simultaneous horizon of the cutting edge. There is what we might want to recognize as a relentless dissatisfaction with *every* method. The humanities, I argue, operate according to what Robert Scholes once referred to as a nihilistic hermeneutics—in short, the search for a grounded meaning that can never be obtained—an impossible practice of reading.[47]

We cannot have a computational digital humanities without critically examining the hardware, software, and social infrastructures and the history of methods that make computation as such possible. The problem of scientific validity that first enables and then obsoletes research within the sciences cannot easily be adapted to humanities research, nor should it be. There is no leading-edge horizon charting out the frontiers of humanistic inquiry that can leave in its wake rejected and obsolete approaches. At the same time, humanities scholars cannot endlessly defer the use of computational methods because of doubts introduced by suspicious and critical readings of these methodologies. This book advocates a third way, a path forward for a critical digital humanities that seeks to combine equal parts critical theory and computational science.

CHAPTER 2

Can an Algorithm Be Disturbed?

Machine Learning, Intrinsic Criticism, and the Digital Humanities

Never act except in such a way that your action may be programmed.

—Jacques Lacan, *The Ethics of Psychoanalysis, 1959–1960*

He who regards poems only as objects to be "processed" according to one or another method should admit to himself that the processing of leather into shoes is more useful to mankind than the processing of poems into interpretations.

—Sigurd Burckhardt, *Shakespearean Meanings*

Within literary and cultural studies there has been a new focus on the "surface" as opposed to the "depth" of a work as the proper object of study. The new focus has been manifested primarily through what appears to be the return of prior approaches, including formalist reading practices, attention to the aesthetic dimensions of a text, and new methodologies that come from the social sciences and pursue interest in modes of description and observation.[1] In arguing for the adoption of these methodologies, some critics have advocated for an end to what many scholars, after Paul Ricoeur, have termed "the hermeneutics of suspicion" and the various forms of ideological critique that have been the mainstay of criticism for the past few decades.[2] While some of these descriptive, surface, or distant readings might begin with what was once repressed through prior selection criteria, they all shift our attention away from an understanding of a "repressed" or otherwise hidden object by understanding textual features less as signifier, an arrow to follow to some hidden depths, than an interesting object in its own right. Computer-aided approaches to literary criticism or "digital readings," to be sure, not an unproblematic term, have been put forward as one way of making a break from the deeply habituated reading practices of the past, but their advocates risk overstating the case and, in giving up on critique, they remain blind to many undertheorized dimensions of computation and computational methods. While digital methods enable one to examine radically larger archives than those assembled in the past, a transformation that Matthew Jockers characterizes as a shift from micro to "macroanalysis," the fundamental assumptions about texts and meaning implicit in these tools and in the criticism resulting from use of these tools belong to a much earlier period of literary analysis.[3]

Stephen Best and Sharon Marcus's well-known essay, "Surface Reading: An Introduction," that introduced a volume of the journal *Representations* from 2009 was dedicated to the topic of "How We Read Now" and examines several variants of surface reading as an alternative to depth or "symptomatic" reading. In their essay, Best and Marcus name the digital humanities and computer-assisted reading as one important and particularly hopeful methodology for the future of humanistic study. They write, "Where the heroic critic corrects the text, a nonheroic critic might aim instead to correct for her critical subjectivity, by using machines to bypass it, in the hopes that doing so will produce more accurate knowledge about texts."[4] Replacing the heroic critic of the symptomatic era with the heroic code, they imagine an objective world of bypassed subjectivity. Without cultural knowledge, biases, political commitments, in other words, without being situated, Best and Marcus believe that the machine and the algorithm can produce more "accurate knowledge" about the world brought into being by subjective human beings. This is to say, that digital or computer-aided readings are imagined as escaping the subjective constraints that draw us to certain passages, figures, or conclusions. An algorithm can be excluded from the hermeneutics of suspicion because it knows nothing of the concept of "hidden" depth. This leads Best and Marcus to claim that digital readings might restore a taboo set of goals for humanistic study: "objectivity, validity, truth" (17).

Heather Love's provocative essay on the surface reading methodology, "Close but Not Deep," takes up some of the challenges to close reading identified by Best and Marcus. Two main concerns with the criticism as now practiced concern Love: first, literary critics have privileged witnessing and empathy and have thus turned literary criticism into an ethical act that draws its power from the charisma of the critic rather than the text. Second, the hermeneutical method of close reading that is the trademark of humanistic disciplines and the methodological lingua franca of most of the criticism of the past fifty years—spanning, one should note, from the New Criticism to feminism to deconstruction—has isolated the work of humanists from other disciplines within the university that do not closely attend to the specificities of language, whether appearing on the page or the screen. While digital humanists like Jockers and Franco Moretti have imagined the only solution to these two problems to be the rejection of reading literature as we read now, to give up on the singular text, the corpus, in favor of collections of texts, that is, corpora, Love wants to keep reading singular objects like the novel but rethink the activity of reading. She suggests that we renounce "depth hermeneutics" in favor of what she provocatively turns into a motto for our moment, to read closely, but not deeply. What keeps Love securely on the surface of her essay is her belief in what she herself terms the "normative view" of science, and in particular the social sciences. She wants to bring literature and humanistic study more broadly into the sphere of the scientific view in order to participate within the currency at present available to this discourse. This supposedly agreeable normative aspect enables Love to reconceive interpretation as description. This is to say that Love presupposes an uncontested descriptive view of literature. This so-called normative view of the sciences links Love's surface reading and Best and Marcus's belief that the digital humanities can deliver "objectivity, validity, truth."[5]

This chapter examines the construction of computational models through the abstracted practices and methods of computer-aided text mining. These text-mining approaches collectively represent what I take to be the strongest form of the digital humanities. They are strong methods in the sense that they are well understood, testable, and from certain quarters defensible. The machine-learning algorithms that enable the majority of text-mining efforts are widely used in other disciplines and thus are less a specific and arbitrary corner of the digital humanities than central to the effort to reposition humanistic research within the bounds of current university research protocols. Matthew Jockers asserts that computational text analysis is "by all accounts the foundation of digital humanities and its deepest root."[6] This "root" of the digital humanities has a long history, one that Jockers connects to the digital concordances of Thomas Aquinas produced by Father Roberto Busa in the

1940s and, as I will show, is attached to the deep dreams of structuralism and its desire for a science of interpretation. I will begin by first discussing in detail several proposed methods of machine reading as possible answers to the call for surface reading. These quantitative methods come to literary studies from outside the humanities and are well understood in certain contexts, especially those within the empirical sciences; my reframing of computer-aided text mining will draw out what I take to be the theoretical assumptions implicit within these models of meaning. I'll then turn to an analysis of structuralism in order to demonstrate the degree to which the digital humanities and machine readings of text have resurrected key structuralist presuppositions. In the process, I will discuss two important critiques of structuralism from within literary studies and what we still have to learn from such interventions. Finally, I will argue that these critiques enable us to call into question the division between the act of interpretation and objective, scientific methodology in the rhetoric of this strong form of the digital humanities.

Objects and Methods of Digital Critique

Many humanists, when confronted with seemingly monumental digital archives and obscure or complicated tools that refuse to fully explain themselves, take refuge in the idea that undirected exploring and poking around might result in novel and unexpected discoveries. A perennial favorite of those teaching the digital humanities—especially to undergraduate students—is Stephen Ramsay's essay "The Hermeneutics of Screwing Around; or What You Do with a Million Books." Ramsay's essay is essentially about the pleasures—although the practical and useful pleasures—of playing with computational tools and digital archives. Library or archival exploration, Ramsay argues, can be classified into two main activities: searching and browsing. Searching is directed and depends on the searcher's trust in organizational and institutional structures while browsing is an anarchically playful activity that is motivated, as it were, by boredom. To take up Ramsay's "screwmeneutical imperative" is thus to imaginatively discard the restriction of catalogs, indexes, and authority and make discoveries. But we need to acknowledge that screwing around, especially with computational tools, always happens within constraints—from the space, real or virtual, in which we explore to our use and even the creative misuse of our tools. It is likely that the larger the space, in other words, the bigger the archive in which we play, the less we feel the need to call into question the constructedness of the space in which we are screwing around. This is all well and good in the transitional or potential space of the classroom, but in order for such experimental results to be useful for research, in order for computational approaches in humanities to grow up, descriptions and considerations of the constraining environment, the playground of the digital humanities, are needed.[7]

Humanists creating and interpreting algorithmically transformed texts will increasingly need to follow the lead of the computational sciences in introducing mechanisms to enable greater transparency for other scholars to examine, critique, and build on their work. Without such articulations of the space and conditions in which they work or play, there is a danger of only a pretense of a scientific methodology—we might call the opacity with which some humanists work a form of methodology cloaking, in that these scholars draw authority from but do not answer to empiricism—in the application of computational tools to humanistic objects. Katherine Bode pinpoints one major and pressing problem: the lack of shared disciplinary standards that might dictate the structure and shape of digital document collections. From her perspective, the lack of clarity with which scholars construct and explain the historical archives from which they make their claims limits the ability of literary historians, like herself, to understand which archives were used and to build on those archives and claims. Bode proposes, although without specifying much detail about the shape, form, and the methods of distribution, a new digital object that would be the equivalent of the scholarly edition for those working within digital literary history. Existing arguments that we need only to combine distant reading with close readings are unsatisfying because they both work under the assumption that the archive is "complete" and "correct."

Noticing the absence of any description of the specific sources and editions of the texts examined or processed and the editorial process used to select texts, Bode mounts a pointed critique of the work of several computational humanists, including Franco Moretti and Matthew Jockers. "What literary history needs," Bode argues, "is not close or distant reading, or a simple integration of the two, but a new scholarly object for representing literary works in their historical context, one capable of managing the documentary record's complexity, especially as it is manifested in emerging digital knowledge infrastructure."[8] Bode's proposed solution places the objects that would become the material through which one generates what she calls a "data-rich literary history" within some historical context, by which I believe she means the publication history of any particular textual objects. Another such scholarly object might look like a standardizing structure, in the form of a shared data standard, that would enable the organization and formatting of humanities data—one that might build on existing standards such as the Text Encoding Initiative and to-be-developed indexing and metadata standards.[9] Such an object, for example, might easily mark the separation between paratext and text, better facilitating the process of selecting text written by the indicated author. Better metadata, descriptive information about information and in this case, standardized formats for registering and sharing publication information and editorial decisions, coupled with open access to the data will enable a greater level of understanding of *some* of the objects of computational criticism. But without also sharing a formalized description of the computational methods, the algorithmic transformations performed on these digital objects, this solution remains a partial fix of the problem created by a lack of shared disciplinary standards.

Stefán Sinclair and Geoffrey Rockwell use the term *object* to name both the scholarly archival object identified as missing within the digital humanities by Bode and the computational tools used to transform these textual sources. An object can suggest something with a shared understanding and it can function as a central focus of critique, but this conceptualization of computation also adds a sense of opacity and a natural self-explanatory givenness. The Voyant text-mining and data-display tools mentioned in the previous chapter and presented by Sinclair and Rockwell as the accompanying computational platform and laboratory for *Hermeneutica* function as this later type of object. These individual Voyant objects, these "hermeneutica," are abstracted Web-based black boxes. This means that the individual tools are linked together in an online interface as opaque digital objects situated within an equally obscure tool chain. Such an approach may make their platform available to novice researchers seeking to experiment with text mining, but the danger of this type of interface is that it can produce unnecessary distance between the researcher and the tools as well as the automatically interpreted text. Highly abstracted or minimal interfaces are typically designed for nontechnical audiences, but the minimal interface, as with any abstraction, means that many decisions are made for the user, hidden behind default settings, parameterization, and preselected options. It is likely that the computational criticism will experience something of a bifurcation, with one set of open-source community-developed and -supported tools intended for researchers working within the field and another set of tools, built on the abstracted model of Voyant, available for teaching as well as general purpose and exploratory use. This split will be necessary as methods become more complex and scholars increasingly work at a larger scale on shared, standardized, and community-developed datasets of the type called for by Katherine Bode.

The best way to add transparency to the computational methods used within the humanities is the open-source model described above. This model tends toward minimal interfaces and simple, modular designs. In an essay titled "Critical Computing in the Humanities," Phillip R. Polefrone, John Simpson, and Dennis Yi Tenen describe such an approach, which they used in a hands-on workshop course in computational methodologies titled "Computing Foundations for Human(s|ists)" that they have taught at several institutions and locations, including the Digital Humanities Summer Institute.[10] The authors make a compelling argument for a minimal interface with computing systems (called "minimal computing" elsewhere) in pursuit of small-scale and human-comprehensible research programs. That this approach appears at the same time as big data and complex machine-learning technology has been foregrounded in other fields seems worthy of analysis. Polefrone and his colleagues argue for an approach to research and pedagogy that "is premised on extended rather than replacing long-standing critical practices of humanistic inquiry" (86). They are right to assert that any critical use of computational systems should expose as much of the computational methodology as possible, but much remains unexamined in any proposed "plain text" computing, including the social and cultural residues found within the selected approaches, algorithms, secondary databases, archives, and other objects of the variety I call text-external referential systems in the next chapter.

The human-scale, minimal-computing model coupled with richly described and openly available datasets answers some of important critiques launched against computational methods as now used within the humanities. The charge of methodological obfuscation, for example, can be answered, even if just provisionally, when it becomes possible to follow and compare the narrative found within the mechanics of the workflow with the description supplied. Because most of the forms in which humanities research is disseminated do not contain or make easily available a separate methods section but rather position a generalized statement of method in relation to the primary objects of critique, a description of a minimal-computing methodology might be coupled with the presentation of computationally derived evidence, an analysis of this evidence, and an auto-critique of the selected method. Minimal computing also presents a compelling answer to a core question of political economy attached to large-scale, big-data projects: who has access to these big computational and data resources and how do these institutions inform the conditions of possibility for research? In making computational methods available to humanities research-ers working in all types of situations—whether the student experimenting on an inexpensive laptop, adjunct and precariously employed scholars without long-term access to institutional research systems, or scholars and teachers working in underfunded colleges and universities—minimal computing and minimal methods might level the playing field of digital humanities research. Yet it is also the case that many of the most compelling applications and find-ings of computationally intensive methods require large datasets. These big-data algorithms, as discussed in the fourth chapter, derive their power from the existence of either many repetitions of data with similar or nearly similar context or a widely diverse mapping of whatever representation space is the subject of analysis. Textual data sources, luckily, can be encoded with minimal storage and memory footprint relative to the requirements of other fields and, once encoded, these sources are highly compressible.

At present, one of best ways of sharing or publishing these workflows might be with the free and open-source Jupyter Notebook. Jupyter Notebooks are experimental, Web-based digital notebooks that locate code alongside its exe-cution. These notebooks are imagined as versions of the paper-based labora-tory notebook, as once used in the sciences, but they offer more than just a record or log of the design and execution of experiments; they contain the com-putational experiment itself. Inspired by the commercial interfaces and envi-ronments found in Mathworks MATLAB or Wolfram Research's Mathematica, Jupyter displays the code in line with the results of that code segment. While there is support for several programming languages and platforms within the notebooks, Jupyter is written in Python and it has the strongest support for this programming language. Jupyter and other, similar tools remediate com-putational methods through the mixing and sharing of code and commentary alongside executed code. Such tools have the possibility of making quantita-tive experiments sharable and collaborative media. The Jupyter Notebook code block, or cell, in figure 2.1 demonstrates the combination of writing and execution of Python code. The code is contained within the boundaries of the gray box and the output from its execution is below, in white:

```
In [1]:   # local Natural Language Toolkit
          import nltk
          print("nltk version: ",nltk.__version__)

          # load scikit-learn
          import sklearn
          from sklearn.feature_extraction import text
          from sklearn import decomposition
          from sklearn import datasets
          print("sklearn version: ",sklearn.__version__)

          nltk version:  3.2.2
          sklearn version:  0.18.1
```

FIGURE 2.1   Jupyter code block

For the critical digital humanist, this tool importantly offers the ability to write comments within the body of the code (here specified with the lines that begin with the # symbol) and to annotate the code blocks with special free-form commentary blocks that explain decisions made by the researcher and limitations discovered within the tools, data, and algorithms. Notebooks are theory—not merely code as theory but theory as thoughtful engagement with the possible theoretical work and implications of the code itself.[11] Disciplinary norms—including contextual framing, theory, and self or auto-critique—need to accompany, supplement, and inform any computational criticism. Revealing as much of the code, data, and method as possible is essential to enable the ongoing interpretative disciplinary conversation. Compiling these together in a single object, one that can be exported, shared, examined, and executed by others, produces a dynamic type of theorization that is modular yet tightly bound up with its object.

The display of code, especially the simplified syntax of high-level scripting languages such as Python, goes some way toward removing the black-box effect of using embedded Web-based tools, closed-source applications, or obfuscated workflows.[12] But while there is greater transparency in what happens when viewing the code, as the above Jupyter cell demonstrates, these modern programming languages are highly modularized and abstracted and thus give the impression of greater clarity than might actually exist. In the above example, two major libraries for text and data mining, the Natural Language Toolkit and Scikit Learn, each containing thousands of lines of code and many calls to load other libraries and modules, are loaded and made available for performing data transformations—all without the programmer or user of the Jupyter

Notebook having an understanding of the whole. There are many important details—including software versions, parameters, and algorithms—that are nested and buried in other loadable modules and functions. An unintended side effect of the "transparent" boxes of displayed code might, in fact, be the obscuring of those buried and embedded elements of computation and the possibilities of critical inquiry into these logics.

The move toward methodological "openness," the standardization and sharing of primary archives and the sharing of copyleft or open-source code, is crucially important for a critical digital humanities. Yet such openness alone cannot ward off theoretical and cultural questions directed at various levels of computation and computational discourse. Stephen Ramsay has argued that programming and algorithmic readings of text can be thought of as a "critical reading strategy."[13] While computational tools can assist in producing new information about text that can be used for critical ends, they are not critical tools on their own. Algorithmic manipulations of text—deformations, distillations, macroanalytical approaches—none of these is free from the existing critical apparatus as found within the humanities. While software environments such as Jupyter enable greater critical engagement with tools and data by joining together code authoring, execution, display, and commentary, the framing device of the notebook makes apparent the limitations of computation. This is to say, digital humanists need to apply both emergent theories and already existing critical reading strategies to the entire computational processes, the entire workflow, by which algorithms might be said to read or otherwise generate their own reading of the text.

There Is No Such Thing as the "Unsupervised"

Franco Moretti's initial work in distant reading was not exactly computational—his founding of the Stanford Literary Lab would later produce a space in which he made what was previously only a set of implicit quantitative methods into an explicit research program—but it has provided the foundations for examining the stakes of the digital intervention being proposed by critics like Stephen Best and Sharon Marcus. Like Heather Love, Moretti has, for some time now, articulated his frustration with close reading. Unlike those critics exhausted with suspicious close reading because these moves have been appropriated by those with different political agendas than the authors of critique (Latour), or because criticism encourages forms of exposure that reinforce the critic's sense of knowing more than the object studied (Sedgwick), or even because critique has just become rote and boring (Felski), Moretti's frustration originates within the limitations of the narrow scope of close reading that complicates his ability to criticize larger forces and systems.[14] Calling the slow, careful, close reading of an individual text a "theological exercise," he accuses literary critics of giving too much attention to a small set of mostly canonical texts. Moretti wants his proposed practice of *distant reading* to enable an understanding of "the system in its entirety."[15] In other words, it is precisely the failure of abstraction foreclosed on by the specificity of the singular close reading that motivates Moretti's desire for a distanced position capable of producing a critique of the entire literary system.

When he puts his distant reading theory into practice in *Graphs, Maps, Trees* (2005), Moretti presents an alternative approach to the digital yet still qualitative methodology imagined by Best and Marcus. What keeps Moretti's claims to systematicity "honest" in his earlier distant reading work that results from his quantitative but not necessarily computational analysis is the fact that his target is not something like a hard, empirically knowable reality, but rather the socially constructed fiction known as the market. Thus, Moretti is able to stake out a stronger position for quantitative research within the humanities: "Quantitative research provides a type of data which is ideally independent of interpretations, I said earlier, and that is of course also its limit: it provides *data*, not interpretation. . . . Quantitative data can tell us when Britain produced one new novel per month, or week, or day, or hour for that matter, but where the significant turning points line lie along the continuum—and why—is something that must be decided on a different basis."[16] Moretti's turn to the scientific quantitative from the humanistic qualitative takes as its presupposition some fundamental distrust of the act of interpretation. The interpretive act of reading, in his account, is too tied up with evidence collection. Literary critics have what social scientists would call a selection bias that always informs the practice of close reading. Moretti, like almost all computational humanists, seeks to address this problem through the separation of his scientific methodology with its accompanying data from the hermeneutic act of interpretation. The substitution of what close reading would call textual evidence with quantitative data—for Moretti, the length of book titles, the number of books within specified categories sold, the number of booksellers—enables his strong claim for a quantitative approach to literature. It is especially important to note that Moretti desires the possibility that one might take as a given not just the raw input data but also the algorithmically transformed output data provided by quantitative research.

But of course there is no such thing as contextless quantitative data. As David M. Berry reminds us, "digital data is also the result of the discrete way in which computers, and digital technology in general, translate the analogue continuous phenomenal world into internal symbolic representational structures."[17] The analog to digital conversion involves a transformation or translation into discrete values. That process involves selections and numerous choices—for example, the sampling rates found in digital audio encoding—as well as potential decontextualizations and recontextualizations. Even in so-called "born digital" data, there are numerous points at which we see the intrusion of subjectivity. Data are imagined, collected, and then typically segmented. Within digital literary studies, texts are usually segmented into some unit prior to algorithmic transformation: period, genre, author, text, chapter, paragraph, sentence, or some arbitrary machine-produced container of words, for example, the ten-thousand-word segments that are popular with computational humanists. The concept of raw data, as Lisa Gitelman and Virginia Jackson have recently argued, is a bit of a misnomer, an oxymoron as they point out in the title of their jointly edited volume.[18] We should doubt any attempt to claim objectivity based on the notion of bypassed subjectivity because human subjectivity lurks within all data. This is because data do not merely exist in the world, but are abstractions imagined and generated by humans. Not only that, but there always remain some criteria informing the selection of any quantity of data. This act of selection, the drawing of boundaries that names certain objects a data set introduces the taint of the human and subjectivity into supposedly raw, untouched data.

Data cannot ever be said to be computed, distilled, and analyzed free of subjective intent—from the selection of data types and structures to schemas and models, situated subjectivity haunts computation. Best and Marcus do not elaborate on the specific digital technologies that they believe will lead to objectivity and they do not differentiate between computer-aided and supposedly completely automated approaches. Even if data were free of subjectivity, the approaches that have been presented as completely automated, unsupervised, and human-free turn out to be even more tainted by subjectivity than the original data-selection process. Machine learning, the name given to a set of algorithms that enable many computer-aided text-mining applications, provides us with an ideal test case for examining the possibility of objective readings of text. Machine learning is a branch of artificial intelligence that builds on and can supplement earlier rule-based or expert systems that provide explicit criteria for the classification of new input data. These techniques uniquely have the ability to address an incredibly large amount of data with various degrees of input from a researcher. They have been used to transform approaches in fields as diverse as economics and cognitive neuroscience. The learning aspect of machine learning suggests the continual repetition of an automated task that can reflexively integrate the results of prior tasks with those encountered in the present. Each repetition, ideally, improves the accuracy with which the algorithm performs the task—this is what is considered "learning."[19]

There are two kinds of machine-learning algorithms: supervised and unsupervised. Supervised machine learning can categorize data—data, in the case of applying machine learning to literary studies, would be segmented units of text and descriptive metadata—into predefined, rather than discovered, categories with predetermined understandings of what constitutes these known categories. Supervised methods are frequently called computer-aided. A program or application using machine learning might, for example, make use of a list or dictionary of key terms that define clusters of words that can be used to index or categorize a collection of documents. Support Vector Machines (SVM) form a major class of supervised machine-learning algorithms, much like the k-Nearest Neighbor (kNN) algorithm examined in the fourth chapter of this book. What makes a supervised machine-learning algorithm supervised is the existence of either (a) a human-labeled, representative, and well-understood training dataset, (b) a set of rules for classification, or (c) reinforcement activity on the part of the researcher to correct mistakenly classified data. In this category of supervised machine learning, there are always two datasets. The human researcher must first chunk and parcel a set of input data—typically this might include measurements, counts, features, or other metadata—into a known and familiar dataset, the training dataset, in which labels are attached to each member object that define its membership within various categories—categories might include genres, periods, or genders. The algorithm then trains itself on the training dataset by learning the distinguishing features or attributes most strongly associated with each category, for example, the words or phrases more likely to occur in one genre than another. After this training phase, it extracts sets of features from these data and uses them to categorize the objects into the researcher-created categories. These features are then used on what is called the test dataset. The texts or measured and counted objects composing the test dataset should be similar to those within the training dataset. The algorithm then attempts to categorize the test dataset into the categories or labels provided by the researcher. There are a number of arguments addressing how one should determine the appropriate size and construction of the test and training datasets. Some users of supervised algorithms modify parameters, selected features, and variables by testing on every object in the training set through a process called "leave-one-out cross-validation" that can produce a highly accurate model of known samples.

If the use of the term *supervised* by computer and information scientists suggests the presence of what Best and Marcus would call "critical subjectivity," then supervision must be understood as the unavoidable presence of the human subject within this area of machine learning. Supervision means that our interpretation of the results, the output from the algorithm, must take into account decisions made by the researcher to establish a set of initial conditions. These conditions might be the existence of labels that, while not providing explicit rules or criteria for categorization, mark each dataset, each text or grouping of words, as unambiguously a member of a particular category. Thus the results of any supervised algorithm contain traces of decisions made by the researcher, precisely the subjectivity this work might be imagined to lack. Unsupervised algorithms would presumably lack any such influencing traces of the researcher. Yet such an unsupervised state cannot be said to exist. The researcher must, as Gitelman and Jackson remind us, necessarily make a set of decisions in forming the original input dataset, even if it is completely unlabeled and considered disorganized. We must also choose an algorithm from the range of available options and then an implementation of this algorithm. Not only will different machine-learning algorithms give different results, but different implementations of the same algorithm may not agree. Reproducible results will depend on the precise replication of the software and hardware environment used. Reproducibility remains an ideal for all computational fields, but in practice it is very difficult to achieve, even more so when we are searching for small yet statistically significant bits of evidence for our claims.[20]

I invoke the above concerns to question some of the assumptions held by those promoting versions of machine reading and to also question the possibility of formalized and fully automated reading.[21] This is to say, there cannot be an automated reading of a text that is free of the taint of subjectivity. Reading,

I would claim, is always situated. Best and Marcus were wrong to imagine and hope for a computational analysis free of subjectivity as digital humanists are wrong to insist on the separation of methodology and data from the act of interpretation.

On Models and Theory

An oft repeated charge against the use of computational approaches in the humanities is that the methods and data are polluted by the existence of major errors or mislabeling—consider, for example, a workflow using the year of printing of a digitized text rather than the date of first publication or including a dataset of genre-tagged texts that contain numerous misclassified texts or one that makes the common categorical error of flattening the distinction between biography and autobiography. Pointing to these errors, insisting on a perfect match between reality and the intersection between program and data, might improve the results or the accuracy of the method but according to Richard Jean So, the existence of these errors does not invalidate the statistical power of a researcher's model. On the contrary, So frames error and uncertainty as "a constitutive part of science" and urges critics of computational humanities work to redirect their criticism away from imprecise methods and data categorization errors toward abstractions of "aspects of an interesting phenomenon."[22] These abstracted aspects are models. They are a compressed, simplified, and formalized structure in which the researcher embeds his or her assumptions about the way in which their object of study should work. These assumptions frequently take the form of stable or ideal conditions—think, for example, of the way in which weather is modeled. Models, as So reminds us, do not need to reflect the world as it is, but instead should be understood to offer up an interpretable and revisable conceptual object for the close examination of the gap between ideals and measured data.[23] Computational criticism, thus, should concern itself with the possibilities that occur in generating accounts of how a researcher's model of literary history, for example, works and how it fails—in other words, producing an *ex post facto* explanation of variation found within the experiment. So produces an inversion of the cultural stereotype of the stubborn and pedantic scientist and the playful humanist by casting the users of computational tools as models of "generosity, curiosity, and openness" (672). Adopting a more scientific or at least a more social-scientific model of research, he claims, will bring about a liberation of the humanities.

It is apparent that the incorporation of quantitative research methods into the humanities requires some grappling with modeling, but the concept of the model itself is increasingly under attack—not by skeptical humanists but by big-data techno-futurists. In 2008, Chris Anderson, at the time editor of *Wired* magazine, argued that the changes wrought by data science were leading not to the transformation of the humanities into the social sciences (as in the figurations of big data offered by Viktor Mayer-Schönberger and Kenneth Cukier), but rather to the obsoleting of science itself. Frustrated with the deliberateness with which modeling takes place, data science has emerged with a data-driven version of something like the blogger dictum of publish first and revise later.[24] Data and correlationism, Anderson argues, have superseded modeling and brought about the end of theory. He argues that the application of machine-learning technologies to large-scale scientific and cultural datasets eliminates the problems with modeling: "Today companies like Google, which have grown up in an era of massively abundant data, don't have to settle for wrong models. Indeed, they don't have to settle for models at all." Models, in Anderson's account, are not the refined, neatly constructed, and alterable statistical models idealized by Richard Jean So but a much larger category of tools for thinking about the world. "Out with every theory of human behavior, from linguistics to sociology. Forget taxonomy, ontology, and psychology," the former editor of top-tier mainstream science journals *Nature* and *Science* argues in a wide-reaching rejection of both the models of empirical science and almost all theories.

It is the rejection of theory, specialization, and nuance that gives pause to many when assessing the big claims of quantitative analysis and the ideology of correlationism. Big data substitutes scale for complexity. The impressive results of machine learning require very large quantities of text—at such a scale that the particular becomes swallowed by the universal. This universalizing tendency can be found in Google's neural network models that require training on billions of words and millions of documents. Bernard Stiegler glosses one such big-data model, Google's universal translation system—a system that does not need any understanding of the local "target" or "source" language but only large datasets containing enough correctly spelled words—as effecting "a statistical and probabilistic *synchronization* that on average *eliminates diachronic variability*."[25] We can find another example in Anderson's account of Google's big-data approach to advertising. He argues that corporate entities such as Google can harness the power of big-data statistics without any understanding of culture, much as they have done with translation, to produce good results and quickly dominate existing markets. "Google," Anderson writes, "conquered the advertising world with nothing more than applied mathematics. It didn't pretend to know anything about the culture and conventions of advertising—it just assumed that better data, with better analytical tools, would win the day. And Google was right." Culture, of course, does matter and unregulated markets and unexamined assumptions have caused a broad range of problems such as the appearance of illegal advertisements for products that exclude potential customers based on identity categories, including race, as well as the spread of fake news.

"All Models are Wrong," Richard Jean So writes in the title of his defense of statistical modeling with a citation of statistician George E. P. Box's famous maxim.[26] So's idea of a model has a much narrower definition than the one provided by Anderson. So takes the statistical model as the only valid type of model or at least the representative type because it provides a framing context for the "nuanced analysis of the data" within the scope of the model that directs attention away from the gap between the model and the world toward the gaps within sample data that reside in the closed world of the model. He defends the use of statistical models in the humanities, although within the larger cultural discourse about technology, models are considered an unnecessary hindrance to the production of meaningful data. Anderson cites Google's research director Peter Norvig, who stated to a group of software developers that "All models are wrong, and increasingly you can succeed without them." So's definition of the model as a tiny statistical testing ground is too narrow; Anderson's broader definition of the model and modeling is correct, but his conclusion about the need for theory and contextual (cultural) understanding is wrong. In neither version of modeling do we find a place for the work of humanities: either for theory or for cultural critique. While Anderson understands that we bring to any computational analysis existing models in the form of preexisting theories, assumptions, and frameworks, he does not consider it worthwhile to engage with these ideas when computational methods can short-circuit the slow work of the dialectic between deductive and inductive reasoning.

Statistical models might not be accurate representations of the world, yet they make many things happen in in the world. Complex computational models enable the rapid trade of stocks and investments. They determine who gets a loan or health insurance and who is denied. Models determine sentencing—they increasingly inform decisions about who goes to prison and who is allowed to go free.[27] Statistical and hypothetical models contain within them another type of model—what we used to call ideology: prejudices, values, and received commonsense. Models might be wrong, but we increasingly cannot do without critically examining them. The optimism of the early years of big data was unchecked by any serious thought of algorithmic manipulation and the possibility that cultural and contextual differences might indeed complicate the free-market fantasy of effortlessly matching sellers and buyers. The methods of the humanities provide the tools by which we can best build and interrogate models—both statistical models and those conceptions of the world that make modeling possible.[28]

The Example of Topic Modeling

There are a number of widely used methods of digital reading making use of machine-learning algorithms that do not depend on either prelabeled data or the assistance of user-created or presupplied extratextual sources. Probabilistic topic modeling, or simply topic modeling, was one of the first computational methods to find some application in the humanities.[29] This method comes to the humanities from the information sciences; to what extent it might still belong to the latter is an open question. Topic models are a way to organize a large and unlabeled collection of documents into computer-generated "thematic" categories. Rather than supply a list of hierarchical keywords to group documents, these algorithms "discover" shared topics from textual features that are used to fit documents into the discovered categories. The "document" unit in a typical application of topic modeling might be a complete text, a fragment of a text, or a standard chunk of a collection of texts. A topic model, like the collocation algorithm introduced in the previous chapter, produces groupings of terms that appear close together in the input set of documents. For some scholars, the words that make up a topic are correlated with possible themes within a collection of documents while for others they serve only as organizational clusters for identifying similar documents.[30]

The method by which one extracts textual features from source documents for this application are quite similar to those used in many other text-mining approaches. The features are essentially tables of word or phrase frequency or occurrence counts. The most frequently repeated terms might have some interpretive value on their own, for example, in the case of Martha Griffith

Browne's fictional *Autobiography of a Female Slave* (1857) the CountVectorizer function in Scikit-learn returns the following term occurrence counts in sorted, descending order:

man 226
negro 196
people 186
great 169
men 162
country 144
slave 144
rev 137
say 135
american 134

In most cases, a complete table with a much larger set of features or vocabulary, with single appearances of uncommon words, is used in the modeling of texts. In some applications of text mining, selected and tabulated features might include an almost unlimited number of textual objects, including punctuation, ordinal numbers, Roman or Arabic numbers, and units of money or time. While rather simple, this so-called "bag of words" method of counting occurrences of words within a document has been used with some success in activities as wide ranging as genre or period classification and authorship attribution.

The term *topic model* covers the use of several algorithms that use variations of what are called term-frequency : inverse document frequency ratios (TF-IDF) to construct models of the supplied documents. Two of the most popular algorithms for extracting a list of topics are Latent Dirichlet Allocation (LDA) and Non-negative Matrix Factorization (NMF).[31] Different algorithms will produce different results. The following word list forms the first single-word or term topic for a fifty-feature NMF model of the entire DocSouth North American Slave Narrative archive using the implementation of NMF found in Scikit-learn:

Topic #0:
people, work, time, way, make, great, come, place, came, say, slavery, home, day, know, went, life, new, long, little, good, church, thought, men, god, free, country, colored, house, left, children, called, years, lord, man, white, took, told, state, soon, slaves, slave, shall, saw, said, old, night, negro, mother, master, away

The choice between competing and alternative algorithms is usually determined by the quality, in terms of interpretability, of the model's output or the overall efficiency, which is mostly measured in terms of total runtime and the use of limited hardware resources such as memory. Using the same preprocessed input dataset, the Scikit-learn implementation of LDA (code displayed in Figure 2.2) produces the following first single-term topic:

Topic #0:
told, colored, race, asked, city, right, think, negro, south, states, land, tell, best, thing, things, wife, money, mind, morning, friend, world, far, kind, state, received, free, large, general, seen, hand, young, black, sent, mother, heart, felt, lord, poor, slaves, present, meeting, school, slavery, church, john, freedom, power, brother, slave, woman

If these terms form a more interpretable or coherent topic, then one might prefer the use of the LDA algorithm over NMF. After examining the single-word

```
# topics to model
num_topics = 20

# features to extract
num_features = 50

print('reading files and loading into vectorizer')
print('generating',num_topics,'topics with',num_features,'features')

# for LDA (Just TF)
lda_vectorizer = text.CountVectorizer(max_df=0.95, min_df=2,
                        max_features=num_features,
                        lowercase='true',
                        ngram_range=(2,4),
                        strip_accents='unicode',
                        stop_words='english')

lda_vectorizer.decode_error='replace'
lda_tf = lda_vectorizer.fit_transform(topic_model_source)

# fit to model
lda_model = decomposition.LatentDirichletAllocation(n_topics=num_topics, max_iter=5,
                        learning_method='online',
                        learning_offset=50.,
                        batch_size=128,
                        max_doc_update_iter=100,
                        random_state=None)
lda_model.fit(lda_tf)

print("LDA Model:")
feature_names = lda_vectorizer.get_feature_names()
for topic_idx, topic in enumerate(lda_model.components_):
    print("Topic #%d:" % topic_idx)
    print(", ".join([feature_names[i] for i in topic.argsort()[:-num_features - 1:-1]]))
    print()
```

FIGURE 2.2 Python code to generate LDA topic model using Scikit-learn

model, one might decide to use multiple words to locate possible topics, the multiple term or token units popularly called "n-grams." The following list of n-grams was produced by the NMF model, our first algorithm, from the same input dataset:

Topic #0:
great deal, colored people, young man, years age, years ago, years old, white people, short time, colored man, baptist church, young men, old man, men women, long time, father mother, thousand dollars, jesus christ, day night, white man, took place, new york, episcopal church, united states, methodist episcopal, read write, methodist episcopal church, good deal, colored men, women children, large number, run away, wife children, black man, white men, old master, north carolina, john brown, negro race, man named, running away, free man, frederick douglass, south carolina, southern states, new england, new orleans, free states, coloured people, slave states, fugitive slave

The n-gram model, it seems fair to say, provides greater possibilities for interpretation than the single-term model: words that appeared isolated in that model are now attached to others, providing some additional context, for example "years" appears as both a marker of historical time and the age of individuals. Some very common stopwords have been removed, which leads to the common appearance of "read" and "write" next to each other.[32]

But even these unsupervised implementations of machine-learning algorithms are subject to some of the critiques outlined above. For example, all machine-learning implementations, both supervised and unsupervised, that are capable of performing text mining need to make some conversion and initial reduction of the string of characters that a text or document comprises. And if a text has been digitized from a print edition, then one has to select the digital edition. The machine-learning package may attempt to convert the text from one encoding to another, for example, from the simple ASCII encoding to the more modern Unicode standard known as UTF-8 or vice versa. In the process, accents, special characters, and other textual features may be removed or translated to equivalent marks. Characters appearing identical on the screen might be encoded with different values. The workflow, or automated set of procedures, might perform what linguists refer to as lemmatization on the string of words, which is to say, the trimming of each word into its smallest meaningful components, as well as remove plurals, capitalization, punctuation, and tense affixes (see figure 2.3). For most humanists,

```
In [1]:   # Display the count and list of stopwords in the NLTK English
          # language stopword list
          from nltk.corpus import stopwords
          stopwords = stopwords.words('english')
          print("total stopwords:",len(stopwords))
          print(stopwords)

total stopwords: 127
['i', 'me', 'my', 'myself', 'we', 'our', 'ours', 'ourselves', 'you', 'your', 'yours', 'yourse
lf', 'yourselves', 'he', 'him', 'his', 'himself', 'she', 'her', 'hers', 'herself', 'it', 'it
s', 'itself', 'they', 'them', 'their', 'theirs', 'themselves', 'what', 'which', 'who', 'who
m', 'this', 'that', 'these', 'those', 'am', 'is', 'are', 'was', 'were', 'be', 'been', 'bein
g', 'have', 'has', 'had', 'having', 'do', 'does', 'did', 'doing', 'a', 'an', 'the', 'and', 'b
ut', 'if', 'or', 'because', 'as', 'until', 'while', 'of', 'at', 'by', 'for', 'with', 'about',
'against', 'between', 'into', 'through', 'during', 'before', 'after', 'above', 'below', 'to',
'from', 'up', 'down', 'in', 'out', 'on', 'off', 'over', 'under', 'again', 'further', 'then',
'once', 'here', 'there', 'when', 'where', 'why', 'how', 'all', 'any', 'both', 'each', 'few',
'more', 'most', 'other', 'some', 'such', 'no', 'nor', 'not', 'only', 'own', 'same', 'so', 'th
an', 'too', 'very', 's', 't', 'can', 'will', 'just', 'don', 'should', 'now']
```

FIGURE 2.3   Default list of "stopwords" included with the Natural Language Toolkit

this process can produce large-scale information loss.[33] In addition, almost all machine-learning implementations used on text include what is called an exclusion list, or stopwords. Stopwords are terms that are considered to be lacking in semantic content. These words are removed before running the text through the algorithm because they are considered superfluous; they are "noise" that would make that task of document classification much more difficult. MALLET ("MAchine Learning for LanguagE Toolkit"), a popular and free topic-modeling package written in the Java programming language and implementing the LDA algorithm, contains a default stopword list of 524 English words.[34] While this set contains words like *you*, *no*, *but*, *and*, and *whatever*, it also contains terms of potential interest to the humanities researcher, like *associated*, *appreciate*, *sorry*, and *unfortunately*. And even the words from this previous list, take *whatever* as an example, might have important meanings and semantic value for some genres and periods. The Natural Language Toolkit (NLTK) provides 127 stopwords, far fewer than MALLET. Each methodological decision in preprocessing involves some aspect of interpretation. Any filtering, preprocessing, or reduction of data dimensionality involves interpretive decisions and influences all later interpretive acts. All this is to say that within humanistic approaches there are no words that do not signify—everything is signal and nothing is noise.

Matthew Jockers deploys MALLET for topic modeling in *Macroanalysis* in order to extract and interpret thematic content from a collection of nineteenth-century novels. Jockers's process is rather complicated—he describes the process by which he transforms a dataset of 3,346 novels into five hundred algorithmically produced topics before clustering and visualizes a selection of the most "interpretable" topics. Figure 2.4 reproduces the workflow described in the "Theme" chapter of *Macroanalysis*. In Jockers's description of his workflow, the words or "tokens" that make up the input and output of the MALLET topic-modeling transformation are nouns that are not automatically tagged as a "named entity" by the Stanford Named Entity Recognition (NER), not popular common names, and not otherwise found within his custom stopword dictionary of 5,631 words.[35] These remaining nouns, according to Jockers, contain the material needed to extract a "pristine thematic signal" (131). Each step within this workflow contains important interpretive choices that shape individual outputs and frame the resulting topic data—from his selection of the MALLET variable that instructs the application to produce five hundred topics to his choice to use the Stanford Named Entity Recognition package

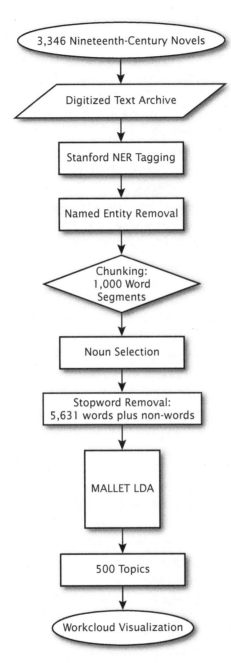

FIGURE 2.4 Matthew Jockers's workflow
from the "Theme" chapter of *Macroanalysis*

and all the historically contingent assumptions about language and meaning embedded within this tool. The example of Jockers's workflow demonstrates the degree to which there is no real notion of pristine data within the humanities—all data are imagined, collected, shaped, and marked even before they are transformed through the application of any algorithmic operation.

As many computational critics and digital humanists have argued, computer-aided reading methods such as topic modeling are just the beginning.[36] Interpretive activities, many argue, take over once the distilled and computed results have been generated. Unfortunately, the division between interpretation and method makes it possible to neglect to interrogate what deconstruction has taught us to recognize as the pretext—the whole range of presuppositions for conducting the reading, including the set of initial conditions or states such as the selection of stopwords, a spelling and internationalization standard, codes, algorithms, and text-encoding schemes. Jacques Derrida has shown the way in which an "outwork" ["*hors d'œuvre*"] functions in Descartes and Hegel to preface the "main" philosophical text by stating methodological commitments.[37] For Derrida, the pretext of these outworks is that they are introductory, that they come before the text; rather, he argues, they are produced after the text and predetermined by the text (20).[38] Likewise, in digital criticism, the task of interpretation cannot be framed as isolated from methodological decision making and all the algorithmic and computational presuppositions. In a recent article examining the history of literary criticism through machine learning and topic modeling, Andrew Goldstone and Ted Underwood attempt a rigorous theorization of the digital methods they deploy. They applied the MALLET topic modeling application described above to a digitized archive of academic journals dedicated to the field of literary studies. They deployed these techniques in order to answer the question of when "criticism" and "critique" came to dominate literary studies. Goldstone and Underwood's project evinces what might come to be recognized as an important turning point in the application of computer reading techniques to literary studies: they bring a sharp and critical account of these tools while using them to produce readings and counter-narratives of their own field formation. Yet there are still some unquestioned assumptions that persist in their methodology.[39]

When Goldstone and Underwood search through their archive of journal articles for the term *criticism*, they depend on an understanding that articles using what they term "*critic*-words" (words beginning with the root-word *critic*) are doing the work of criticism and those that do not are not "critical." Perhaps recognizing this would not alter the story told by their model, as they claim that the model only adds nuance to an already familiar account of the "emergence and subsequent naturalization of the discourse of criticism over the whole course of the twentieth century" (370). But a nuanced reading of the qualitative difference between critical practices and the specific language of criticism that self-referentially invokes *critic*-words is foreclosed by the rejection of reading practices resulting from theoretically informed close reading. There is a risk of creating categorical errors through a reliance on the self-evident stability of these categories.

Structuralism and Systemic Criticism

Heather Love's turn to the social sciences and Goldstone and Underwood's use of topic modeling are both part of a larger movement that advertently or inadvertently functions to reposition literary study as a science. Goldstone and Underwood explicitly place their work in "the recent tendency for literary studies to develop stronger connections to social science" (379). This movement tends toward sharing the desire to answer to Best and Marcus's call for "objectivity, validity, truth" in literary criticism. There are, to be sure, dissenting voices within the digital humanities; while arguing that all criticism is algorithmic, Stephen Ramsay suggests that, rather than longing for a scientific criticism, "we would do better to recognize that a scientific literary criticism would cease to be criticism" (15). Yet all these different approaches can be understood to be part of a retrograde movement that nostalgically seeks to return literary criticism to the structuralist era, to a moment characterized by belief in systems, structure, and the transparency of language. The Stanford Literary Lab's quantitative formalism is as indebted to structuralist linguists as it is to Russian formalism, and Ted Underwood has produced for himself a genealogy that originates in social-scientific methods and neatly bypasses the critique of these methods while disarticulating distant reading from the digital humanities.[40] It was well before our present concern with retheorizing the surface of the text, prior even to the advent of "symptomatic reading," that those working within literary studies dreamed of the possibilities of a scientific criticism. Northrop Frye's *Anatomy of Criticism* (1957) serves as one such early work. Frye made the polemical case for a systematic and scientific criticism derived from an inductive reading of literature that could encompass all of literature. He outlines the expansive scope of his approach by creating a theory of criticism, explicitly modeled after Aristotle, "whose principles apply to the whole of literature and account for every valid type of critical procedure."[41] This approach would work, he argues, because, like a scientific investigator, he assumes the existence of an order of nature, an order of words that lies behind the enterprise known as literature and exists as a coherent whole. Discovering the laws governing this order becomes the task of the critic. This understanding enables Frye to read widely across numerous literatures, to extract major modes and archetypes, and to produce a categorization of all these into a single organizing schema. Individual texts are then brought, either by Frye or a future critic, into the law of the schema and used to establish minor variations on a theme. This is what Frye believes makes his system scientific: each revision made by critics and scholars builds progressively on the entire body of prior humanistic research. Above all, Frye's schema works in pursuit of what he sees as a set of unalterable structural principles that can guide future criticism and reading. It is a "genuine" mode of criticism—to be differentiated from the accretion of judgments made by literary taste makers—or what he calls "meaningless" criticism—that follows the research models provided by science and "progresses toward making the world of literature intelligible" (9).

Frye's *Anatomy* creates what he calls a "conceptual universe" in which all of literature can be plotted, located, and mapped. His schemata are ultimately less rigid than we might expect, and one particularly important feature of Frye's system is its open-endedness: he intended that categories beyond those major labels that have made his book famous—the mythic, generic, and archetypal—would come to improve and even obsolete his theory. Yet, as Geoffrey Hartman notes in an important critique, the mythic holds a central place in Frye's system. Hartman selects this category because he believes that myth occupies a blind spot in Frye's system. Like our present moment, the possibility of a scientific criticism was deployed as a surface against the concept of depth. This leads Hartman to call Frye's method a "flattening out" of literature in opposition to the "depth criticism and depth psychology" of their shared historical moment. Frye's *Anatomy* is ultimately spatial. The *Anatomy* charts and maps the literary terrain and, in so doing, it drops what Hartman believes to be an important dimension: time. Claiming that "literature unfolds in time rather than quasi-simultaneously in space," Hartman criticizes Frye's understanding of temporality and literary history.[42] The system evades the question of historical development by treating all literature as essentially co-occurring and by finding little use for concepts like tradition, influence, and inheritance. These characteristics lead to Hartman's greatest concern. He worries that such "archetypal analysis can degenerate into an abstract thematics where the living pressure of mediations is lost and all connections are skeletonized" (30–31). Without the literary-historical network, the system that takes its place finds a series of dead-end nodal points.

But this network is precisely what myth requires and what it reworks. There are no pure forms of myth in Frye's system, only multiple appearances of historically situated myths. Hartman writes, "a writer does not confront a pure pattern, archetype, or convention, but a corpus of tales or principles that are far from harmonized" (37). Hartman was right about the disappearance of history from Frye's system as a cause for concern. History is, after all, one key to humanistic inquiry. Without the nuanced understanding of the ways in which ideas and representation unfold throughout time, literary critics would be the social scientists that Frye seeks to distance himself from. Thus, Frye explicitly rejects the sociological reading advocated by critics like Heather Love and the work of contemporary digital humanists like Goldstone and Underwood: "I understand that there is a Ph.D. thesis somewhere which displays a list of Hardy's novels in the order of the percentages of gloom they contain, but one does not feel that that sort of procedure should be encouraged. The critic may want to know something of the social sciences, but there can be no such thing as, for instance, a sociological 'approach' to literature" (19). In this fascinating passage, Frye explains that he would reject what is a common enough computational task for the present, the creation of a "gloom" topic with topic modeling tools and the categorizing and ranking of novels containing this topic, not because the approach categorizes and counts units of language, but because he believes this project is dedicated to the extraction of not literary but sociological values.

In 1989 Northrop Frye was invited to give a lecture to the first joint annual meeting of the Association for Computer and the Humanities and Association for Literary and Linguistic Computing at the University of Toronto. This annual conference would eventually become the Digital Humanities conference sponsored by the Alliance of Digital Humanities Organizations. In Frye's talk, "Literary and Mechanical Models," he reflected on the history of literary criticism and speculates on how the new computer-assisted methods that were being discussed in the conference might have enabled him to have refined and extended the work of his *Anatomy of Criticism*. He explains to his computer-savvy audience how when he used *science* in the "Polemical Introduction" he intended the word as a placeholder for a schematic approach to the study of literature:

> I have never been impressed by the "hard" and "soft" metaphors applied to science, nor did I care two pins that the conception of science I invoked was as soft as a marshmallow. But such conceptions as "software programming" and "computer modelling" were as yet unknown, and if I were writing such an introduction today I should probably pay a good deal of attention to them and talk less about science. Ballads and folk tales are an obvious area for computer assistance, and an approach to literature through its recurring conventional units might be equally so. Again, I had always suspected that the basis for the prestige of judicial and evaluative criticism was social snobbery: for it, criticism was a gentlemanly, and therefore an unsystematic, occupation. But that was only an intuitive hunch, which the coming of computers has done much to clarify.[43]

Northrop Frye, at what would become the primal scene of the digital humanities, gives this revisionary account of his method to imaginatively place computers and the "word-crunching" (8) computational methods at the founding center of his structuralist project.

What seems most interesting about the many contemporary digital humanities projects when compared with prior forms of scientific criticism is the deep focus on history. Indeed, these projects seem to have incorporated critiques such as the one Hartman makes of Frye and make the temporal dimension central to their inquiry. Very large archives such as HathiTrust and Google's "Google Books" enable heretofore impossible readings across the *longue durée* of literary history. Tools like the "Ngram Viewer" make the historical tracking of word or phrase genealogies through almost all of print history a trivial task. Thus, these projects could be understood as answering Hartman's main complaint about the systematic and scientific approach to literature. And yet I want to argue that the hermeneutical critique of what Hartman calls the "sweet science" remains helpful advice to the would-be scientific literary critic.

Disturbing Criticism?

Frye's archetypal system shares much with structuralist criticism of the 1960s and 1970s. Both approaches seek to organize all of literature into well-defined categories and take as a founding assumption the existence of an ordered world that could be illuminated through progressive critique. Like Frye, the structuralists explicitly referred to their practices as a science. This was in part because structuralism came to the humanities from the social sciences, but also because of its status as a classificatory methodology. In his well-known 1967 essay "From Science to Literature," Roland Barthes describes the structuralist commitment to taxonomy: "Structuralism, by virtue of its method, pays special attention to classifications, orders, arrangements; its essential object is taxonomy, or the distributive model inevitably established by any human work, institution, or book, for there is no culture without classification; now discourse, or ensemble of words superior to the sentence, has its forms of organization; it too is a classification, and a signifying one."[44] For many, structuralism was essentially a formalism. Like Frye's system, it erased history and, like the new historicism that would eventually follow structuralism, it operated synchronically rather than diachronically. It formed schemata based on the presupposition of a closed world of meaning that enabled the taxonomization of texts and the components of a text. The forms or categories, however, were not necessarily considered objective, and arguments over selection and categorization prevented the production of any truly definitive readings.[45] It understood itself as an improvement upon what has become known as the New Criticism primarily through the introduction of Ferdinand de Saussure's division between *langue* and *parole*. Understanding each individual textual object, the closed world of the poem as theorized by the New Criticism, as an individual instance of enunciation, what Saussure called *parole*, and its object of criticism as the system, the *langue*, which produces the grounds of possibility for the individual poem, structuralists desired a larger object of critique and common language to be used by a community of scholars. They realized that certain formalist methods that depended on close reading would not, to use one of today's popular terms within computational fields, "scale."

Barthes's turn from structuralist to poststructuralist hinges on his discovery that there is no "neutral state of language" that would allow literary criticism to become a scientific enterprise; structuralism cannot "call into the question the very language by which it knows language" (7). Contra the wish of the structuralists and New Critics, there were no closed worlds and no "common language." Barthes argues that the descriptive language of scientific discourse is not a metalanguage, a "superior code," but merely one code coexisting and layered among many others. Deconstruction, the most prominent mode of poststructuralist thought, called into question the stability of the spatial features that enabled Frye's charts and maps by drawing attention to what could be thought of as the continental drift active underneath the surface. Deconstruction questioned the oppositional forms that enable structuralism to establish categories. In pushing aside this fundamental insight from deconstruction, as well as the various forms of political critique that remain linked with this project, the digital humanities work described in this chapter repeats the categorical errors of structuralism.[46]

While literary critics were still engaged in forms of critique influenced by Frye and the structuralists, Sigurd Burckhardt produced a strong critique of the mechanical tendencies found in these methodologies. Burckhardt's "Notes on the Theory of Intrinsic Interpretation" appeared as an appendix to his *Shakespearean Meanings* (1968). This essay sought to revitalize literary criticism primarily through the division of intellectual labor into two categories: explanation and interpretation. His own categorizations enable him to make an unusual defense of hermeneutics by arguing against the normative understanding of interpretation as the description of the way in which a work of literature "works." Interpretation is not the accounting for why a text follows certain mythic laws or archetypes but a mode of discovery that takes as its primary object the text itself. At the same time, if the surface reading and digital readings of the present reject the conception of "depth hermeneutics," so too does Burckhardt's theory. For what calls his reading practice into action is not the deeply buried symptom, the sense of deep meaning to be revealed by the critic, but something on the surface that troubles our ability to give a structuralist account of the text.

Burckhardt argues that insofar as it has a methodology capable of supporting a theory, science is intrinsic. By this Burckhardt means, like Northrop Frye, that science understands the universe as ordered and organized by a set of discoverable laws. Like the religious belief that science has made obsolete, the entire world postulated by empiricism is subject to intrinsic analysis. Everything must have a place and meaning. Interpretation, according to his account, "would mean the attempt to know the law of a poem *solely from the poem itself*, on the necessary assumptions of the infallibility of the poem. Explanation, on the other hand, would mean the attempt to demonstrate how parts of a poem obey an already known, established principle."[47]

Interpretation and explanation map onto, respectively, intrinsic and extrinsic analysis. Frye's conception of the "order of words" necessitates an intrinsic approach and this shares some assumptions with those of Burckhardt.

Burckhardt, however, places his emphasis on the hermeneutical act called into being by the intrinsic method. While the residual New Critical focus on poetry and the single poem draws Burckhardt toward the poem as his unit of interpretation, there is no reason why this procedure should be limited to a single poem, to poetry, or even to a single novel. Indeed it seems entirely likely that Burckhardt's hermeneutical approach is exactly what we need for the large archives studied with digital approaches. One does not have to necessarily follow Burckhardt in his belief that each textual object is a "unit" or world with knowable rules in order to understand the force of his critique of certain strains of structuralist thinking. What I mean to say is that Burckhardt's conception can revitalize the digital humanities-cum-structuralist reading practices that we find at the present moment.

Returning to Goldstone and Underwood, we might want to think about ways in which they invoke the concept of the hermeneutical circle as it relates to digital reading. They invoke a soft hermeneutics when they write "in the end we must always close the hermeneutic circle with human interpretation" (10). I agree with them that the digital humanities cannot function without "human interpretation," but I resist the division between interpretation and method that renders method totally free from interpretation. In their version of the circle, the human interpreter comes after; interpretation, according to their logic, proceeds from algorithmic output. They want to extend "human interpretation" over very large archives, over collections of documents and texts that would be too large for a human interpreter. Yet in an important way the circle remains incomplete. When Hans-Georg Gadamer produced a definition of the hermeneutic circle he made the point that the concept "is based on a polarity of familiarity and strangeness."[48] The poles in Gadamer's circle are less rigidly defined than allowed for by much work in the digital humanities and "strangeness" extends all the way through the project of criticism, not just to an examination of the results.

Yet there are ways to turn the major presupposition of digital reading techniques such as machine learning back against itself. Classification, whether machine or human derived, fits observed data or objects into distinct categories.[49] The important difference between human and machine classification, however, is what draws us to categorize data into categories and our doubt about this categorization. The algorithm assumes that all data will "fit." Within machine learning there are concepts to label the degree to which data fits into categories: we call any potential uncertainty within classification "confusion" or simply error. The outlier, that peculiar object not belonging to the domain of one law or another, might present some difficulty to categorize for the algorithm, but it is of high interest to the human interpreter because it represents a problem. Burckhardt draws our attention to the way in which when we are reading we encounter something that he calls a "stumbling block" (289) that becomes the occasion for analysis:

> What occurs, then, when I really do interpret? Something which in principle is very simple. I read a poem and the poem "speaks to me." At the same time, however, or perhaps only after several readings, I get the impression that I have not yet grasped its true significance. Something 'disturbs' me. What it is that will 'disturb' me is never predictable. It may be a 'discrepancy' (a contradiction, sometimes purely factual, which seems to reside in the poem itself); it may be an apparent whim of the poet or a seemingly inappropriate word; it may be configuration whose meaning is obscure; or it may be (as with Hölderlin's late hymns) that the coherence of the whole completely escapes me. Finally any conception of the poem which contradicts my own may also disturb me in this sense. (301)

Burckhardt's "stumbling block" functions much like the effect of the *punctum* in Roland Barthes's account of the photographic image. For Barthes, what disturbs the interpreter is the appearance of a "sting, speck, cut, little hole" within the field of the image, what he calls the *studium*.[50] The *punctum* produces the occasion for interpretation: "The photographer's *punctum* is that accident which pricks me (but also bruises me, is poignant to me)" (27). Burckhardt here faults the dominant contemporary theory during this time, structuralism, for not paying enough attention to those objects that do not fit within preexisting strategies. This critical science has pushed these difficult-to-categorize elements aside in favor of generalizations and categorizations.

To return to this chapter's titular question: can an algorithm be disturbed? In the case of computer-aided text-mining and machine-learning algorithms, the ever-present risk is that they cannot. Digital readings resist and reduce disturbance—it is only when they fail to be properly iterative that they might be said to be "disturbed." Algorithms, of all kinds, are recipes for success. They are a description, an ordering of operations, which can be iteratively executed to produce a "correct" result.[51] Algorithmic failure, as opposed to algorithmic success, might be the special province of humanists. It is in another essay in *Beyond Formalism* that Geoffrey Hartman describes interpretation as requiring either the location of a space in between the text or the opening of that space by the critic: "Interpretation is like a football game. You spot a 'hole' and you go through. But first you may have to induce that opening. The Rabbis used the technical word *patach*, 'he opened,' for interpretation" (255). For Hartman, literature is special because it has the capacity to sustain the hole. Interpretation exists within a space that might be thought of as between the "bits" of language. When we allow our algorithms to overly familiarize that which is fundamentally ambiguous, we risk turning our work, the project of literary criticism, into what Burckhardt would call explanation. This activity of explanation risks too quickly closing down the disturbing possibility of texts. In privileging explanation over interpretation, digital humanists might be tempted to exploit the cunning of empiricism to ideologically suppress interpretive moves and in the process marginalize a certain kind of questioning of the critical "pretext." Perhaps we can use machine learning and other computer-aided reading techniques to open holes by deploying the algorithm against itself, but ultimately interpretation is an interesting and compelling narrative of how one deals with being "pricked" by a text, by being disturbed.

Throughout this chapter I have argued that the present movement in criticism that seeks to reposition literary studies as a social science is resurrecting the project of structuralism. The computer-aided text-mining practice of the digital humanities provides us with an important case study through which we can examine the stakes of this swerve away from much of the contemporary critical discourse. This discourse remains, as Rita Felski shows us, quite suspicious.[52] But these suspicious interpretive practices have enabled a whole range of important political projects that have made visible what was once invisible and have moved what was once on the margins to the center. An entire generation of critics disturbed by absences and tightly constricted categories that reinforced ideological thinking about difference has rightfully questioned the self-assurance with which prior critics deployed what they conceived of as politically neutral methodologies. A criticism that, once again, seeks to authorize itself through an appeal to the social sciences cannot ignore the insights of these political projects, nor can it so easily push aside the deconstructive critique of the first literary science, structuralism.

CHAPTER 3

Digital Historicism
and the Historicity of Digital Texts

> Thus founded on the rupture between a past that is its object, and
> a present that is the place of its practice, history endlessly finds
> the present in its object and the past in its practice. Inhabited by
> the uncanniness that it seeks, history imposes its law upon the
> faraway places that it conquers when it fosters the illusion that it
> is bringing them back to life.
>
> —Michel de Certeau, *The Writing of History*

How do we engage with historical texts in a responsible fashion? Do we recognize them as offering just a slightly different form of a familiar narrative that can speak to our concerns in the present moment? Do we read them alongside other contemporaneous documents as evidence of widely circulating dominant ideologies? Do we search these strange historical objects for similarities and differences between the past and present? Or do we understand these texts and their historical context as radically other than the present? These questions have long troubled literary scholars. But what changes in our treatment of the past and the historical archive have been wrought by the digital revolution? Has the combination of sophisticated computational methods with the capacity to dig deeply and locate connections and similarities with big (historical) data altered the previous assumptions and positions of literary scholars? The digital humanities and the digital turn within literary studies has appeared simultaneously with calls for a posthistoricism and other, related forms of postcritique discussed in the previous chapters, yet it seems likely that computational methods might have much to contribute to historically oriented research questions. This chapter takes up several important theoretical problems and complexities introduced by text mining and datafication into historical research in order to think about the problems and promises of a digital historicism. The chapter concludes by examining the methods and practice of extracting and analyzing emotional or affective content in texts through what is called sentiment mining. Functioning as a case study, sentiment mining demonstrates the need for quantitative and computational literary scholars to give greater attention to the historical dimensions of both text and affect.

Digital archives and digital methods, of course, make it possible for humanities researchers to produce much larger collections of objects and documents and to launch different kinds of inquiries than those made by scholars in the past. This does not mean, however, that scholars are asking better questions or that their queries are capable of returning better answers or that newer, larger archives have superseded past collections. Yet these new capabilities and abilities have renewed or reactivated long-held imaginings and desires on the part of many for a "complete history," for an archive without gaps and without any loss. Because of the large and rapid increase in size of these queries and objects, digital projects have the worrisome ability to draw attention away from certain questions by fetishizing the archive and imagining its objects as mere repositories of the past. Archival projects making use of sophisticated computational systems for the collection, interpretation, and dissemination or display of historical objects and data—and even those projects organized by those who have strategically limited their claims as a form of auto-critique— risk participating in what might be called the fantasy of total history through the use of tools and methods that conceive of archives as a closed and complete source of knowledge, that operate on and can only address objects residing in the digital archive.

This particular orientation to the past is not just a risk of interpretive humanistic projects in literary studies. When historians reflect on the changes to their discipline introduced by contemporary methods and practices found within the digital humanities, they tend to notice, and in some cases reinforce, the ways in which these discussions of the digital foreground those tools that have been of greatest use to literary critics. Stephen Robertson argues that "in almost all cases, what is labeled digital humanities in those critiques is in fact digital literary studies, effectively casting the big tent as housing only a single discipline."[1] In the 2004 *Companion to Digital Humanities* volume that gave the digital humanities its name, William G. Thomas explains the use of computation and digital methods in the field of history. Thomas argues that "the goal for historians working in the new digital medium needs to be to make the computer technology transparent and to allow the reader to focus his or her whole attention on the 'world' that the historian has opened up for investigation, interpretation, inquiry and analysis."[2] Thomas's explicit desire to make technology transparent is connected with the primary use of computational systems, at the time he is writing, to display and distribute digitized artifacts. In calling the created or curated digital collection a "world," Thomas gestures to his understanding of interpretation as directed toward the collection, not the subjective act of collecting. Questions about the way in which computational systems might produce limiting conditions in their use function of enabling this "worlding" of the archive are foreclosed by the goal of making computation itself transparent. Eight years after Thomas's account of the digital history, Tom Scheinfeldt, a historian of science, argues for a similar utilitarian understanding of computation. For Scheinfeldt, the entrance of computation into history marks a "sunset for ideology" and a "sunrise for methodology," by which he means a shift in focus from theoretical and critical concerns, those concerns that he glosses and groups with a concern with ideology, back to the concerns with "methodological refinement and disciplinary consolidation" that were present in late-nineteenth- and early-twentieth-century scholarship: "The new technology of the Internet has shifted the work of a rapidly growing number of scholars away from thinking big thoughts to forging new tools, methods, materials, techniques, and modes or work that will enable us to harness the still unwieldy, but obviously game-changing, information technologies now sitting on our desktops and in our pockets."[3]

To some degree, the discipline of history is different from those humanities and humanities-adjacent disciplines undergoing a transformation as a result of the field's position between the social sciences and the humanities. History has previously undergone a quantitative turn and thus addressed many of the questions that are now becoming pressing methodological and theoretical issues in humanities fields. There are, however, many similarities between the ways in which digital historians and digital humanists discuss the incorporation of technology and specifically computational methods into their practice. There are even those within history departments who believe in archival completeness, a total history to come that will be revealed by digitization and computational techniques. In a conversation with a group of historians titled "The Promise of Digital History" and published in the *Journal of American History*, Daniel J. Cohen describes the "prospecting and analysis that a future historian will be able to do with digital archives . . . once more of the past is digitized." He then makes the startling claim that "within the next decade we will be able to generate a very accurate and complete database of every single use of the Bible in the Victorian era. Scholars will be able to take a comprehensive look at the use of the Book of Job or of the Old versus the New Testament across the entirety of Victorian publications."[4] Cohen, like Thomas and Scheinfeldt, takes an uncritical position about the ways in which digital technologies alter the past in their frame of the database or archive.[5]

Even if there was some way to produce "a very accurate and complete" digital archive of any past moment, it would still be functionally incomplete. Such an archive would be unable to provide the materials by which one might answer many of the important critical questions about the past asked by humanists.[6] At the same time, there are numerous questions about how digital archives and digital methods participate or add new dimensions to what Scheinfeldt casts as the past emphasis of the "framing knowledge in a theoretical or ideological construct" (124) within a historical field. Laura C. Mandell's notion of "countlessness," a name for the representation of those objects occupying a considerable percentage of big data, helps us understand how digital archives not only reproduce but intensify the historical systematic devaluing of certain types of texts. "[I]n the absolute biggest datasets," Mandell argues, "the number of women is dwarfed in comparison to every man who ever wrote and becomes a small if not insignificant subset of the data stream."[7] This is true not only because of past sexism that prevented women from becoming writers and the centuries of editorial and publication practices that produced multiple editions, printings, and anthologies of work by the same male authors, but also because of the numerous women writers who wrote privately in one form or another. The valuation of big humanities data, Mandell argues, "threatens to eradicate the history of women writers altogether" (521). This same claim can be made about texts written by other categories of writers, writers who we understand to be minor writers in absolute, countable terms within the digitized archive, but who are crucially important for recovering any sense of the past.

All historical research will be subject to some sort of archival difficulties— it is the nature of any historical record that the record will be incomplete. But some archives or potential archives present insurmountable problems to scholars. Saidiya Hartman examines one such archive. She argues that the archive of American slavery is an especially provisional archive, and accessing the everyday experience of those who lived under slavery is complicated by numerous factors. Her project, she argues, "requires excavations at the margins of monumental history in order that the ruins of the disremembered past be retrieved, turning to forms of knowledge and practice not generally considered legitimate objects of historical inquiry or appropriate or adequate sources for history making and attending to the cultivated silence, exclusions, relations of violence and domination that engender the official accounts." Nonetheless, Hartman continues and gathers her fragmentary accounts of past lives lived under the unimaginable and mostly unrepresented subjection and terror, acknowledging that she must work against the "constraints and silences imposed by the nature of the archive." These issues related to working through the incomplete and suspect archive, though, are not the only problem for the historically minded scholar, for present concerns always impress themselves on the scene of research. "A totalizing history," Hartman argues, "cannot be reconstructed from these interested, selective, and fragmentary accounts and with an acknowledgement of the interventionalist role of the interpreter, the equally interested labor of historical revision, and impossibility of reconstituting the past free from the disfigurements of present concerns."[8]

Computational methods might, however, also enable researchers to identify important gaps in the (digital) historical record. Lauren Klein argues that visualization tools and network analysis can be one method by which we can illuminate "archival silence," those missing records or unrecorded data that are the result of suppression or indifference. She takes up absences in the archive of American slavery invoked by Hartman through an investigative search for references to Sally Hemings in the correspondence of Thomas Jefferson and his circle. Rather than a close reading of archives directed toward to the recovery of the unrepresented, Klein asks us to "look to the pathways of connection between persons and among groups, the networks of communication in which these men and women engaged, and the distributed impact of the labor they performed."[9] Embedded textual references to Hemings and her family within the archive enables Klein to trace dependencies between Jefferson and the enslaved people in his household. Her approach takes the incompleteness of the archive as a given and uses visualization to call attention to the known absences. But what about those unknown absences? While not a large archive—Klein uses a total of fifty-eight letters—the methods used on these data privilege entities or people who "count," to use Mandell's formulation. Hemings and other enslaved people were not absent from the archive—absent, perhaps, as correspondents, but still counted by virtue of mentions within the content of the archive.

Historicism and Posthistoricism

Given the problems involved in the concept of countlessness raised by Mandell and the need to turn to those "legitimate" objects of historical research identified by Hartman, how should digital humanists address the constructedness of the history presented by archives and tools for digital humanities? For the past several decades, the answer to addressing archival inequality and issues of devaluation has been a deeper turn to history that expanded what was understood to constitute an archive. In the 1970s, critics, especially feminists, developed nuanced understandings of the conditions of historical print culture that recognize uneven access to printing technology and the public sphere. Later critics, deploying ideological and theoretical critiques, examined the making and remaking of literary canons and the historical legacies that have privileged and reproduced preferences for certain modes, genres, and author identity categories. To some degree, both responses are forms of historicism. Historicism has a long history, beginning in the late nineteenth century, as an interpretive practice that seeks to produce varieties of connection, from determining conditions to suggestive links, between humanist objects of study and their historical context. In the United States, prior to the widespread institutionalization of literary studies in the midtwentieth century, a version of historicism was the dominant reading practice or methodology. This historical criticism read a fairly small selection of canonical literary works against the background of a historical narrative and a set of historical facts. The New Criticism that emerged after this moment promoted a mostly decontextualized reading practice; texts, mostly poems, were read closely, in isolation from supplementary biographical information related to the author and historical facts. Focusing on the words on the page, close reading did not allow information to flow across the margins of the page. This practice served to produce a distinction between the way scholars in the recently created English departments and those in history read historical texts. Jane Gallop argues that it was the close reading practice that was promoted by the New Criticism in English departments that "was the very thing that made us a discipline, that transformed us from cultured gentleman into a profession."[10] The New Criticism's ahistorical close reading practice, however, tended to preserve the existing focus on a small set of well-known authors who were, almost as a rule, white and male.

Following theoretical interventions of the 1970s that were made by feminists, Marxists, psychoanalytic critics, and poststructuralists, the types of textual objects were destabilized and expanded. Most of these critical movements preserved close reading, but some desired a renewed contact with the past, with history. Frederic Jameson's injunction in *The Political Unconscious* to "always historicize!" was rooted in his insistence that "the traditional issues of philosophical aesthetics: the nature and function of art, the specificity of poetic language and of the aesthetic experience, the theory of the beautiful, and so forth . . . themselves need to be radically historicized."[11] For others, a fuller account of the historical context, the cultural context, was necessary to understand the specificity of literature. Building Clifford Geertz's anthropological "thick description," these humanists invoked history not as background, but as another culturally produced object of critique. The "new historicist" methodology, as used within literary studies, emerged during the early 1980s as a posttheoretical version of the earlier "old" historicism.

As a crude gloss, the new historicism generally takes a pairing of a literary text with some nonliterary text circulating at the same point in time to make larger claims about this particular temporal slice of time and culture—this is why the method would later come to be known as cultural poetics. The new historicists argued for a synchronic understanding of history in which a singular determining cultural logic would inform a number of texts in different ways—from the emergent middle-class conduct book to the Victorian novel of manners. Stephen Greenblatt opens his *Shakespearean Negotiations*—the book that more than any other inaugurated what Greenblatt himself termed the new historicism—with "I began with the desire to speak with the dead," expressing his wish to make contact with something more "real" within the text and the past than the many layering and mediated readings produced by academic discourse.[12]

New historicist reading practices have been used in concert with other academic and political commitments to disarticulate present understandings of particular concepts and cultural formulations from those in the past. In the introduction to his edited essay collection *The New Historicism*, H. Aram

Veeser defines a set of key assumptions that he argues are shared by most practitioners of the new historicism:

1. that every expressive act is embedded in a network of material practices;
2. that every act of unmasking, critique, and opposition uses the tools
   it condemns and risks falling prey to the practice it exposes;
3. that literary and non-literary "texts" circulate inseparably;
4. that no discourse, imaginative or archival, gives access to unchang-
   ing truths nor expresses inalterable human nature;
5. finally, as emerges powerfully in this volume, that a critical method
   and a language adequate to describe culture under capitalism participate in the economy they describe.[13]

Veeser's enumeration of these assumptions are not definite and have been contested by those who call themselves new historicists, but together they provide
some sense of the dominant concerns held by those scholars seeking a renewed
connection with the past. The new historicism, at best, was a defamiliarizing
technique that attempted to evaluate the literary past on its own terms or
at least remove the accreting influence of successive critical reevaluations of
the past. As a methodology, it enabled scholars to call into question received
common sense and to continue the recovery work of earlier cultural critics.

The primary mechanism or methodological device by which new historicists
attempted to produce a connection between context and text was the anecdote. Anecdotes, or rather the anecdotal account, provided access to history
without resorting to the grand narratives or facts of the "old" historicists. Joel
Fineman defines the function of the anecdote in new historicist practices as
such:

> The anecdote, let us provisionally remark, as the narration of a singular
> event, is the literary form or genre that uniquely refers to the real. . . .
> [T]here is something about the anecdote that exceeds its literary status,
> and this excess is precisely that which gives the anecdote its pointed ref-
> erential access to the real; a summary, for example of some portion of a
> novel, however brief and pointed, is, again, not something anecdotal. These
> two features, therefore, taken together—i.e., first, that the anecdote has
> something literary about it, but second, that the anecdote, however liter-
> ary, is nevertheless directly pointed towards or rooted in the real—allows
> us to think of the anecdote, given its formal if not its actual brevity, as a
> historeme, i.e., as the smallest minimal unit of the historiographic fact.

And the question that the anecdote thus poses is how, compact of both literature and reference, the anecdote possesses its peculiar and eventful narrative force.[14]

Anecdotes are historicizing objects—a compressed store or minimal unit of information about the past that provides a shock of something outside the text to the hermeneutical scene of reading, the intrusion of history-as-the-real in Fineman's account. Yet anecdotes are not data, as the common caution in the sciences that reminds us to avoid an overreliance on a single report. Too often these single reports, these interesting anecdotes, were used to stand in for all of culture and in the process to help in imagining culture as consistent, contained, and self-evident to the critic from the knowing perch in the present.

Along with the rejection of symptomatic readings and ideological critique, a growing number of literary critics have called for a posthistoricism that would enable both more complex accounts of history and culture in the past and for a suspension of the linear, progressive temporality that underwrites familiar understandings of the unfolding of time and history.[15] The reasons for this particular turn away from historicism, both the new historicism and a broader historicism, are multiple. Some of these concerns with the place of historicism in literary studies are shared by those critics who have rejected the modes of reading that have been animated by the hermeneutics of suspicion. Arguing that "context stinks," Rita Felski rationalizes the use of Bruno Latour's actor-network-theory to revitalize literary criticism by pointing out that *"History is not a box*—that is to say, standard ways of thinking about historical contexts are unable to explain how works of art move across time. We need models of textual mobility and transhistorical attachment that refuse to be browbeaten by the sacrosanct status of period boundaries."[16] Felski seeks to release texts from the boxes established by historicists—more important, from those period boundaries that stand in for various commonplaces about the past and culture. In seeing texts as actors and not just repositories of determining ideologies, Felski can pose questions about how texts act in the world—specifically, how they affect readers in the present. Searching for a way to account for the "transtemporal liveliness of texts" that escape the conditions present at the publication of text, that "move across time" to touch readers in the present, Felski places central importance on the affected reader in the present. Her argument, in part, is a strategic response to questions about the value of studying literature by revaluing texts themselves rather than their contexts, but it is also a recognition that what she calls "slice of time" thinking has produced disconnected containers of the past that do not resemble dynamic, lived social attachments.

The interventions made possible by the use of the various computational methods described in this book could be made in service of a version of the desire that a newly formed academic collective, the "V21" group of Victorianists, has expressed, with their rallying cry and motto "strategic presentism."[17] The field of Victorian studies, at least within the United States, has been generally a historicist field with many of the major works of new historicism coming out of the study of the Victorian novel and the culture of the Victorian period. Strategic presentism takes its name from the "strategic essentialism" of Gayatri Spivak and acknowledges the limitations but necessity of the second term, essentialism for Spivak and presentism for the V21 Victorianists.

But even going forward in time, with the so-called born-digital text or electronic literature, critics might want to give some attention to marking and reading the historical import, the historicity of our present moment, within texts. What exactly this means might be rather hard to say.

The New Digital Historicism

It seems readily apparent, within the very wide scope of what constitutes the digital humanities at present, that there is a split emerging between the way in which the past and history are invoked and deployed in archival projects and the way in which they function in computational criticism, within text and data mining. Katherine Bode gestures to one possible explanation for this split in her account of the declining role of textual scholarship in the digital age. Bode argues that there has been a longstanding neglect of the tradition of textual scholarship and editing within digital literary history, a subset, to be sure, of digital literary criticism and the digital humanities. She claims that this neglect is the result of the prominence of certain computational methods that implicitly or explicitly draw on the legacies of the once dominant New Criticism. The New Criticism was centered on the practice of close reading, a topic discussed more fully in the first chapter, and famously trained critics and students to focus on the text itself, ignoring or devaluing extratextual sources of potential information about a text. Despite almost a century now of critique and rejections of major new critical presuppositions, Bode argues, literary scholars have, in the main, continued to treat literary works as enclosed texts and to assume that these texts are "single, stable, and self-evident entities."[18] Those using computational methods, as her argument goes, inherit these assumptions from the field at large. Bode's critique points out the way in which some digital humanists, particularly those deploying computational methodologies for text analysis, have started from potentially troubling assumptions about the status of the text that might have profound impacts for the arguments made by these scholars.

Much of the work that falls under the banner or "big tent" of the digital humanities has been thought of as constructing archives: digital projects that take advantage of the multimedia capacities of Web browsers, the dynamic nature of knowledge organization or digital ontologies, and large storage capacities to present and organize large numbers of digital and digitized objects that were previously difficult to access, index, and search. For Amy Earhart, digital humanities methods, specifically the pairing of the database and end-user-oriented display and presentation technologies, enable what she refers to as a new "era of the archive."[19] The version of the digital humanities that is of interest to Earhart, however, develops out of the field of textual criticism and thus her examination focuses on those context-thickening archival projects that use technology to store, archive, and present literary texts alongside other historical material. Digital environments, for her, are not a tool to produce something categorically different but an improved and richer experience of existing historicist practices—"a mechanism," she argues, "for refining the archive" (40). Drawing on Jerome McGann's *Radiant Textuality* (2001), Earhart offers an understanding of the digital (new) historicist impulse as directed mostly toward the collection of archives that would enable literary scholars—digital or otherwise—to examine these objects and texts in order to unpack and examine context.[20] Unlike the historians mentioned above, Earhart argues that digital humanists should not consider the enabling technologies used in constructing archival projects as transparent but rather constructive: "Scholars who engage in digital archive creation also refused to view the archive and the technology used to create it as naturalized or organic and remained self-reflexive about all aspects of the archive, from the materials selection, to metadata, and to interface design" (55). Earhart's concern with context, however, remains bound within the space or tradition of the archive itself, and thus she is unable to apply her otherwise theoretically astute account of historicist practices to *method* itself. Digital methods, the computational process that are the subject of this book, are themselves also subject to a historicist critique and the posthistoricist critique. While Earhart asserts that "the most enduring legacy of new historicism is digital literary studies' rejection of the innate meaning of both individual objects and the structures in which they function" (55), her application of this conceptual framework to method or approach falls flat.

At the same time, those deploying computational approaches to literary studies in the form of text and data mining, as I have argued in the previous chapters, tend toward reproducing earlier, structuralist approaches to texts and bring with them a ahistorical interpretive framing. This is due to a number of factors, including the nature of computational approaches, the ideological coupling of what are seen as "newer" up-to-date computational methods with the desire to connect to something meaningful in the present, and the result of importing these computational methods from other fields, mostly the empirical social sciences, with less of an investment in the historical dimensions of human culture. Computational linguists and others developing natural-language-processing techniques might care about the specificity of the languages studied, but for the most part they ignore the historicity of their source corpuses. The wealth of data generated in the present easily overwhelms the historical archive and thus textual sources like Wikipedia or collections of articles from the *New York Times* are typically used in the modeling and training of text-mining methods. The use of machine-learning algorithms in text categorization, to take one simple example, depends on a split between a "learning" archive that is labeled by researchers and an unorganized collection of "target" documents. Many of the approaches used within text mining also deploy secondary textual archives—dictionaries, thesauruses, and other forms of human-constructed schemata—that have tended to capture categories, topics, and semantic relations that are dominant in the present and may not be appropriate to historical target documents. I'll shortly be discussing the historical dimension of this type of data and the way it functions, intentional or not, as a historicizing object. When these computational digital humanists do consider the cultural or historical situatedness of the digital archive, it is typically through labeling their assembled set of texts in terms of genre, fiction almost exclusively, the nationality of the author, and the rough historical period in which the text was printed, frequently making using of broad century markers.

Of course, one of the major shifts in interpretive practices produced both by the new historicists and other challengers of the canonical situation of literature in the twentieth century was a radical leveling of the literary field.

Using the term *text* or *object*, for example, to describe all historical textual artifacts enabled these critics to reconfigure the relation between major and minor literature, between a literary text and those textual objects previously considered as lacking literary qualities. Using the previously privileged term *text* loosely also enabled scholars inspired by the work of Michel Foucault, Roland Barthes, and other socially minded theoreticians to enact a dislocation of the analysis of discourse and social concerns from the construction of certain types of texts, those privileged canonical texts, to the entire social field.

Reading practices originating in the interdisciplinary field of cultural studies, for example, apply critical analyses of culture from the "text" of athletic events to complex material objects like a Sony Walkman.[21] Much existing use of computational methods does not take the narrative ordering or structure of even a single text into account, never mind the difference between canonical and noncanonical texts. The so-called bag-of-words approach, insofar as it can operate widely across textual sources with no adjustment needed to take account of generic differences between fiction and poetry or between newspapers and governmental reports, might be a particularly apt way to study culture in a synchronic fashion—as long as we have some assurance that these textual objects were created in the same slice of time as our primary objects.

If history and the new historicist method functions differently in text mining than in digital archival projects, it might be the case that this is because the unstated goals of new historicism have become fully embedded within the digital humanities. In a polemical critique of the so-called distant reading computational methodologies used in the digital humanities, Andrew Kopec describes what he calls the "surprising affinity" between the new historicism and these approaches. Kopec argues that new historicism was already engaged in something like a data-driven approach and that the application of computational methods to texts delivers on the perhaps unstated promise of the earlier reading method: "literary history, no longer mined for the luminous detail that, like a skeleton key, unlocks the shared logic of cultural discourses, becomes instead a field of pure information that should be managed by a computer."[22] For Kopec, the new historicist notion of "text" renders all documents of the past not barbaric and individual objects of critique, but flattened into database-ready form that he calls "pure information." There is, of course, no such possibility of "pure information" and it seems unlikely that any historicist, new or old, would accept treating data as a cultural discourse without some historical specificity. At the same time, he is correct that text mining does have the capability to unsettle inherited hierarchies, which would supposedly be the problem with treating literary texts in a different manner from other historical objects. Yet there is no compelling reason why digital humanists using computational tools should not approach their archives and collections with the same contextualizing concerns as those building archives.

Digital humanists might instead invert present discussions in which textual archives become data by asking questions of data that are traditionally directed toward textual sources. At present, the lack of an agreement about data, file format, and archival or database standards presents several problems to those who would use computational tools to approach data as text. Determining the status—most important for the question of historicism being the edition and origin—of all the texts and objects within any large digital corpus has been rather difficult, and the hesitation or outright refusal to share these objects has made further scholarship and criticism based on earlier work impossible. All of this is to say that some of the various historicist methods that have been long available to humanist scholars and computational text- and data-mining methods are not necessarily in opposition—they might even supplement each other.

Text-External Referential Systems

Any digital method operating on historical texts should take seriously the historicity of the primary texts and the secondary objects that are used by computational processes to assist in interpreting the primary texts. Existing digital humanities work that address the problem of text encoding, to take just one important example, has produced a number of solutions including the use of look-up tables for roughly equivalent terms and a wider variety of training data, to address the use of historical typefaces, variant spellings, the long *s*, the presence of multiple languages, diacritical marks, idiosyncratic textual features such as Emily Dickinson's long dashes or her alternate words, and a number of other historical complexities present in the body of the text.[23] This text encoding work has functioned well in the creation of sophisticated annotated scholarly digital editions, but there has been little effort, as Katherine Bode suggests, to bridge this work with text-mining tools that are primarily designed to work on the simplest of texts, the unmarked-up, plain-text digital sources. In addition, the rapidly expanding use of secondary digital sources, data sources that because of their nature or idiosyncratic structure fall outside the carefully edited and annotated textual apparatus, are also removed from any detailed attempt to record bibliographic metadata. These secondary objects—for example, databases, dictionaries, statistical models, and maps—are potential sources of knowledge about the world, but insofar as they are cultural objects, they cannot be treated as ahistorical repositories of truth.

Another obvious example of the need for attention to historical sources and data can be found in the presently popular method of projecting historical spatial data on present-day maps. It is not clear what the interpretive value might be of the simple geographical projection of place names within an archive or a single text.[24] While the Google Maps API, as just one provider of mapping data, makes it trivial to drop "pins" and "geolocate" historical data on their mapping system, these contemporary maps do not come with the historical boundaries that are required to make much spatial and geographical historical data meaningful. While examining present-day geopolitical boundaries, for example, we might be drawn to certain interpretations about the existence of particular clusters of data or the lack of data in what would seem, from such boundaries and configurations, as important points or nexuses. Borrowing the notion of thickness to connote a "cultural analysis trained on the political, economic, linguistic, social, and other stratifactory and contextual realities in which human beings act and create"—as suggested by Clifford Geertz's use of thick description—Todd Presner, David Shepard, and Yoh Kawano suggest that mapping in the digital humanities can provide a corrective to the postmodern inflected way in which scholars describe digitally rendered spatial relations as a hyperspace.[25] Thick digital maps, they argue, are a way of drawing out dynamic relations—mapping is a process, not a static and stabilizing operation—that can help scholars resist the temptation to use them, as one would use the nonliterary text in various versions of historicism, as corrective objects: "Maps are a representation of a world, which reference other such representations. When we georeference historical maps, we are not 'correcting' them or making them 'accurate'; instead, we are keying one representation to another representation (not to reality)" (15). Tracking the historicity of the representational objects placed on the various layers of these thick maps, however, remains quite important in any attempt to understand the import of what Presner and his colleagues call their "keying" operation. Keys open doors and provide access to interiors; in this case, what is called a keying operation functions to expose or highlight the spatial network of meaningful objects mapped and established by the digital humanist.

Alan Liu has connected historicism, specifically the new historicism, to modern relational database systems through the previously mentioned figure of the anecdote. If anecdotes provided new historicists with methods by which they disrupted the privileging of certain objects and certain histories, Liu finds something analogous in the "random access" of a database search or query.[26] "If the New Historicism is a kind of relational database," Liu explains, "then the anecdote is its query" (259). In reconstructing the history and theory of the relational database, Liu demonstrates the capacity within this system for storing and quickly retrieving large amounts of indexed data. Databases require structured data—neatly organized, named, and datatyped tables and columns—but this structure, according to Liu, enables one to conduct unstructured queries: "anyone other than a cutting-edge cultural critic (and even the latter when engaged in the act of querying a library database or quickly verifying a date via Google or Wikipedia) knows what the anecdote really is. It is random access" (259). Liu, as Maurice S. Lee argues, "is brilliant on database theory, but when generated by electronic searches, historical anecdotes are far from random."[27] Lee observes that it is typical to find what you have queried, particularly in search engines, and thus the search for information about the past is already somewhat predetermined. In a manner, this is also the structure of Liu's own historical framework in *Local Transcendence: Essays on Postmodern Historicism and the Database*. As Liu recounts the history from Charles Babbage to Microsoft's archival project, Liu traverses what he himself refers to as "well-established relays" (249). The apotheosis of database fever in Liu's account is Microsoft's large-scale storage system for archiving all the information produced by and about an individual. The experimental technology called "MyLifeBits" aspired to make all this data instantly searchable. There was only one user of MyLifeBits, Microsoft principal researcher Gordon Bell. The explicit goal of MyLifeBits, according to Microsoft and Liu, was "total history" (255). Later called "Lifeblogging," the MyLifeBits project ended silently when Gordon Bell, the only participant, decided that his project "wasn't something that was bringing a lot of value to my life."[28] The digital project for total history was terminated not because of privacy concerns or limited storage but because it was boring.

There might be some possibility for a historical method, a cultural poetics or something other, that does not historicize to a single object as in, for example, the model of the anecdote, but one that produces more complex relations between historical artifacts. Brook Thomas gives special attention to what he called "that favorite new historicist figure—chiasmus" in his historicist account of the new historicism.[29] The chiasmus as a figure makes possible exchanges, but are they enclosed within this same structure? The new historicists, Thomas argues, deployed the figure of the chiasmus in order to produce balanced connections between literature and history. These connections, as Thomas notes, are usually synchronic. If there are exchanges of ideas and energy from a literary work and the historical moment, they tend not to escape from the slice of time marked out by the four-cornered and mirrored chiasmus. The addition of some nuance to historicizing reading might be enabled by multidimensional devices that make possible multidirectional flows between the objects of critical analysis.

The use of secondary digital resources and databases produces a complication for the new historicist desire to treat all textual objects equally—Veeser's claim that "literary and non-literary 'texts' circulate inseparably" can be incorporated into computational methodologies, but as references, these resources work something like the use of a historical dictionary in understanding how language was used during the period in question. Any new digital historicism must contend with the repeated historical disruptions created by comparisons, lookups, and queries originating outside the assembled digital archive. These secondary, external resources might function as a background through which one might project data, or a space in which one might reorient data, such as with the use of present-day Google maps with historical data that I have mentioned above. These maps might be thought of as feature spaces, constructed in the present, into which historical data is remapped. Any projection, and indeed almost any visualization, is a distortion of data, but that does not necessarily mean that it is "wrong" or without any interpretive value. The realignment or altered projection of historical data or text into the present can be understood as a special case of what Stephen Ramsay, following Jerome McGann and Lisa Samuels, calls "deformation."[30] For Ramsay, the algorithmic deformation of a text or data enable viewers, readers, and others to encounter a defamiliarized version of a text, object, or archive. These deformations, he argues, are central to the mission and function of the digital humanities. In deforming text, in taking it out of its otherwise self-enclosed framing, the database, the file, et cetera, we expose various dimensions and resources to the present. These new encounters can produce dramatic reinterpretations of the past and enable interruptive or disruptive encounters in the present.

Many of the existing computational methods used in text mining and text analysis, generally speaking, do not draw on resources outside the boundaries of the text or texts in question. The corpus is generally treated as a self-enclosed body. The process of generating collocated word lists, for example, does not need any external sources such as a supplementary dictionary because the collocation algorithm uses context within a document or collection of documents to produce lists of words frequently appearing near each other. While some preprocessing steps used in collocation, for example, the selection of stopwords, might be contingent on historical language use or regional dialects, the process itself can be understood as essentially an intrinsic—meaning internal to the text—operation. This method has some appeal for the literary critic interested in addressing historical sources and treating them as such—since texts are not generally compared with other objects, this approach might be capable of treating the text, much as the New Critics would have it, in isolation. But many tasks, especially those that incorporate or leverage machine-learning approaches, require additional textual resources and break what has been imagined as the seal of the closed text by invoking these as either containing prior formulations of the inquiries to be applied or to draw on categories contained within the textual resources to help make sense out of the new textual object.

To understand some of the implications of external data sources, think of how you might, for example, have organized and browsed music on a hardware-based MP3 player, such as the original Apple iPod, or a simple software-based MP3 player. You, as a user of this device, might browse across an existing music collection that was organized through metadata (the information about the information stored within each MP3 file). This type of searching and data retrieval is restricted to the standardized formatting of the supplied metadata: the artist, composer, album, genre, year of release, et cetera. If you were enjoying a specific genre, you might explore other albums or songs labeled as belonging to this same genre. The same goes for the year of release, if you were listening to and enjoyed several songs produced in the 1980s, you might try to listen to others within your collection from that same decade. These are all metadata operations. Following the success of these relatively simple systems, more sophisticated packages and devices examined the data objects directly. Labels could then be applied from the sound files themselves, from the data or the signal encoded within the MP3 format. These labels would provide an algorithm with some "features" to help identify—it is important to note, these features are not based on human-supplied metadata—collections of songs that share selected features. These correspond to a specific set of textual features extracted from the body of a textual source, while a metadata search would correspond to an index of encoded catalog entries, including information extracted from title pages and paratexts. Although genre classifications might be subject to change or perhaps even questions of authorship, it would be safe to assume that much of this information is static and linked to the object itself. Now, to return to my music player analogue, contemporary devices and many popular music services draw on another type of data to make recommendations. These data are supplied, directly or indirectly, by other, contemporary listeners. Their decisions and behaviors are used to determine categories and groups that enable classifications and recommendations. If you enjoyed listening to music produced by this artist, you may enjoy this other song. The databases that store and retrieve data for these algorithms are secondary in that they are once removed from the primary data, the store of digital objects and their associated static metadata. These databases are dynamic; they are the product of historically contingent subjective choices and behaviors made and performed in the present.

Secondary databases within computational criticism function, in perhaps several senses, as heuristic aids for making meaning of the analyzed texts. Secondary databases do not rise to the same level, to the primacy as an object of attention or critique, as the major objects under examination because secondary databases are imagined as functioning only to assist in the interpretation of another digital object. The primary use of secondary sources at present is to assist in locating objects in space and in time, even if users do not recognize that this is how they are using them. Think of how a scholar might make use of specific historical translations of foreign texts to better understand the way in which figures or events referenced in another object, for example, a novel, were the result of specific translation practices that were circulating contemporaneously with the primary text. At the grammatical level, linguists sometimes call references such as these—references within a text that point to something outside the text—as exophoric or text-external references. While not a perfect analogy for the way in which secondary databases function within text mining, the concept provides a way an entire network of relations is activated by the critic in resolving these detached and dereferenced pointers.[31]

Lexical databases are one such type of text-external referential system. WordNet is one of the more popular lexical databases used in computational research, particularly in computational linguistics.[32] Providing programmatic access to sets of synonyms or "synsets," WordNet enables researchers, initially those working in the field of psycholinguistics, to conduct searches for similar terms and to locate semantic distances between supplied pairs of words. The paper introducing WordNet acknowledges that the database was developed in opposition to diachronic dictionaries such as the Oxford English Dictionary. Assuming the primacy of a "contemporary (synchronic) structure of linguistic knowledge," WordNet can provide humanists with access to synonyms and, through other interfaces, the automatic tagging of sentences and individual words into parts of speech, but these are all limited to the historical moment and cultural context within which WordNet was created. Other lexical databases, such those containing or trained to identify locations and names, are compiled from labeled and marked-up training textual documents. Nancy Ide notes potential problems with using these type of reference systems: "most of these tools have been developed using existing corpora which consist of newspapers and government reports and are unlikely to perform well on the kinds of data that interest humanists, such as literary works, historical documents, etc."[33]

In the first chapter, I examined the ways in which Geoffrey Rockwell and Stéfan Sinclair have theorized computational tools as objects or things that assist humanities scholars in their inquiries much as laboratory instruments enable scientists to conduct experimental research. Rockwell and Sinclair call these computational things hermeneutica. The category of hermeneutica that I am calling text-external referential systems are deeply embedded within specific cultural moments and, because they are constructed and highly curated systems, they carry with them the assumptions, preferences, and prejudices of their creators. These systems capture, contain, and direct discursive features of language toward other objects. They function, as I have argued, as potential sources of knowledge about the world but they are not closed systems; they are fully subject to the same lines of critique as those used on primary textual objects. They are an example of what Jennifer L. Fleissner calls "digital prostheses"—digital objects equipped with a supplemental interpretive horizon that perform their own historicizing operation, either with the programmer or operator's intention or not, as they are imported into and referenced by computational workflows.[34] Digital prostheses instantiate an alternative meaning system but cloak much of this system through the abstraction of datasets, dictionaries, libraries, and system calls. If the term *text* in the now infamous question "is there a text in this class" raised, for Stanley Fish, the problem of the interpretive community and evidence that the target of this utterance was already installed within what he called a "situation," then text-external referential systems gesture toward the situatedness of all data. That that situation might not be the same as the one occupied by the person executing and interpreting results of the computational operation returns us to the problem of making sense, to what Fish called "systems of intelligibility."[35]

Mining Sentiment

Following the rather sudden availability of large-scale and rich digital corpora through end-user- or consumer-generated activity on social media and other locations offering free-form commentary in the early years of the twenty-first century, computer and data scientists began to quickly develop methods that could analyze and categorize this otherwise disordered flow of linguistic content. Working with some existing procedures, tools, and data from the field of natural language processing, an interdisciplinary field involving computational linguists, sociologists, and computer scientists, researchers began to mine new digital repositories and social media for a particular type of textual content that they refer to as sentiment. Knowing what, for example, consumers think about a particular product, especially when they imagine that they have some agency in posting their own opinions rather than responding to a survey, has an incredibly large value to marketers and business executives. When taken in the "big data" aggregate, their thoughts or opinions might offer some average sense of what people think about a consumable good or aesthetic object and maybe even offer some nuance about the attributes or aspects of this object.

Sentiment analysis, as used widely within various computational fields, including the digital humanities, has an empirical and deeply ahistorical understanding of sentiment and sentimentality and yet introduces assumptions from the present into the understanding of what constitutes sentiment and feeling. (See figure 3.1.) This paradox emerges through the creation and use of dictionaries and lists that score, rank, and categorize affective language. These dictionaries alter the horizon of interpretation and are a prime example of what I have been calling text-external referential systems.

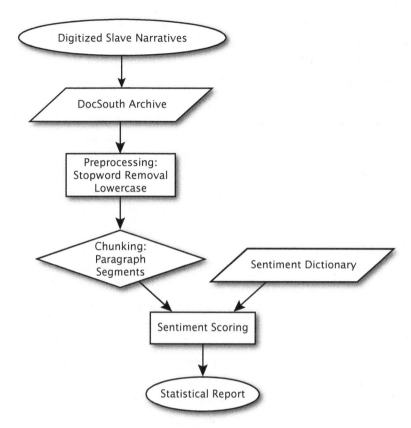

FIGURE 3.1   Sentiment analysis workflow

For Bing Liu, a computer scientist and an early developer and proponent of the sentiment analysis method, the sentiment in sentiment analysis does not name emotional response or affects but subjective opinions held by a person about an object—so much so that in his definition of this subfield and his own project in a survey of the state of the art in sentiment analysis, Liu uses these two terms as synonyms: "Sentiment analysis or opinion mining is the computational study of opinions, sentiments and emotions expressed in text."[36] Liu and his colleagues have developed several computational methods to determine whether a given subjective review of a product is positive or negative on the basis of the free-form textual content, the descriptive language, used by the author of the post. Sentiment, for Liu and other researchers working on this type of text mining, remains anchored to an object. Opinions are always opinions about an object. Objects, for Liu, are entities: "a product, person, event, organization, or topic" ("Sentiment Analysis," 630). Sentiment arises from subjective interaction with objects. Liu differentiates objective from subjective sentiment about an object through differentiation between "factual information" and the expression of "some personal feelings or beliefs," although he does make it clear that objective language can contain implicit opinions (633). Liu explains that once sentences have been classified as subjective, the object and sentiment can be extracted and the type of opinion can be computationally identified. What he calls "opinion orientation" is the process through which a researcher can attempt to computationally determine, through what he refers to as a lexicon-based approach, whether a given opinion is positive or negative. In this method, the researcher scores a sentence or section of text with a single value that will determine the degree of subjective positive or negative orientation a sentence expresses about an object.

To determine the orientation of a segment of text, in units like a sentence or a paragraph, scores of individual words are required. The lexicon approach, as Liu explains, requires a supplemental dictionary of prescored words that express positive and negative opinions or affects—a special type of heuristic aid that I have called a text-external referential system. What makes Liu's dictionary or dataset a system is the split structure that divides in half the semantic space constructed and mapped by the dataset. Liu published and made public the dataset that he uses in his sentiment-analysis routines. This dataset contains a binary classification of the indexed words—each word is either positive or negative—with 2,006 positive and 3,007 negative terms. Armed or rather supplemented with this labeled dataset of terms, Liu's procedure moves through supplied input textual units, scoring first the individual words and then calculating a total score along with the determined affect orientation, positive or negative, for the entire unit.

The lexicon-based approach of scoring and sorting text used by Liu and others assumes much, including a certain stability of the larger sentiment classes or categories. The more complicated sentiment dictionaries add greater levels of specificity and additional assumptions for those making use of scales or degrees of sentiment or dictionaries organized by affective categories. Chosen categories, classifications, rankings, and the key terms themselves cannot be considered ahistorical or universal; all are necessarily the product of any dictionary's historical moment and cultural milieu. A notable example of this situatedness of a sentiment dictionary can be found within what is called the "psychology dictionary" that forms part of the sentiment-analysis dictionary distributed with one popular commercial text-mining package, ProvalisResearch's QDA Miner/WordStat.[37] WordStat's psychology dictionary contains 3,150 terms that align concepts and phrases into groups associated not with contemporary psychological terms but with those derived from the language of psychoanalysis. Not just any "dialect" of psychoanalysis, however: Colin Martindale, the author of this dictionary, chose to organize his terms into areas associated with the popular practice of the 1970s, Jungian psychoanalytic analysis.[38] One slightly idiosyncratic group in the dataset "Icarian Imagery" demonstrates the limitations of the model used by this dictionary. Martindale identified these terms, and also those terms making use of these root-words, with the subcategory "ascension." They have been grouped together within the larger Icarian category:

```
ICARIAN_IM
ASCEND
ALOFT*
ARIS*
ARISEN*
AROS*
ASCEND*
ASCENS*
```

Of course, psychological concepts from more widely accepted strands of psychoanalysis, including Freud's own theories, as well as the field after the influence of the cognitive and brain sciences, have no representation in the dictionary. Thus, this dictionary would enable one to locate potential sources of evidence for reading Jungian imagery and associated categorizations of sentiment within a text but not, say, the terms used by the New Psychology of the 1890s that preceded psychoanalysis as the dominant discourse or those from the present that reflect an understanding of the mind derived from empirical studies of the brain.

Matthew Jockers builds on the sentiment-analysis work of Bing Liu and others in his development of an automatic method of evaluating sentiment. Jockers uses these methods not to examine the assumed nonliterary language of social media, but rather to extract sentiment from canonical literary texts. Jockers and his colleagues developed an open-source toolkit for the "R" statistical package called Syuzhet that he uses to analyze literary sentiment. While Liu uses a binary dictionary with either positive or negative terms—any particular positive term is no more or less positive than another positive term—Jockers provides several independent mechanisms for scoring sentiment, including Liu's dictionary, three other databases, and Jockers's own coded dictionary with scaled, variable values for the positive and negative terms.[39] The "R" code for Syuzhet contains source-code comments (discursive text embedded within or alongside the code) that provide some basic explanation of the default Syuzhet sentiment scoring mechanism: the function "iterates over a vector of strings and returns sentiment values based on user supplied method. The default method, 'syuzhet' is a custom sentiment dictionary developed in the Nebraska Literary Lab. The default dictionary should be better tuned to fiction as the terms were extracted from a collection of 165,000 human coded sentences taken from a small corpus of contemporary novels."[40] This routine or function returns a list of 10,748 terms that have been scored with values from -1.00 to 1.00. The average score of the words in Jockers's "human-coded" sentiment dictionary has what Liu would term a negative orientation, with a value of -0.2129606. There are 3,581 words with positive sentiment (values greater than 0.0), 7,161 with negative (values less than 0.0), and none with a neutral sentiment. The median word in a sorted list of negative to positive terms is "unintentionally" (scored -0.40) and sorted positive to negative, bloodless (also scored -0.40).

To see how sentiment analysis functions, we can examine several well-established textual structures that have served as case studies in the published research in this subfield. The following shows the calculated sentiment scores produced by Jockers's Syuzhet tool on Bing Liu's sample "opinion orientation" sentences:

> get_sentiment("The picture quality of this camera is not great, but the battery life is long")
[1] 0.5
> get_sentiment("The picture quality of this camera is great and the battery life is long")
[1] 0.5
> get_sentiment("The picture quality of this camera is great and the battery life is good")
[1] 1.25
> get_sentiment("The picture quality of this camera is great and the battery life is excellent")
[1] 1.5

Liu provides these sample sentences to show two difficult problems for determining sentiment orientation. The first problem is separating sentiment directed toward primary and secondary objects. Liu's primary objective is to determine whether a particular free-form textual review of an object is positive or negative. These objects are often complex with multiple features. The above sentence includes two separate options about two different features of the main object, the camera. The positive opinion about the camera's battery life is not given any value, either positive or negative—the only words given a score in this example is "great." If we were to change "long" to an explicitly positive term without any specialized or domain knowledge about cameras and batteries, the total score changes. A negative opinion of a feature might not mean that the subjective opinion of the larger unit is also negative. The second difficult problem is addressing what Liu describes as negations and *but*-clauses in the sentiment-mining context.

The lexicon-based approach to sentiment analysis, as I've already mentioned, counts only the words listed in the dictionary—all other words are discarded or ignored. The sentences shown in figure 3.2 display Syuzhet sentiment scores for another pair of sample sentences used by Liu: "This drug reduced my pain significantly" and "This drug increased my pain significantly." Because "reduced" is not listed in the dictionary, the raw count of "sentiment" found in the first sentence (–0.85) is higher than the second (–0.35). The Syuzhet dictionary contains scores for three words found in the second sentence, the one that expresses what might be called, to follow Bing Liu, a stronger negative orientation: drug –0.10, increased 0.50, and pain –0.75. (See figure 3.2.)

As these examples show, using external sources for information about a text—what I have been calling a text-external referential system—introduces

```
In [9]:  get_sentiment_raw("This drug reduced my pain significantly")

         drug -0.10
         pain -0.75

Out[9]:  -0.85


In [10]: get_sentiment_raw("This drug increased my pain significantly")

         drug -0.10
         increased 0.50
         pain -0.75

Out[10]: -0.35
```

FIGURE 3.2   Raw word scores

numerous assumptions from the cultural and historical perspective of the system's designer and curator. Examining the reduction of text in running the first paragraph of the main body of Harriet Jacobs's *Incidents in the Life of a Slave Girl* (1860–61) through sentiment scoring demonstrates additional problems. This paragraph, like many slave narratives, begins with a statement that aligns the author of the narrative with the first-person narrator and establishes her voice as the voice of a former slave: "I was born a slave; but I never knew it till six years of happy childhood had passed away." There are 795 words in the first paragraph. A simple preprocessing routine, the same as used throughout the examples in earlier chapters, removes 468 stopwords and nonalphabetical characters or words, leaving a total of 327 words available for sentiment mining. Jockers's sentiment dictionary contains only 69 of these 327 words, but several of them are repeated in this paragraph, thus leaving a set of 96 words (including those repeated words) with scored "sentiment" values from the original text. The total sentiment score of these remaining 96 words is 27.95.

The following is a textual representation of the scoring of the sentiment in the concluding sentences of the first paragraph of Harriet Jacobs's *Incidents in the Life of a Slave Girl*. The terms recognized and tagged as positive are indicated with underlined typeface and the negative terms are in bold:

> My grandmother remained in her service as a slave; but her children were divided among her master's children. As she had five, Benjamin, the youngest one, was sold, in order that each heir might have an equal portion of dollars and cents. There was so little difference in our ages that he seemed more like my brother than my uncle. He was a bright, handsome lad, nearly white; for he inherited the complexion my grandmother had derived from Anglo-Saxon ancestors. Though only ten years old, seven hundred and twenty dollars were paid for him. His sale was a terrible **blow** to my grandmother; but she was naturally hopeful, and she went to work with renewed energy, trusting in time to be able to purchase some of her children. She had laid up three hundred dollars, which her **mistress** one day begged as a loan, promising to pay her soon. The reader probably knows that no promise or writing given to a slave is legally binding; for, according to Southern laws, a slave, being property, can hold no property. When my grandmother lent her **hard** earnings to her **mistress**, she trusted solely to her honor. The honor of a slaveholder to a slave!

Seventeen words in the above segment are listed in Liu's sentiment lexicon. There are thirteen positive and four negative words, which produces an overwhelming positive sentiment score for this paragraph. Some curiosities of this lexicon include "work" as a positive term (as in, "this camera works well") and the categorization of "master" as positive and "mistress" as negative; in this context, the terms should have the same categorization.

Plotting Sentiment

While Jockers's scoring mechanism, a selection of ten thousand words that he claims are common in contemporary novels and score by members of his laboratory, might represent some improvement of the binary positive-negative scoring system used by Bing Liu, Liu demonstrates a much more complex understanding of sentence structure. A small group of mathematicians and social scientists—Andrew J. Raegan, Lewis Mitchell, Dilan Kiley, Christopher M. Danford, and Peter Sheridan Dodds—interested in examining the relative happiness expressed by textual systems have also deployed a scaled scoring system to automatically score sentiment in text. Calling their system "The Hedonometer," they initially directed their analysis at social media, including Twitter.

This group, like Jockers and Liu, compiled a list of words for which they wanted to score with some measure of readerly affect. They call this list or dataset labMT 1.0 (Data Set S1) or "labMT" for short. They collected 10,222 unique words and recruited subjects on Amazon's Mechanical Turk platform to rank these words, on a scale from 1 to 9 and marked with sad to happy faces, on the basis of how each word made them feel. They collected fifty scores for each word, breaking the dataset into lists of one hundred words for each task. The labMT term with the largest standard deviation between happiness scores (suggesting the greatest disagreement about the happiness value of this term) was "fucking" with an average happiness score of 4.64 and a standard deviation of 2.9260. The least happy terms provided by this dataset, in descending rank toward least happy, are cancer (1.54), death (1.54), murder (1.48), terrorism (1.48), rape (1.44), suicide (1.30), and terrorist (1.30). Some oddly located terms that tell us something about the subject population recruited for this social experiment include that fact that "reasoning," "salvation," and "sciences" as terms all share a 6.30 average happiness ranking.

Following some success in scoring sentiment with this mechanism, the researchers then turned to examining novels. Reading, as numerous literary theorists have argued, is a profoundly social activity and individual acts of reading happen within interpretive communities that provide the reader with strategies, schemata, contexts, and existing interpretations of other related narratives that help to frame each act of reading. For many critics, one of the major problems with the historicist turn in literary studies was the assumption that all historical subjects share the same sense of simultaneity, that "culture" circulated and spread evenly in a synchronically shared understanding. Even more damaging, many critics point to the problem with the assumption that there is even a single culture, national or otherwise. Even if one were to assume that there is a single national culture with a simultaneous and shared understanding of semantics, cultural references, and meaning, then the labMT dataset would *still* present a problem, as we do not know the nationality of the respondents. The curators of this dataset are not the least interested in sharing the demographics of the subject pool alongside the data; not because they are hiding something, but because the identity and national belonging of their Mechanical Turk respondents do not matter to them. The authors assume, as many social scientists might, a universal psychological subject who participates, perhaps somewhat paradoxically, in the author's own culture.

Responding to Jockers's attempt to yoke emotion to plot, Andrew Reagan and Peter Sheridan Dodds applied their Hedonometer and their labMT database of sentiment scores. They explicitly claim that their research does not reveal the plot of a text but the shift in emotional experienced by a reader: "The emotional arc of a story does not give us direct information about the plot of the intended meaning of the story, but rather exists as part of the whole narrative (e.g., an emotional arc showing a fall in sentiment throughout a story may arise from very different plot and structure combinations)."[41] Jockers prefers the social psychological term "emotional valence" to the more restricted notion of positive or negative sentiment as found in Liu and others. While Andrew Reagan and Peter Sheridan Dodds constrained their understanding of shifts in sentiment throughout a novel as the emotional arc of a particular narrative, Jockers insists on the predictive capability of his Syuzhet method and argues that "shifts in emotional valence may serve as a reliable proxy for plot movements in novels."[42]

These experiments suggest that methods such as sentiment analysis might not be appropriate for every text. Computational techniques that assume that language operates the same in every situation throw out some of the major assumptions of literary analysis—not just the historicist assumptions articulated above. The "reading" in machine reading does not resemble anything like a human reading, but should it? Surely there are important insights for the humanities to be gained from the application of strongly quantitative, pseudo-empirical, and neuropsychological methods to literature.

Sentiment analysis, as the above examples demonstrate, most frequently takes the form of what Matthew Jockers calls microanalysis in that this method treats the words provided by the secondary dictionary as the only available "signal" to find within the supplied input text, which, as the above examples demonstrate, is typically used on a single text rather than a larger "macro" collection of texts. While Bing Liu discusses solutions for addressing some of the context surrounding these dictionary words, the signal terms are frequently just simply converted to recorded values through the dictionary, and all the other words within the text are rejected as valueless noise. Sentiment analysis is just one of many limiting and filtering processes used in computational text analysis that reduce data and, in the process, create new datasets. Sentiment analysis is properly sentiment mining, as the text is mined for those terms that have already been determined to possess some value to the text miner. The "bag of words" approach found in many other text-mining activities "disembeds" and decontextualizes all the words and simultaneously produces a bag of unused words. When some form of "chunking" of the data into smaller groupings is performed, the methods operate exactly as above but within a smaller container or "bucket," such as a chapter, a paragraph, or an arbitrarily measured number of words. Despite the expressed goal of computational work in the humanities as being the addressing of "big data" through the large scale of distant reading and macroanalysis, the existing use of sentiment analysis has also returned digital humanists to treatments of a single text. Perhaps this is because the method at this time is relatively new, and new methods require some comparison for validation of the method with existing approaches or even a commonsense account of an object (note how Jockers depends on his readers comparing how they recall the plot of a book and with the visual plot of graphed sentiment values) or because processing sentiment at the macro level just does not make much sense.

But in the aggregate, as part of a model, these plots might have some value. Matthew L. Jockers and Jodie Archer, a graduate of the doctoral program in English at Stanford, where Jockers once worked, teamed up to turn Jockers's previous work on large-scale text mining and smaller-scale sentiment analysis into what they refer to as "the bestseller code"—a "code" that is both a collection of statistical code and the heretofore "secret" code of the book-publishing industry. In a book of the same name, Archer and Jockers offer an extended and commercial-friendly account of Jockers's computational methods. They make the provocative claim that they have successfully decoded the formerly hidden narrative structures required for a commercially successful novel. They write, "Traditionally, it is believed that there are certain skills a novelist needs to master in order to win readers: a sense of plot, compelling characters, more than basic competence with grammar. Writers with big fan bases have mastered more: an eye for the human condition, the twists and turns of plausibility, that rare but appropriate use of the semicolon."[43] They claim to be able to identify "an uncanny number of latent features" that are used in commercially successful fiction, features that will enable them to identify and help shape potential bestsellers (6). Their emphasis on "latent features" references the hidden or otherwise undisclosed formal features that can be delivered back to authors to help them craft a narrative and a plot that will land their manuscript on the bestseller list. While algorithmic criticism or other digital humanities approaches are often aligned with the turn to surface reading and other non-symptomatic or antisymptomatic reading methodologies, examples such as this provide evidence that computational methods, especially those methods making use of large numbers of undisclosed variables and features, can also invoke the same sense of depth and obscurity as found in the demystifying logics of Marxist and psychoanalytic approaches. In obscuring and explicitly calling the model that contains what they call the "DNA" of the bestseller "the black box," Archer and Jockers produce an argumentative context in which their claims cannot be contested.

Their particular black box turns out to be a potentially profitable site. On the accompanying website created to promote *The Bestseller Code*, Archer and Jockers posted an advertisement for their manuscript-review services: "Since the release of *The Bestseller Code* in October 2016, we have been overwhelmed with requests for individual manuscript reviews. We are pleased to be able to offer this service beginning in September 2017. Please add your name to our mailing list, if you want to work with us on your manuscript."[44] The advertisement promises to close the circle on the computational analysis of the bestseller by building on their model of past bestselling novels to help their clients revise their manuscripts into well-positioned candidates for publication. The service provided by Jockers and Archer, however, does not promise access to the algorithms and data used, which remain proprietary. Instead, one might imagine, the results of the algorithm—to what degree the manuscript matches the bestseller model—can be given back to the author or perhaps passed along to agents and editors.

In sentiment analysis, as the methods exist at present, algorithms query or reference recorded or scored language norms to invoke a response, an average human account of the meaning of the information indexed by the table. In querying these text-external referential systems, these computational tools perform a one-way historicizing gesture that yokes text to context without the possibility of exchange. All the above methods of sentiment analysis extract the affect of the words in question through what are essentially empirical studies performed in the present or near to the present. Language, especially words assumed to have a high affective charge, is embedded within a particular cultural and historical moment, and some attempt to historicize these meanings, with both the secondary list of terms and the "primary" text archive, needs to be done to ensure that the algorithm is not "misreading" the text. Language and connotative meanings drift over time.

. . .

It was still the early days in the institutionalization of literary studies when William Wimsatt and Monroe Beardsley issued their statement on the difficulty of reading a poem on the basis of the affect produced in the reader. Their coauthored "Affective Fallacy" paper was one of the founding documents of midtwentieth-century literary criticism. Arguing against the "neuro-psychological poetics" of I. A. Richards, Wimsatt and Beardsley sought to clear up what they present as a "confusion" between what a literary work is and what it does.[45] Appearing between the "old" and the "new" historicism, their essay takes issue with both the psychological criticism put forward by Richards, in which he produced what Barbara Herrnstein Smith has called "traditional empiricist-normative accounts" of poems and the historicist who asks readers to interpret a poem within its context.[46] Thus, they write "[if] the exegesis of some poems depends on the understanding of obsolete or exotic customs, the poems themselves are the most precise emotive evaluation of the customs" (54). In other words, the poem itself should deliver, to the present reader, everything one needs to give an account of how the poem works. Wimsatt and Beardsley's argument would find fault with the practice of sentiment mining in both the empirical uses described above and in any attempt to historicize affect, to engage in what they call "affective relativism, the cultural or historical, the measurement of poetic value by the degree of feeling felt by the readers of a given era" (39). Raising up the value of "great poets" who produce works that do not require deep historical knowledge, "antiquarian curiosity," (39) or an appeal to "romantic reader psychology," they attempt to reorient literary criticism and in the process free it from what was a common concern at this moment: a parasitic relation to other disciplines. "There is," Wimsatt and Beardsley conclude, "no legitimate reason why criticism, losing sight of its durable and peculiar objects, poems themselves, should become a dependent of social history or of anthropology" (54).

Responding to new research about affect and feeling in the cognitive sciences, Jane Thrailkill makes an argument for revitalizing the reading of affect in historical literature by arguing that Wimsatt and Beardsley's affective fallacy is itself a fallacy. Wimsatt and Beardsley's rationale for withholding consideration of the way in which a poem makes the reader feel depended on their understanding of affect as culturally contingent. "The actual corporeal architecture of emotional experience," Thrailkill argues in response to this claim, "has evolved so slowly over the course of millennia as to be, in the limited timeframe of human history, practically stable."[47] Emotion, she argues, cannot be fully explained by either biological accounts, which she links with the New Criticism of Wimsatt and Beardsley, who understand it as located in private experience, or the accounts offered by cultural critics who argue that emotions are shared and socially constructed. Instead, Thrailkill argues for an "embodied but not mindless" (16) understanding of affect that takes what she argues are the universal aspects of emotional response along with the historical manifestations of literary representation. Her interdisciplinary reading of late-nineteenth-century novels seeks to connect empirical accounts of emotion and feeling, the literary representation of these affects, and a range of historical science and medical accounts. Thrailkill's reading of affect, both in the present and in the past, corrects for the overly rapid dismissal of feeling from criticism, but, like Wimsatt and Beardsley, she rejects an empirical presentism that positions criticism as a "dependent" of the sciences.

Sentiment analysis is one such mode of empirical presentism. It was in a subtle jab at the "protocols," the student-generated reports on poems collected and interpreted by I. A. Richards, that Wimsatt and Beardsley made their argument for the rejection of criticism as a science. "The critic," they argue, "is not a contributor to statistically countable reports about the poem, but a teacher or explicator of meanings" (48). Reacting against Richards as a "tabulator of the subject's responses" (47–48), Wimsatt and Beardsley seek to mark a clean line between the experimental social sciences and the work of literary criticism. Thrailkill and others working in the emerging field of cognitive literary studies trouble some of these distinctions—indeed, a communication and collaboration among the disciplines is Thrailkill's explicit aim in *Affecting Fictions*—but while she aims to take the science seriously, Thrailkill argues that literary criticism should "not abandon its essential concern with literature, interpretation, cultural practice, and historical contingency" (16). Sentiment, affect, feeling—whatever it is called and however it is theorized, has value to the humanities and especially to the study of literature, but depending on scored, tabulated, and averaged values of reported feeling in interpretative acts, machinic or hermeneutical, ignores the contingency of history and the situatedness of human culture.

Prospects for a Digital Historicism

Oddly enough, the scholars paying close attention to such problems are not digital humanists but those computational scientists interested in the quantitative analysis of culture, or what they call "culturomics." Provocative questions are asked and interesting computational methodologies used, but their undertheorized and uncritical understanding of culture and literature leads them to some weak conclusions. Take, for example, the research article that accompanied the release of Google's Ngram tool and brought the term *culturomics* into being. With free and unfettered access to the five-million-object Google Books archive of scanned books and documents, Jean-Baptiste Michel and his colleagues set out with the highly ambitious and suspect goal to examine "trends in human thought."[48] They collected word frequencies and the publication of year of the scanned objects to generate the multiple-word (*n*-gram) trajectories that became, for a moment, widely popular in presentations to demonstrate quantitative evidence in historical humanities research.

James Hughes and his colleagues, for example, open their analysis of "stylistic influence" in literature with the claim that "literature is a form of expression whose temporal structure, both in content and style, provides a historical record of the evolution of culture."[49] Using a filtered set of texts in the Project Gutenberg archive, only those written in English after 1550, with more than five works available in the archive, and with known birth and death years, the authors examined the use of what they call "content-free words"—three hundred and seven prepositions, articles, conjunctions, common nouns and pronouns, and the verb "to be"—over time. Hughes and his colleagues present their quantitative analysis as proof of what they call the "anecdotal" theory of a literary "style of a time." Hopelessly naive about the construction of digital archives and the literary archive, the authors of this study approach Project Gutenberg as if it were representative of literature as such or at least what they assume to be historically representative canonical classics. This approach to literary history starts from the mistaken assumption that the inherited archive is *the* archive.

The prominence of text mining and other tools that search across large historical archives within the emergent toolbox of the digital humanities has resulted in scholars adopting a position that we might call, after Dominick LaCapra,[50] documentary realism. In an earlier period, LaCapra critiqued history, and especially the field of intellectual history, for its tendency to treat the objects and texts of the past in an uncritical fashion. In his magisterial *History and Criticism*, LaCapra writes of the scholars using this approach as pursuing an "archivally based documentary realism that treats artifacts as quarries for facts in the reconstitution of societies and cultures of the past" (46). Computational methods might imagine directing queries into big data quarries but only a naive understanding of history could imagine these databases as a transparent repository of culture and the returned results as facts. LaCapra's critique of this "total history" model is entirely apt for the age of computational criticism. He reminds us that not only is the scholar's dream of a complete digital archive suspect and misplaced, but that these dreams themselves are performing important work in structuring the entire project of cultural criticism. The wishes and desires of humanists, in other words, unavoidably shape the way in which archives are assembled and the questions posed.

CHAPTER 4

The Cultural Significance of *k*-NN

We pre-suppose labour in a form that stamps it as exclusively
human. A spider conducts operations that resemble those of
a weaver, and a bee puts to shame many an architect in the
construction of her cells. But what distinguishes the worst
architect from the best of bees is this, that the architect raises his
structure in imagination before he erects it in reality. At the end
of every labour-process we get a result that already existed in the
imagination of the labourer at its commencement.

—Karl Marx, *Capital*

In the computer age, the question of knowledge is now more than
ever a question of government.

—Jean-Françoise Lyotard, *The Postmodern Condition: A Report
on Knowledge*

In the previous three chapters, I have argued that humanists need to give critical attention to the methods and the historicity of all primary and secondary
sources used in any computational activity, especially those directed at the
understanding of historical cultural artifacts. This chapter takes up the subject
of one of the core mechanics of all digital computing, the abstract yet crucial
concept known as the algorithm, in order to provide a framework for understanding and situating these minimal units, what might be best thought of
as the major building block of more complex computational applications and
workflows. This analytical framework, in opposition to the mostly formalist
or phenomenological approach used by most humanities scholars researching
and critiquing algorithms, takes the form of a cultural and historical critique.
In this chapter, I reconstruct and critique the partial genealogy, the intellectual

history, of an algorithm known as k-NN or "k-nearest neighbor" that was key to sense making in the midtwentieth century and has found continued life in our so-called "big data" present. In the process of situating the k-NN algorithm within the larger field containing other residual and emergent statistical methods, this chapter seeks to produce an intervention within the developing critical theory of what is variously called "algorithmic culture" or "algorithmic governmentality."[1]

Understanding the scope, utility, and function of the rapidly multiplying algorithms used by businesses and governments that are hidden, embedded, or present in almost all areas of everyday life is necessary for any account of how culture and power work in the present moment. Consumers now are perhaps more familiar than ever with the ways in which they are targeted by advertisements based on their prior purchases, their location, and automatically determined demographics. Savvy users of information search-and-retrieval systems understand that the results returned from most queries are in some way individualized or customized by algorithms and data collected from other, similar users.[2] While these forms of algorithmic classification and manipulation are at least partially visible, many others are hidden and, in almost all these encounters, the rationale for these decisions—the logic that produces what can appear fittingly appropriate or widely off the mark—remains obscure. The political import of data mining and large-scale applications of a particular class of algorithms, the machine-learning approaches that have been the subject of much of the critique offered by this book, have much, much more profound entanglements with our lives than some of the places in which we see algorithms deployed, for example, the results of our Google searches. I have serious reservations about whether voters in two major 2016 elections, the US presidential election of Donald Trump and the United Kingdom's EU Referendum or "Brexit" vote, were influenced as a result of directed Facebook advertisements, but the inquiry into the corporate and government connections and the psychological operations of big-data consultancy Cambridge Analytica suggests that there is at least the desire on the part of some to deploy sophisticated computational techniques to profile and persuade.[3]

Algorithms, those miniature bits of computational logic, are also playing a larger and larger role in the reconfiguration of knowledge in the twenty-first century. The use of algorithmically driven prediction and preemption tools, according to a number of theorists, threatens to take the mostly benign recommendation engine that suggests movies, music, people you might know or like and turn it into a widespread and saturating ideology that disables due process and installs a logic of anticipation.[4] In their introduction to a special issue of the *European Journal of Cultural Studies* on the topic of data-mining algorithms, Mark Andrejevic, Alison Hearn, and Helen Kennedy explain the scope of algorithmically driven computational "analytics" and the necessity for a critical account of our data-saturated present: "Data analytics involve far more than targeted advertising, however, they envision new strategies for forecasting, targeting and decision-making in a growing range of social realms, such as marketing, employment, education, health care, policing, urban planning and epidemiology. They also have the potential to usher in new, unaccountable and opaque forms of discrimination and social sorting based not on human-scale narratives but on incomprehensibly large, and continually growing, networks of interconnections."[5] Insofar as the creators and users of algorithms present them as "unaccountable and opaque," they can reconfigure the distribution and discourse of power by representing, to the potential addressee or subject of big data, any decision-making process as just the rational analysis of objective data. While information about the past informs these automatic sorting mechanisms, they are mostly used for their predictive capabilities. Alison Hearn calls this "the pre-figurative work of algorithms" and warns that their "anticipatory affects . . . interpellate us into a pre-constituted future every day."[6]

Computational processes and algorithms are two distinct concepts that have some overlap in their functions and how they are used in discourse, but they are not identical. Simply defined, algorithm names the formal description of any repeatable set of steps or procedures. In formalizing the description of an algorithm, scholars can compare designs and approaches used to solve a particular problem and assess algorithms on the basis of their efficiency, speed, and even the elegance of the result. Tarleton Gillespie argues, probably correctly, that algorithms are designed in response to an abstract model of a problem and that these models are "the formalization of a problem and its goal, articulated in computational terms."[7] An algorithm that has proven itself as the correct solution for a particular abstract goal is then embedded in larger computational systems, the workflows or pipelines introduced in the earlier chapters of this book, which may contain many other algorithms and stacked input and output datasets. Additional modification and tuning might then be performed to ensure that the algorithm works correctly outside the model environment and with "real world" data.

It is no longer enough to say that we have specific and contained encounters with algorithms—it is not enough to imagine the constraints of the input box into which you enter your search terms as the primary site in which algorithms operate—for we are now in constant contact with algorithmic processes: we are data for algorithms, we are informed by algorithms, we are interpellated by algorithms. In examining the genealogy of one particular sorting and categorizing algorithm, this chapter follows David Golumbia's *The Cultural Logic of Computation* (2009) in asking how "the rhetoric of computation, and the belief-system associated with it, benefits and fits into established structures of institutional power."[8] What follows is not a larger-scale reading of the cultural impact of the species of computational logic known as algorithms—there is already a growing body of work on this topic—but instead a critique of one specific algorithm and the cultural context in which it was created and the ways in which aspects of its context can be found residing in the contemporary discourse surrounding the algorithm and how assumptions present at the moment of the algorithm's creation inform and shape its use in present digital humanities research.

Too much contemporary so-called digital humanities discourse is really less about the now trendy topic of "algorithms" than what we might consider the various inputs and outputs for algorithms: user interfaces, data-collection systems, and training systems. Not that there is anything wrong with these, but in giving up on the possibility of a critique of the actual algorithm, in treating what is presented as a black box as if it were a true black box, digital humanists lose much interpretive power and wind up treating complex, multilayered corporate trade secrets as unknowable and inevitable.[9] Each of the previously mentioned levels of computation—input, transformation, output, rendering—have associated critical vocabularies and methods by which we can frame, historicize, and produce suggestions or make demands for correction. The cultural context within which an algorithm is imagined, formalized, and first implemented establishes the condition of possibility for the algorithm but, as Adrian Mackenzie reminds us, "all algorithmic processes blend historically disparate practices, knowledges and conventions."[10] Algorithms might be a thing, but they are a special type of discursive object that is shaped by the limits and affordances of the digital materiality in which computation takes place.[11]

In understanding and critiquing the operation of computational processes—from the complex, multistage workflows of digital humanities to the workings of one particular algorithm—we might be tempted to follow some of the framing and critical approaches used with science and technology studies. The descriptive approach to understanding the experimental sciences offered by Bruno Latour and Steve Woolgar in *Laboratory Life* (1979) has some potential for critical use in the digital humanities, but unlike the line that separated the biologists in the laboratory from Latour and Woolgar, humanists making use of computational processes cannot view themselves from a distance.[12] The introduction of scientific concepts and computational methodologies into the humanities disrupts the division between critical observation and research, in the Latourian paradigm, as the production of facts. The emergent work of what has been variously called the new materialism, object-oriented ontology, or speculative realism provides a potentially useful set of terms that are related to those used in science-technology studies but add a theoretical dimension that might be better suited to examining the intersection of culture and computation.

Ian Bogost's notion of the "unit operation," for example, comes out of his studies of the construction not of the facts generated by scientists in labs, but of video or computer games. His preferred ontology and grammar centers on small, configurable objects that he calls units. Thinking in terms of units enables him to break free from what he sees as the residual attachment to subjects found in the object-subject relation. Bogost has spent the better part of almost a decade refining the relation between complex systems and units. He first outlined the concept of the unit in *Unit Operations: An Approach to Videogame Criticism* (2006). His approach to computation and games is mainly formalist; he describes his reading practice as a method of examining and unpacking supplied configurations of units to reveal the enclosed and modular smaller units or artifacts: "I wish primarily to encourage the use of criticism as a tool for understanding how videogames function as cultural artifacts, and how they do so along with other modes of human expression. I am specifically interested in the intersection between criticism and computation; in particular, I am concerned with videogames as a type of configurative or procedural artifact, one built up from units of tightly encapsulated meaning. As such, the present study does not try to situate itself generally within the history of games or the history of play."[13] Arguing that the figure of the network, such as the one found in Latour's actor-network-theory, "is an overly normalized structure, one driven by order and predefinition" (19), Bogost remains intently focused on the smallest configurable units, those that have "encapsulated meaning."

Almost a decade later, in a short and playful book titled *Alien Phenomenology*, Bogost refines his concept of the unit operation in an attempt to accept both a philosophical view rejecting the dominant anthropocentricism of science studies (including, for him, the work of Bruno Latour who Bogost argues preserves and brackets the human agent) and the fact that some things are "complex structures or systems crafted or used by humans."[14] He offers readings of the configuration of multiple units as the site through which critics can examine the construction of digital objects, including algorithms. Examining the way in which these computational things work by taking them apart and rebuilding or recrafting, to use one of his key terms, enables Bogost to argue for the mutability and reconfigurability from the perspective of these computational things: "Things are not *merely* what they do, but things *do indeed do things*. And the *way things do* is worthy of philosophical consideration. Units are isolated entities trapped together inside other units, rubbing shoulders with one another uncomfortably while never overlapping. A unit is never an atom, but a set, a grouping of other units that act together as a system; the unit operation is always fractal" (28, emphasis in original). The notion of carpentry is central to Bogost's account of understanding the logics of fusion and connection that are central to the unit operation. Drawing on Graham Harman's notion of "vicarious causation," a way of understanding the relation between objects outside the lens of human consciousness as less a mode of direct interaction than a vicarious influence that works through a mediating relation of a third object, Bogost sets out to speculate on the operation of algorithms through the practice of software carpentry.[15] Carpentry, for Bogost, is a phenomenological activity directed toward replication: "the phenomenologist who performs carpentry creates a machine that tries to replicate the unit operation of another's experience" (100). We can think of software carpentry as a practice enabled by the use of human-readable and human-comprehendible text and code written and shared in workflows designed around transparency, such as the Jupyter environment. But users of such systems are in the minority, and in the corporate and government use of many complex machine-learning algorithms, there is no transparency. Software carpentry cannot account for the intentional obscurity built into and added onto the closed-source use of algorithms in all too many applications. Finally, in building there is understanding, but carpentry is a decontextualizing operation that risks treating the history that produced the "found" constructed unit as inevitable, and it may also depend on too simple of a model of construction.[16]

The formal study and even the phenomenological study of what we call the user experience of algorithms can take us only so far.[17] Consider Apple's Siri, that bit of voice-operated logic that only partially resides in the local storage of the iPhone. The Siri application operates algorithmically, but these baseline algorithms are supplemented by various rules, exceptions, and workarounds that filter input and amend or modify output. Ed Finn's *What Algorithms Want: Imagination in the Age of the Computer* provides an account of how Siri's initial response to the voiced request for the nearest abortion provider would, for some users, provide directions to an "anti-abortion crisis pregnancy center" (54). In response, Apple updated Siri's logic to not to suggest just the closest facility connected with the term "abortion"—the "crisis" center—but a faculty that would actually provide the requested service. Finn reads this moment as demonstrating the ways in which "business logic, legal agreements, and licensing schemes" supplement supposedly algorithmic operations—a mystifying supplement possible only through the black boxing of the trade secret operation of Siri.[18] Siri, of course, is not an algorithm but a complex hosted or "cloud" application that is made up of numerous other algorithms, including neural network models. Any attempt to critique—and by my use of the term *critique* I mean to gesture to the classical sense of critique as a tool of understanding and comprehension, to the ways in which the various techniques of governmentality operate as modes of subjection or subjectification, to the various versions of our shared and familiar forms of cultural critique—any attempt to critique, that is, how Siri functions needs to account for both the rule-abiding algorithm and its partially obscured exceptions. Attempts to understand the algorithmic operation of Siri, as software carpentry would have it, through the replication of the tool, will not be able to successfully recover these exceptions, for they are not algorithmic. Any critique of algorithms, especially those used within corporate or governmental applications, cannot be directed solely toward the formal operation of the algorithm if it is to describe the output of algorithmic operations contained within black boxes.[19]

It is becoming increasingly clear that we need some additional—not wholly new, but additional—critical language by which we can better understand the historical trajectory of big-data governance and the ways in which technologies are altering the modes by which we are and are not addressed and rendered subject to these forms of control. Alexander Galloway's *Protocol: How Control Exists after Decentralization* gives what I believe to be the best accounting of the shift from sovereign to discipline to control societies. Despite the appearance of neat lines of demarcation between these periods, Galloway argues that "when history changes, it changes slowly and in an overlapping, multilayered way, such that one historical moment may extend well into another, or two moments may happily coexist for decades or longer."[20] Building on Michel Foucault's account of sovereignty and discipline and Gilles Deleuze's "Postscript on Control Societies," Galloway's critique deflates the pretension of technological evangelists who believed that the distributed nature of computing in the early years of the twenty-first century freed us, along with our Web browsers, from the effects of centralized power.[21] He does so by recognizing that the protocols that were supposed to liberate computing are themselves discursive forms and that they are intimately connected to traditional command and control networks. Galloway's critique of the protocological is exemplary digital studies and digital humanities work—an early form of what I am calling critical digital humanities—in that he grounds his analysis in the long history of not just computing, but the slowly morphing practices of governing.

Belgian legal theorist Antoinette Rouvroy has recently been developing the concept of "algorithmic governmentality" as a way of naming a new regime of governmentality, a new system that for her produces a break with prior norms of subjectification and discourse. What differentiates algorithmic governmentality from prior modes of governmentality—including the much discussed biopolitical governmentality—that exercise control through rows and columns is that these modern, statistical modes of governing depend upon individuation. This to say that while statistical methods manage populations, they address a subject and are contestable by this subject. Disciplinary practices are directed toward the body of the subject; biopolitical modes address the population with norms, averages, and standard distributions; algorithmic governmentality does not seek to forcefully fit the subject to norms or require the subject to reform him or herself but instead operates through the prediction of anticipated behaviors based on profiles, not people. Rouvroy's account of algorithmic governmentality is not necessarily an argument against the use of data or even systems of quantification. "The quantification process," she argues, "binds individuals together within a given system of evaluation and constrains them to use the 'language' of quantification in comparing their respective merits, needs, etc."[22] Quantification as used in governing, in other words, produces comparable "epistemic communities" that are open to evaluation and interpretation by those individuated and addressed subjects. The body politic has a body, perhaps in aggregate, perhaps in the form of an "average" person or demographically defined groups, but this bound collection of embodied public bodies is addressed by modes of governing. Individuals within these collections can contest these forms of address and the categorization that produced them as subjects. Algorithmic governmentality, in Rouvroy's account, depends on the suspension of epistemology and any correlation between the body public and the behavior described and predicted by the algorithm. Again, statistical governmentality operates according to quantitative benchmarking of the public; algorithmic governmentality has no relation to the subject. It does not need, like neoliberalism, hyper-"becoming" subjects who have internalized the demand to know, expand, improve, and market the self (153). Algorithmic governmentality, Rouvroy claims, does not even need subjects; it needs only people affected—not called, hailed, or addressed—by the "alerts and reflexes" of predictive algorithms.

What Rouvroy calls "data behaviourism" (149) is an anticipatory algorithmic logic that produces a "probabilistic subject" as opposed to "the actual, experiential, present and sentient subject" (153). Rouvroy's valorization of the "actual" subject, however, does not mean that she wants to return to the idea of an autonomous self, to some notion of possessive individualism, for Rouvroy follows a mostly deconstructive understanding of the subject. She instead wants to reenchant "the commons" by turning to language and scenes in which subjects, following Judith Butler's account of subjectivity, perform authorship and are given "authority to speak, to give account of themselves" (161). In becoming subjects, in turning away from the impossible confrontation with algorithmic profiling to spaces that Rouvroy characterizes as "heterotopic spatio-temporal spaces interrupting digital and capitalistic flows—such as the judicial, theatrical, literary, laboratory scenes," these unaddressed create scenes in which there might be some possibility of due process and critique (160). Rouvroy privileges these spaces because they "guarantee a certain heterogeneity of the modes of construction of realities" that are foreclosed by the anticipatory and decidedly virtual logics of the "probabilistic subject."

While we can treat "the digital" as an abstraction and inquire into the philosophical ramifications of the move from analog systems to digital systems along with the accompanying concepts of sampling and discrete data, in practice digital systems have specific and historically contingent material forms. David M. Berry and Anders Fagerjord have argued that critical approaches to digital studies and the use of digital methods within the humanities requires critics to become familiar with the history of digitality and the digital computer systems that make present computations possible.[23] By digital materiality I mean, for example, that humanists are well positioned to give an account of the changing forms of digital encoding and processing—see Jonathan Sterne's *MP3: The Meaning of a Format*, Aden Evens's work on the object-oriented programming paradigm, Wendy Chun's critique of the "software effect," and Matthew Kirschenbaum's accounts of "forensic materiality."[24] Digital materiality, however, also prompts us to ask about the ways in which there have been few substantial changes to many aspects of computation, for example, the virtualized computer for which almost all contemporary software has been written is also, despite its status as virtual, deeply historical and contingent on specific decisions made by major commercial computer-system vendors during the 1980s. All this is to say that scholars need a method by which they can encounter, examine, and critique the various histories—and there are several—of digital systems and computation.

In a recent interview with Joy Buolamwini, a researcher at the MIT Media Lab, discussing racial bias within facial recognition algorithms that appeared in *The Guardian*, Buolamwini claimed that "Our past dwells within our algorithms. We know our past is unequal but to create a more equal future we have to look at the characteristics that we are optimising for. Who is represented? Who isn't represented?"[25] In her response, Buolamwini points out one major level of "pastness" within any contemporary machine-learning algorithm: the presence of existing "training" data that is used for future decision-making processes, but there are other ways in which the past dwells within our algorithms. Properly speaking, training data, in the machine learning world, are algorithm-agnostic; shortly we'll see an example of this, but for now it is enough to say that they remain deeply historical insofar as they are, at minimum, a created and "curated" sampling of whatever phenomena requires analysis. Algorithms are imagined and produced alongside data—Gillespie's formalization of an abstract model might encompass both—and like a historical recipe and its ingredients, data and procedure might share a certain way of thinking, a paradigm, or something like that. The degree to which we can say that an algorithm or a more complicated model composed of multiple algorithms has succeeded is determined by a framing informed, if not determined, by the creator's desires. In her cautionary account of big data and what she terms "weapons of math destruction," Cathy O'Neil calls such models "opinions embedded in mathematics."[26] Algorithms are cultural, and how we link history, culture, and technology remains, for me at least, a complicated question. Humanists have, if nothing else, a responsibility to think historically—for who else is going to take the past seriously?—yet some of the historicism deployed in studies of digital culture or the digital humanities is remarkably simplistic.

Computing history, as Donna Haraway has taught us, is inextricably tied up in some of the worst crimes of the twentieth century—and almost all of this work was funded and supported by the US government—but, at the same time, the fracturing opened up by technology might enable us to perform "garbage collection" on some damaging myths and ideologies.[27] If digital humanists are not bothered by the question of the historicity of the tools, methods, and fields, the multiple entanglements of the computer industry with the military-industrial complex, and the ways in which the world in which these objects and abstractions were developed to function might not be the world we actually inhabit or the world we want, then they are not paying adequate attention. Yet the work of understanding the way in which the histories of computing—from workflows to algorithms—cannot rest on a form of historicization that results in overcontextualization, a too-neatly-yoked-together example of a technology and its determining historical moment. In reconstructing the origins and tracing the development of a technology or a computational method, it becomes possible to shed light on both the ways in which prior cultural formulations and ideologies were registered within the models, functions, and description of these tools and methods—for our present concerns, how machine learning methods were historically constituted—and how these histories create the conditions of possibility for the present moment.

Bayes and Modernity:
The Birth of Probability Theory

The theory of probability, the major theoretical concept that was essential for the birth of the modern science of statistics and today makes contemporary artificial intelligence and machine learning possible, emerged in the seventeenth century. Like the midcentury algorithms that provide statistical backing for pattern recognition and categorization tasks, probability did not appear *ex nihilo*; it required a certain amount of mathematical knowledge to steadily build and accumulate. In order to begin any critique of the machine-learning approaches used within the various computational fields and especially within a methodologically self-aware critical digital humanities, some understanding of the history and fundamentals of statistics and probability theory is needed.

The set of methods collectively known as Bayesian statistics were central to the emergence and popularity of probability theory, and they are crucial to understanding discourse about prediction and uncertainly in the present big-data moment. Bayesian statistics are widely popular and widely contested. In some fields, they provide a comparative baseline for evaluating more complex methods. In others, and especially in niche areas of data analysis, these methods are the dominant tool for filtering and assessing probabilities and likelihoods in an uncertain future.

Ian Hacking makes a strong case for examining the historical conditions that made thinking about chance and developing a theory of probability possible. Dissatisfied with existing explanations of the emergence of probability, Hacking argues that the important question to ask is not how any individual theory of probability came into existence, but rather to reach an understanding of "a quite specific event that occurred around 1660: the emergence of *our* concept of probability."[28] In tracing the contours of an ongoing, developing idea, in creating a conceptual history rather than a restricted account of a single theory, Hacking wants to show the ways in which this concept comes to the present loaded with residues of past thinking that have become difficult to recognize as rooted in the past: "I am inviting the reader to imagine, first of all, that there is a space of possible theories about probability that has been rather constant from 1660 to the present. Secondly, this space resulted from a transformation upon some quite different conceptual structure. Thirdly, some characteristics of that prior structure, themselves quite forgotten, have impressed themselves on our present scheme of thought. Fourth: perhaps an understanding of our space and its preconditions can liberate us from the cycle of probability theories that has trapped us for so long" (16). It is precisely this third dimension of Hacking's inquiry that bears repeating one more time: the appearance of new paradigms, such as the turn to big-data computational methods, are merely imagined as displacing past modes or structures of thinking. Not only do these new paradigms contain residues of their site of origins and the conditions that made possible their emergence, but assertions of a ruptural break with the past, a total displacement, should be treated with suspicion, for these clearings can foreclose any inquiry into the commonalities between what came before and what has come cloaked as wholly new. If the past lingers on in the form of biases embedded within the input data selection and the dataset curation process, it can also be found as a presence in conceptual models and an absence in the displacement of prior structures. The discourse of computation is loaded with the assumptions of what it displaced and its midcentury site of origins.[29]

Bayesian statistics have as their origin in the midseventeenth century, a simple solution proposed by a member of the clergy to what was then known as the problem of chances. Bayes's rule, the shortened name of this formulation, is named after its originator, the Reverend Thomas Bayes, a college-educated—Bayes studied theology at the University of Edinburgh before being ordained—"gentleman" or amateur mathematician. It was in the middle of the eighteenth century when Bayes developed a solution to address what was known as the problem of the doctrine of chances. This moment required philosophical approaches and mathematical models that were capable of bridging two vastly different ways of thinking: one in which the world was understood to be divinely created and ultimately ordered and knowable and the other, which was secular, filled uncertainly, and groping for new descriptions and scientific rules to explain the disorder. Bayes approached the problem of chance in a manner that would seem quite typical of his early Enlightenment era. His rule depends on what we might call a hedge, a slight hedge, that grants slightly higher probability to an outcome derived from the past. What happened in the past, in other words, may have some predicative capacity for determining what might happen in the future.[30] Bayes's rule emerged from this historical moment that was right at the cusp of a scientific modernity but held some minor hesitancy and doubt about the truth of the coming world.

This notion that I am describing as minor hesitancy and doubt is manifested in Bayes's rule through what is called a "prior." Priors are subjective beliefs that lack any objective proof, any data or accounting based on empirical observations. These prior subjective beliefs linger into an empirical and objective present within Bayesian statistics, as much as this eighteenth-century statistical approach itself lingers into our present. In her engaging history of Bayes's rule and the history of Bayesian statistics, Sharon Bertsch McGrayne succinctly describes how Bayesian priors work:

> Bayes combined judgments based on prior hunches with probabilities based on repeatable experiments. He introduced the signature features of Bayesian methods: an initial belief modified by objective new information. He could move from observations of the world to abstractions about their probable cause. And he discovered the long-sought grail of probability, what future mathematicians would call the probability of causes, the principle of inverse probability, Bayesian statistics, or simply Bayes' rule.[31]

Bayes's essay introduces and defines his problem as "Given the number of times in which an unknown event has happened and failed: Required the chance that the probability of its happening in a single trial lies somewhere between any two degrees of probability that can be named."[32] Bayes's theorem, published and introduced by his friend Richard Price in 1763, states that by starting with a subjective belief or proposition and modifying this belief with objective statements of fact one can develop a better proposition. In his introduction to Bayes's essay, the introduction and publication that first brought the rule to the attention of mathematicians, Richard Price writes the following of his interpretation of the value of Bayes's rule: "The purpose I mean is, to shew, what reason we have for believing that there are in the constitution of things fixt laws according to which events happen, and that, therefore, the frame of the world must be the effect of the wisdom and power of an intelligent cause; and thus to confirm the argument taken from final causes for the existence of the Deity" (373–74). While Price's application of Bayes's rule in support of an argument for the existence of God seems supported by Bayes's own biography and some of his exposition of the rule, Bayes did not introduce theology directly into the section of the essay identified as written solely by him.[33]

Sharon Bertsch McGrayne acknowledges the incredibly long life of this simple rule in the title of her book *The Theory That Would Not Die*. Despite its simplicity and the irreducible problem of the subjective prior, Bayes's rule has lived on much longer than the period boundaries of what Alain Desrosières calls "the Bayesian moment."[34] While Desrosières sees Bayesian statistics as the origin of a number of important statistical ideas, including inverse probability, he claims that Bayes's rule and its eighteenth-century moment of "encoding and its particular constraints" have long been forgotten and that "Bayesianism has long been rejected from statistical thinking" (60). Robert Mitchell has suggested that literature and in particular the Victorian novel, "with its emphasis on beliefs, partial but revisable knowledge, and a complex plot" was a crucial cultural location for preserving the assumptions and the approach of Bayesian statistics.[35] Either way, the appearance of big data and machine learning has brought new life to Bayes's rule. Although some methods and forms have shifted, notably in the method known as naive Bayes that takes little more than its name from Bayes's rule, the performance and error rate of Bayes's rule has become the standard by which researchers and data scientists judge the efficacy of contemporary machine-learning algorithms.

k-Nearest Neighbor

The algorithm known as k-nearest neighbor or k-NN is a historically important algorithm—the first, according to field experts, to be proven universally consistent.[36] Rather than a formal reading of the algorithm and the statistical logic that makes it consistent, what follows sketches out a cultural and historical critique of both the genesis and operation of this algorithm. This algorithm experienced initial success and remains quite popular with researchers because it is trivial to implement in various programming languages and it is easy to comprehend the governing logic of the algorithm. This logic, the decision-making rule at the heart of the algorithm, has been described by some commenters and programmers as almost innately familiar and obvious. Yet the obviousness of k-nearest neighbor, the model motivating the algorithm, reflects not the world as it is, but the world as imagined in a specific context, in a particular place and time. In both its formalized description, its exposition in the papers introducing and refining the rule and its implementation in algorithmic form, and in its actual use, the k-NN algorithm draws on dominant mid-twentieth-century ideologies and tropes, including partitioning, segregation, suburbanization, and democratization. In more than one way, k-NN is a representative twentieth-century algorithm and meaning-making tool.

First imagined and given a formal description in the early 1950s and late 1960s, the pattern-matching technique has survived into the present. Like Bayes's rule, a method we could, following Raymond Williams's tripartite schema for historical analysis, cast as residual to k-NN's status as dominant, within algorithmic culture, k-NN continues to thrive despite the development of far more advanced methods.[37] A number of well-understood solutions to statistical problems are available in what some call the software ecosystem or market of ideas. Some fit certain problems better than others and sometimes methods are combined in multistage processes or workflows. It is not uncommon to find software packages or code bases containing hundreds of algorithms. Methods that extend and build upon k-NN have thus become heavily incorporated into many tools and applications across widely different application domains. This algorithm, in an important way for this book, plays a major role in the recent turn to machine-learning algorithms that accompanies our era of big data. Among other uses, it has been recognized as an excellent tool for face and object detection. While k-NN, as I mentioned above, has been to some degree superseded by more complex algorithms and layered approaches, it was the dominant algorithm for many years and remains a benchmark to which to compare new approaches, including neural and deep-learning networks.

The k-nearest neighbor algorithm, like most machine-learning algorithms, promises to produce order from disorder. It operates on a spatial metaphor and is known as a distance-based learning method. There are five major require-ments for using k-NN: (1) a target dataset that includes, by necessity, a finite number of samples, (2) a predetermined set of classes, (3) existing class mem-bership and labels for the data, (4) some method of feature selection by which known and unknown, meaning properly classified and unlabeled, data can be compared, and (5) some split of the labeled, known data into training and validation datasets by the operator. The labels are removed or hidden from the test dataset and the algorithm tests its classification accuracy by com-paring the supplied and the algorithmically determined class labels. There are other requirements for using k-NN, including the important variable k for the number of nearest neighbors to tally in determining class member-ship of the tested sample. There are some rough guidelines for selecting this number, but it is usually determined *post hoc*; one selects the number that returns the best or most desirable results after experimentation and names that the k variable. The k-NN algorithm, as I mentioned, locates each known sample within a multidimensional space using the supplied data from the fea-ture selection step. Distances between points, between samples, are typically calculated using Euclidean distance—the shortest path from point to point. In almost all applications, k-NN works by calculating the distance between descriptive information about objects, not between objects themselves. This information is typically of the metadata type—mostly qualitative features and measurements. Boundaries between supplied classes are automatically produced using a method called Voronoi tessellation. The lines of the Voronoi diagram (see figure 4.1) cut through the transformed data, slicing across rep-resentation space. These boundary lines define the algorithm's sense of the supplied classes by grouping data from the dataset into tessellated parcels, in other words, into neighborhoods.

The five basic requirements specified above are shared with many learn-ing algorithms. Good-quality learning data is perhaps the most important of these requirements. It is only through the features selected from these training data that an algorithm can have confidence in correctly classifying new, unseen data. In the case of the type of humanities data discussed in

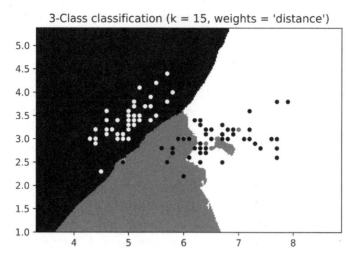

FIGURE 4.1   Voronoi classification of iris dataset from Scikit-learn package

this book, having too many outliers within the learning dataset will lead to poor results. This means that the operator of the algorithm, the researcher intent on classifying data, needs to be sure that the labeled learning data are indeed representative of the type and variety of data that is likely to be used as testing data. Too many features or "noisy" features will also produce a condition in which data points are plotted in sparsely located spaces rather than tidy and organized regions or neighborhoods. This condition is called the curse of dimensionality in machine-learning scholarship. In short, the curse of dimensionality means that the greater the number of dimensions used to compare objects added to the machine-learning analysis, the less reliable the algorithm will be in correctly classifying data. Because *k*-NN operates essentially on all data at once, without a distinct learning or training phase, it can also quickly consume computational resources, most crucially random-access memory for holding the entire set of relations between data from the dataset in memory.

The best-known and most popular dataset for developing and fine-tuning many classification algorithms, including most implementations of *k*-NN, was created decades before the algorithm was developed. A quick glance at the construction and use of this dataset will help us understand both the power and limitations of all classification methods and especially the *k*-NN algorithm. This particular dataset was created and published in 1936 by Ronald A. Fisher, a British statistician, in the scientific journal *Annals of Eugenics*.[38] Fisher's dataset, as it is commonly known, contains measurements from three varieties of the iris plant: setosa, virginica, and versicolor. There are fifty samples from each of these three varieties and each contains four measurements or features: sepal length and width and petal length and width (see figure 4.2). There are several assumptions that need to be accepted before one might make use of this dataset for classifying iris flowers: (1) that the existing set of samples is representative and inclusive of enough variety to cover the possible range of measured irises, (2) that the three varieties represent the total number of known iris varieties, (3) that the existing fifty samples have all been correctly labeled into the three classes, and (4) that the four measurements of features are appropriate to distinguish between the three varieties.

Fisher used this dataset to develop his own method of statistical discrimination, one known as linear discrimination. He pioneered and developed many important statistical methods, including the Analysis of Variance or ANOVA test. Fisher, like Karl Pearson, the Galton Chair of Eugenics at the University of London, was a proponent of eugenics—he held the position Professor of Eugenics at University College—London. His research was supported and tainted by tobacco companies. Sharon Bertsch McGrayne explains Fisher's position on the relation between cigarette smoking and cancer: his first argument, "believe it or not, was that lung cancer might cause smoking. The second was that a latent genetic factor might give some people hereditary predilections for both smoking and lung cancer." "In neither case," McGrayne writes, "would smoking cause lung cancer" (113). He was also engaged in the long and ultimately failed fight against the use of Bayesian statistics. His iris

```
In [1]:  # load Scikit-Learn Fisher Iris dataset
         from sklearn import datasets
         iris = datasets.load_iris()

         # display first five measurements
         print(iris.data[1:5])

         [[ 4.9  3.   1.4  0.2]
          [ 4.7  3.2  1.3  0.2]
          [ 4.6  3.1  1.5  0.2]
          [ 5.   3.6  1.4  0.2]]
```

FIGURE 4.2 Measurements for sepal length, sepal width, petal length, and petal width in the Fisher iris dataset

dataset, which as a dataset of the dimensions of highly cultivated flowers is a cultural dataset, continues to be quite popular. The dataset is also bundled with the test suite and documentation provided by the currently dominant open-source machine-learning package for the Python programming language, Scikit-learn.

Because of the design and function of k-NN, it has found some use in the humanities or humanities-adjacent work, primarily as a tool to determine membership of unknown cultural objects. In the essay "Visual Digital Humanities: Using Image Data to Derive Approximate Metadata," four researchers, Hannah M. Dee, Lorna M. Hughes, Lloyd Roderick, and Alexander D. Brown describe how they used k-NN in an attempt to date undated paintings. The authors describe their research as "the first work that attempts to date the work of an artist by year." Building on the notion of visual stylistics, the authors of this essay examine descriptive metadata including "colour, edge orientation, and texture measures"[39] from a dataset of 325 images of paintings along with "genre, original painting size, painting materials, and image size" (98). The researchers had dates for 102 of the 325 paintings and used them to verify their results. Here is how the authors describe the function of k-NN as they use it in their research: "k-NN is a fast, non-parametric classifier which makes no assumptions about the underlying patterns in the data, merely that paintings from around the same time will be similarly located in our feature space(s)" (99). Testing the algorithm, they claim that they were able to "guess the date of paintings to within 15 years in 71% of cases" (105). "Whilst this result is not yet good enough," they note, "it is promising" (105).

Computational stylistics, a subfield of the area of research formerly known as humanities computing, has long made use of a number of algorithms and text-mining tools in the attempt to identify the author of a text with unknown, questionable, or disputed authorship. In their evaluation of classification algorithms for a stylistics task, determining authorship in the *Federalist Papers*, Matthew L. Jockers and Daniela Witten use methods similar to the above scheme that is used with identifying undated paintings.[40] They first produced a set of classes—simply the name of three authors, Hamilton, Madison, and Jay—and assigned texts with known authorship to these classes. They then preprocessed texts downloaded from Project Gutenberg. Next, they selected a method of feature selection from the entire textual archive of eighty-five texts to use in their comparative analysis. They used both what they call "raw" features, single-word and two-word-phrase (bigram) counts, and a common method of dimensionality reduction, principal components analysis (PCA).[41] The raw number of shared features was perhaps excessively large for good classification results and performance with some algorithms—they identified 2,907 shared words and bigrams shared among all the texts—thus necessitating a small number of extracted "principal" PCA components. With these existing classes, shared features, and prelabeled data, they were able to remove the label from known authors and text for classification accuracy. Jockers and Witten evaluated the performance of five machine-learning algorithms, Delta, k-NN, support vector machine, nearest shrunken centroid (NSC), and regularized discriminant analysis (RDA). They demonstrate that all the methods worked well, meaning produced the fewest errors in classification of known data, with the best performance being from the RDA and NSC algorithms. Jockers would later use k-NN with some reported success as part of his work on the "best-seller code" with Jodie Archer to classify texts into a "best seller" or "not best seller" category.[42]

We can also make use of k-NN in combination with some simple text-mining tools to think about the prospects and problems in using these approaches for automatic literary periodization (see figure 4.3). The classification of the 295 digitized texts in the "Documenting the American South," or DocSouth, North American Slave Narratives into major literary periods is possible if not also a little fraught. The DocSouth archive includes a paltry amount of metadata—certainly in comparison with the painting database; among this metadata, we have the year of publication for most of the texts. If one were to follow the norms of US literary studies and classify texts published before 1865 as antebellum and those after as postbellum, then one could create a simple two-class categorization problem to solve with k-NN. A number of texts in the DocSouth archive have unknown or uncertain publications, and such a classification task could at least indicate the period. A trivial and hopelessly naive method of feature selection for classification would be to extract just a list of words or tokens appearing in each text and their count—this is similar to the raw-feature-selection method used in the Jockers and Witten project and an approach used in the classification of many types of textual objects. These textual features, the word counts, can then be used to produce a very high dimensional representation of the shared vector space. From here we can take a text with a known date and ask the algorithm to generate a classification and, if this produces satisfactory results (see figure 4.4), attempt

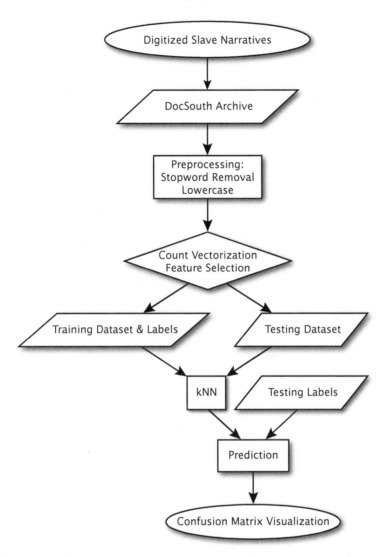

FIGURE 4.3   Periodization workflow

to classify, or in terms of this experiment, periodize, a text with an unknown publication date.

The k-NN algorithm, like many algorithms, builds upon an earlier and simpler statistical rule, which was initially known just as the nearest-neighbor rule. The rule was theorized and developed during what statistician Erich L. Lehmann describes in his field memoir as "a period between two revolutions:

121

```
In [6]:  # display file counts
         print("training data:")
         for period in ['postbellum', 'antebellum']:
             print(" ",period,":",train_labels.count(period))
         print("test data:")
         for period in ['postbellum', 'antebellum']:
             print(" ",period,":",test_labels.count(period))

         training data:
           postbellum : 77
           antebellum : 75
         test data:
           postbellum : 32
           antebellum : 68
```

```
In [7]:  # run kNN and fit training data
         knn = KNeighborsClassifier(n_neighbors=13)
         knn.fit(training_data,train_labels)

         # Predict results from the test data and check accuracy
         pred = knn.predict(test_data)
         score = metrics.accuracy_score(test_labels, pred)
         print("accuracy:   %0.3f" % score)
         print(metrics.classification_report(test_labels, pred))
         print("confusion matrix:")
         print(metrics.confusion_matrix(test_labels, pred))
```

```
accuracy:   0.800
              precision    recall  f1-score   support

   antebellum      0.88      0.82      0.85        68
   postbellum      0.67      0.75      0.71        32

  avg / total      0.81      0.80      0.80       100

confusion matrix:
[[56 12]
 [ 8 24]]
```

FIGURE 4.4   Periodization with *k*-NN

that of Fisher, Neyman, and Pearson, which laid the foundations for the classical statistical theory of that period; and the second revolution, forty years later, brought about by the advent of the computer, which turned statistics in new directions."[43] The boundaries of what Lehmann, perhaps a little too humbly, presents as a statistical interregnum mark, on one side the foundational work produced during World War II and, on the other, the early years of the Cold War era. While Lehmann demarcates this period as just after the one dominated by his doctoral adviser, Jerzy Neyman, and immediately prior to the computer revolution, the rules and procedures developed by statisticians are rather entangled with computational thinking. Consider the tasks performed by human computers—usually women—designed by army scientists, engineers, and university statisticians operated at large scale. While we might be tempted to say that these tasks anticipated the moment in which digital computers would carry out more complex computations, it would be more correct to say that much of the statistical work of the 1940s and 1950s developed alongside the development of high-speed digital computers.

The nearest-neighbor rule, as with almost all things computational, is a direct product of military research. The rule was invented and refined by university- and military-funded researchers employed by a major statistical institution: the University of California—Berkeley. Lehmann describes the transformation of the Berkeley Mathematics Department in response to the emergency needs of the US military: Jerzy Neyman "set up a statistical laboratory as a semiautonomous unit within the Mathematics Department. However, soon America's entry into World War II in 1941 put all further academic development on hold. Neyman took on war work, and for the next several years this became the laboratory's central and all-consuming activity. The work dealt with quite specific military problems and did not produce results of lasting interest."[44] While Lehmann claims that the wartime work of these early Berkeley statisticians did not produce generalizable insights, his own account of his service for the air force and the development of the nearest-neighbor rule suggests that his statement was not exactly true.

Encouraged by Jerzy Neyman, their adviser, a number of Berkeley mathematicians, including Erich Lehmann and a fellow graduate student by the name of Joseph Hodges, signed up to become statistical advisers to the US military. The air force asked them to "track and analyze bombing accuracy" (28), among other tasks. Stationed on Guam, an island that had only recently been captured by the United States, the two, working with the Twentieth Air Force, examined reconnaissance photographs taken to document the physical damage and casualties produced by US aircraft bombing of Japan. Lehmann describes what he regarded as his most important assignment, the only one in which he worked alongside Hodges: "The bombing campaign was . . . not achieving its mission. A principal cause of the lack of accuracy was the high altitude at which the planes were instructed to fly in order to avoid antiaircraft fire" (31). The statisticians were tasked with estimating the change in accuracy and vulnerability if military bombers were to fly at a lower altitude. Shortly after Lehmann and Hodges made their report, on March 9, 1945, Twentieth Air Force general Curtis LeMay launched his notorious "Operation Meeting-house" raid. Lehmann writes, "We did not know about this raid until the next day and then knew little about the appalling toll in Tokyo of over eight hundred thousand dead. Even so, thinking back I am surprised that we were not more disturbed by such an attack on an urban target" (31). Curtis LeMay used more than three hundred B-29 bombers with incendiary weapons with the explicit goal "to start a conflagration" (31). What was called "area bombing" depended on the close proximity of the targets, a large number of the fire-producing bombs, and low-flying aircraft. Area bombing was enabled by the interpretation of aerial reconnaissance photographs and the marking of dense groupings of buildings. While I wouldn't want to suggest Lehmann and Hodges's report and the subsequent area bombing strategy employed by LeMay led directly to the development of classification algorithms used in machine-learning technologies, they share, in disturbing ways, a set of spatial logics.

FIGURE 4.5   Aerial photograph, Tokyo, March 11, 1945.
Courtesy National Archives, photo no. 342-FH-3A3851-56542ac

The earliest description of the nearest-neighbor rule appeared as a technical report printed and made available in 1951 by the Air Force School of Aviation Medicine, located at what was then called Randolph Field and is now known as Randolph Air Force Base, in Texas. The authors of this technical report, which remained otherwise unpublished until 1988, were two young academic statisticians, Evelyn Fix and Joseph L. Hodges Jr. Fix, like her colleagues Erich Lehmann and Joseph Hodges, was a UC Berkeley student of Jerzy Neyman. During the war, Fix worked as a research assistant in the statistical laboratory working on a project known as "Applied Mathematics Panel of the National Defense Research Committee," in which she calculated (all calculations had to be performed using a desk calculator) probabilities for various military plans and tactics related to what was most likely the European front.[45] Fix and Hodges had earned their PhDs only three and two years prior to their inventing this groundbreaking statistical rule. In their paper, Fix and Hodges describe a statistical method for what they refer to as a "discrimination problem," in which a researcher wants to categorize an unknown variable within a multidimensional space into one of two categories. Fix and Hodges describe each of these two previously known categories as "a stated (small) neighborhood" and individual data points as "neighbors," thus establishing what would become the dominant spatial metaphor that continues to the present in this and other classification algorithms. At this point, the algorithm contains no mention of digital or even digitized data. The nearest-neighbor rule defined by Fix and Hodges attacks the subproblem in which a statistician has at hand two populations in which both are "completely unknown, except for assumptions about existence of densities, etc." (239).

The solution to the so-called discrimination problem outlined by Fix and Hodges was refined and expanded in 1967 by two Stanford University researchers, Thomas M. Cover and his doctoral student Peter Hart. Their research on this problem and others was supported by contracts from the US Army and the US Air Force. Cover and Hart's paper on "Nearest Neighbor Pattern Classification" appeared in *IEEE Transactions on Information Theory*. In their paper, Cover and Hart extend Evelyn Fix and Joseph Hodge's nearest-neighbor rule into the "k_n-nearest neighbor rule," or k-NN for short, while simultaneously converting it into an algorithm, for the authors assumed the use of a digital computer to process the data.

Cover and Hart gloss the problem that they have inherited from Fix and Hodges: "The nearest neighbor decision rule assigns to an unclassified sample point the classification of the nearest of a set of previously classified points."[46] This is because, as Cover and Hart argue, "it is reasonable to assume that observations which are close together (in some appropriate metric) will have the same classification, or at least will have almost the same posterior probability distributions on their respective classifications" (21). They restate the major premise of the k-NN algorithm in simple English: "samples which are close together have categories which are close together" (22). This is a version of what Wendy Chun, in her recent work on network algorithms, critiques as homophily, which is "the assumption that birds of a feather flock together." This assumption is not unlike the presence of the subjective prior in Bayesian statistics; it is a model or belief about the world that leaves a trace through the algorithm and the transformed data. The logic of homophily, for Chun, produces homogeneous groupings that, when they are used, for example, to profile Internet users or construct social networks, result in virtually gated communities.[47] If the concept of relatively homogeneous neighborhoods or density of homogeneous groupings within diverse neighborhoods that provided the major spatial metaphor of k-NN is rooted in certain historical and cultural assumptions, the description and operation of the mechanism that produces decisions about membership is even more a product of a particular constellation of ideologies. "The rule of decision by the plurality of votes is so familiar in the daily life of men in modern societies," Satosi Watanabe claims in his wide-ranging account of pattern recognition, "that they will be ready to accept it without hesitation."[48]

In their explication of the algorithm, Cover and Hart drop the language of discrimination in favor of "classified" and "unclassified" for known and unknown data. They develop a solution capable of classifying much larger datasets, those that require the use of digital computers. These datasets are large enough that the operator or statistician cannot possibly have complete knowledge, only some inferences made from a small set of samples. The Cover and Hart k-NN approach seeks to utilize "the information contained in the set of correctly classified points" (22). These samples, the "correctly classified points," are then used to determine the membership of unknown, unclassified data. They gloss this procedure in fascinating terms: "If the number of samples is large it makes good sense to use, instead of the single nearest neighbor, the majority vote of the nearest k neighbors" (22). Cover and Hart invoke the pseudo-democratic logic of virtual neighbor voting against virtual neighbor at the same time as actual neighborhoods were becoming increasingly segmented and fenced off—tessellated, if you will—and were rapidly driving towards homogeneity. Cover and Hart write of this decision-making process to determine where to place x, a newcomer to the dataset: "each of the nearest neighbors casts conditionally independent votes as to the category of x" (26).

John MacCormick calls k-NN one of "the most powerful and useful pattern recognition techniques ever invented."[49] In his examination of key algorithms that "changed the future," MacCormick introduces and explains the operations of this algorithm through a relatively simple task that he claims can predict "which party a person is *most likely* to donate to, based only on a home address" (84, emphasis in original). MacCormick's party problem comes directly from the midcentury suburbanized context of Cover and Hart. Using data from the residential College Hill neighborhood in Wichita, Kansas, provided by the Huffington Post's Fundrace project, MacCormick shows how the nearest-neighbor "trick" can classify, with good results, an unknown neighbor into either one of two classes, either Democrat or Republican. This particular classification task, of course, depends on an understanding of neighborhoods as relatively segregated according to some mechanism that correlates with political party membership and throwing out data that does not fit into either one of the two major political parties. In a similar descriptive account of a neighborhood classification task, the documentation for OpenCV, a popular open-source computer vision package, glosses the mechanics of k-NN thus:

> [T]here are two families, Blue Squares and Red Triangles. We call each family as [*sic*] Class. . . . Now a new member comes into the town and creates a new home, which is shown as [a] green circle. He should be added to one of these Blue/Red families. We call that process, Classification. What [do] we do? Since we are dealing with kNN, let us apply this algorithm. . . . One method is to check who is his nearest neighbour. From the image, it is clear it is the Red Triangle family. So he is also added into Red Triangle. This method is called simply Nearest Neighbour, because classification depends only on the nearest neighbor. . . . But there is a problem with that. Red Triangle may be the nearest. But what if there are lot of Blue Squares near to him? Then Blue Squares have more strength in that locality than Red Triangle. So just checking nearest one is not sufficient. Instead we check some k nearest families. Then whoever is majority in them, the new guy belongs to that family.[50]

While MacCormick uses his simple voter classification problem and OpenCV offers this sorting of a newcomer example to simply illustrate the workings of the algorithm, the assumptions in both examples and the assumptions of the algorithm itself are remarkably simple and at the same time deeply problematic, especially when the algorithm is deployed to make decisions about people and actually existing neighborhoods. All this is to say that the drive toward homogeneity and simple "democratic" voting from mid-twentieth-century thinking permeate the discourse of machine learning and artificial intelligence and require the application of critical analysis in order to understand their consequences.

The development and exposition of k-NN marks a shift in the logics of statistical agency: we have moved from the world in which we understand the implication of subjective decisions in the creation of categories and the assignment of labels, at least within much extant explications of these algorithms, to "granting" decision-making power directly to underlying data. This transformation involves a bit of a mystification. In claiming that data make decisions, scientists and others displace multiple forms of ideologically influenced subjectivity that are heavily involved in the curation of datasets, selection of available codes, algorithms, parameters, and the labeling of known data. This displacement enables the operators of such algorithms to claim a supposedly subjectless decision-making capability, one in which data points are imagined as casting free and independent "votes" for the membership and classification of new data.

In their 1968 request for an extension of a research contract from the Office of Naval Research, Nils J. Nilsson and Richard O. Duda, two of the most important figures in the development of machine learning and artificial intelligence, define the goal of "pattern recognition" as "the discovery of regularity in the midst of confusion."[51] Seeking the comforts of a hidden regularity, artificial-intelligence and machine-learning algorithms appeared at a distinct point in time, when confusion and uncertainty were accelerating. Pattern recognition gives name to theological beliefs in algorithmic form that were deployed on behalf of those seeking to restore order and regularity in the twentieth century.

Governmentality and Critique

I want to conclude by returning to Antoinette Rouvroy and the theoretical dimensions of machine-learning technologies, especially in their application to the management of people. Rouvroy is a Foucauldian. Her notion of critique that underpins the stakes of her engagement with the concept of algorithmic governmentality depends on the existence of a discursive space in which subjects can call into question the operations of power and governmentality. Rouvroy thus approvingly cites Foucault's account of critique as "a practice that suspends judgment and an opportunity to practice new values, precisely on the basis of that suspension. In this perspective, critique targets the construction of a field of occlusive categories themselves rather than on the subsumption of a particular case under a pre-constituted category" (146). Rouvroy understands the new regime of algorithmic governmentality to have limited the scope of critique through the effects of what she calls the virtual probabilistic subject. These effects, as previously mentioned, remove contestable categories of the targeted individual. Technocrats and pattern-matching theologians want machine-learning algorithms to be read as if they have magically produced categories from the bottom up. They desire the output of these algorithms to be interpreted as if the naming of the produced categories or classes were entirely the consequence of data and algorithms, as if there were no labeling or training of code, data, and classifiers, and as if the prior assumptions of these algorithms were uncontestable.

The history of our algorithms and computational culture matters. An understanding of the ideologies that have made the shift from contestable narratives of causation to profiling through correlation is essential both to our use of these algorithms in humanities research and to everyday life in the twenty-first century. Theory, rather than being obsoleted by big data, has an increasingly large role to play in accounting for the transformation of power within the algorithmically driven present. One cannot isolate and distinguish interpretive and computational methods. The humanities provides a space in which scholars can bring these two practices together and understand how each informs the other and through that process humanistic inquiry makes it possible to address the new forms of power. Unpacking the reflexive complexities of a model in which the human is increasingly preceded or anticipated by machine-generated ideas of the human while the concepts powering these model humans have been created by prior humans will require sophisticated theoretical frameworks and historical self-consciousness.

Critical theorists play a crucial role in creating alternative fields in which computational critique can flourish and have uptake. Here, in these heterotopic and discursive spaces, the selection of known and unknown data can be contested, feature selection choices can be questioned alongside the labeling of the known data and the names of the originary classes. In combining expertise in the hermeneutics of culture, text, and computational patterns, such theorists can toggle or switch registers and pull in a wider range of evidence.[52] Critical digital theorists can ask whether the data are representative and provide enough of the range of possible data found in the phenomena under examination. They can contest the assumption that there is a natural order in which like belongs with like. And, finally, they can understand that classification itself is biased because while a list of samples must be finite, the range of possible objects is infinite. From the cosmic scope of Satosi Watanabe, a theoretical physicist, philosopher, and pattern-recognition expert, "any pair of nonidentical objects share an equal number of predicates as any other nonidentical objects, insofar as the number of predicates is finite. That is to say, from a logical point of view, there is no such thing as a natural kind."[53]

Conclusion

The previous chapters charted out a critical approach to the digital humanities that involves a recursive walking down of what I referred to in the preface as the "stack" of any workflow making use of computation. I have argued that from the selection and assembling of input archives to the invocation of an algorithm, any humanities method using computation must apply reflexive thought to all stages of computation, iteratively applying an interpretive frame to those filters, functions, tools, and transformations that would otherwise obscure the interpretive work embedded within these building blocks of computation. The specific implementations of the computational methods described and demonstrated in the preceding pages will no doubt quickly change and evolve into different forms, but the hermeneutical orientation that appears alongside framing—inquiring about assumed origins, looking over the shoulder, under the hood, investigating the scene of execution—these tools, used throughout this book, are among the many enduring contributions of the humanities.

To produce one final and clarifying loop back through this critical approach, I will now to turn to an emerging computational approach, the modeling of semantic space through the use of word embeddings produced by neural network models. Taking their name from the biological model to which they have only a partial resemblance, neural networks are an emergent and relatively sophisticated computational method with the potential of producing major improvements in existing data- and text-mining workflows.[1] These neural network algorithms are adaptive in the sense that they generally utilize what has been called deep learning to explore and locate patterns in very large datasets and databases. Although the discourse around neural networks and deep learning assumes an air of being the cutting edge of computation and although, in fact, their use in humanities applications has just begun, the major concepts and theories involved in these algorithms were already being discussed and developed in the 1940s, and the fundamental technologies used in these models have been available since the 1960s.[2] The greater storage capacity and speed of computers, along with the widespread availability of multicore processing, has enabled the construction of high-performance computing systems with thousands of CPUs that, when coupled with some major improvements in the design of neural networks, can now execute very large multilayered neural network models in parallel.

Developers of neural network models sometimes refer to the individual computational units as "neurons."[3] These neurons are "connected" in multiple layered networks that enable each neuron to pass output to another neuron. Borrowing the concept of activation from neuroscience, computer scientists describe neurons as either "activated" or "deactivated" by the computational operation executed by the neuron on its small part of the input object. Like the network of reasonably specialized neurons in a brain, these computational neurons are trained, or train themselves, to recognize small patterns that form part of the whole of a large object. In most computational neural networks, the output from the neurons is passed along to others in another layer where this output becomes the input for another set of computing units or neurons. These multiple layers sometimes function in a "feed-forward" manner, moving through the network, or use loops to introduce what is called "backpropagation" as a mechanism to improve the performance of the algorithm through an optimization based on the errors generated by prior executions.

Feed-forward and backpropagation are two advanced forms of machine learning. Machine learning, as the concept is used within the discourse of the field, involves some alteration of what we might think of as the temporality of computation. Take, for example, Bayesian approaches in which one introduces the "prior," the initial subjective guess, as one small remnant of the past before moving on to handling empirical observations in the present. Or, in the case of the *k*-nearest neighbor algorithm that is the subject of the fourth chapter of this book, the presence of training data. *k*-NN is frequently mentioned as an example of "lazy learning" because the algorithm does not exactly learn from prior executions, from the presence of accumulated learned training data. In its standard implementation, the *k*-NN algorithm reads all available data and plots the location of unknown data in relation to known, labeled data. Everything available to the algorithm exists in the same form at the same time, all in memory. History or the past belongs to *k*-NN primarily in the form of the collection and organization of the dataset. Neural networks learn through training and optimization and, once considered trained, the "learned" input data no longer needs to be available to the algorithm. These trained and tested networks can then be incorporated into complex applications, for example, services such as Apple's Siri or Amazon's Echo, both of which take new input, compare it with trained models, and then apply various rule-driven operations to deliver the desired output. Neural networks might be said to learn through the preservation and transformation of the past.

In chapter 4, I described a number of prerequisites or requirements for the *k*-NN algorithm, all of which involved the intervention of what we could call researcher or operator subjectivity. The list of requirements included a target dataset with a finite number of samples, a set of classes, class membership or labels for known data, a method of feature selection, and a testing dataset. These decisions and choices, along with the base assumptions of the algorithm and its implementation, are all fully open to critique. To this list neural network algorithms add, according to one software developer, "that an application developer specify the appropriate network learning algorithm, define an interpretation for the *signals* that will be propagated through the network, and provide a set of application-specific data patterns that collectively represent the desired behavior of the network."[4] The majority of these subjective decisions are present regardless of whether the algorithm is supervised or unsupervised.

Unlike supervised machine learning algorithms and models, including *k*-nearest neighbor, which use some human-labeled training data containing specific and marked identifying features, unsupervised neural networks recognize potential patterns within input data on their own.[5] Models like this one can classify supplied unlabeled input images, for example, into what are basically large numbers of learned features corresponding to what would have been the supplied image categories or labels. The limited selection of features required by *k*-NN and other algorithms of the same category enables research-ers to understand classification outcomes, provide feedback, and trace deci-sions back to concrete details. Neural-network models do not make available decision criteria that are based on selected features and thus are more difficult to critique. It is only after the learning phase, when these machine-learned features can be tested against a set of labeled and unlabeled data (a test set) to detect the components of the neural network, that some limited understand-ing of the outcome can be derived. The collection and preprocessing of objects as both training and testing data, as we have seen, are prime candidates for critical analysis—so too are the implementations of the neural networks, the parameters used, and the selection of activated neurons.

Building on his doctoral thesis on neural networks, in 2013 Tomas Mikolov and his colleagues at Google published a conference paper titled "Distrib-uted Representations of Words and Phrases and Their Compositionality" that detailed work on their recently introduced model, called the continuous skip-gram model, for extracting syntactic and semantic relations from very large textual datasets.[6] Word vectors or word embeddings are similar to the colloca-tion method used within natural-language processing discussed in chapter 1. Their task was to move from single-word models to bigram or phrase-based models and in doing so improve the performance of the skip-gram model for "predicting the surrounding words in a sentence or document." As with other tools used in text mining, including topic-modeling applications and sentiment-analysis techniques, using a well-known or at least a well-described corpus might lead to interpretable results for digital humanities scholars. The word2vec model has no labeled training data or specified feature selection. The model is instead "trained" by running through very large textual datasets that define the extent of the semantic space available to the algorithm. The word vectors and what the authors call the "language understanding" extracted by the word2vec algorithm are highly context-dependent—the larger the dataset, the better the results. But while large datasets produced from contemporary textual sources might be helpful for many applications, they might have lim-ited uses for more specialized and historically contingent humanities research. Mikolov and his colleagues used an archive of contemporary news articles collected by Google that contained one billion words before they removed words with fewer than five appearances, leaving them with just under seven hundred thousand words, or what they call their "vocabulary" in the mapped semantic space.

Simple calculations can be performed on the trained vectors to extract relations as a measurement of distance, within the semantic space, between sets of vectors representing modeled words. These computable vectors of word relations are the major difference between lists of collocated words and algorithms searching for similar context. The relations are comparable to something like a very-high-dimension semiotic or Greimas square, with terms connected through scaled differences rather than binary relations. The computed vectors generated by the word2vec model can be used like these other tools to locate clusters of words or concepts, but they can also help locate oppositional terms through mathematical manipulation of the vectors. In the same paper in which they introduce word2vec, Mikolov and his colleagues present an application of vector arithmetic through what they call "analogical reasoning tasks." Analogical reasoning was initially used to validate their model, but the rather easy interpretability of the results suggested additional uses. They describe the operation of the analogical reasoning task as "A typical analogy pair from our test set is 'Montreal':'Montreal Canadiens'::'Toronto':'Toronto Maple Leafs'. It is considered to have been answered correctly if the nearest representation to vec('Montreal Canadiens') – vec('Montreal') + vec('Toronto') is vec('TorontoMaple Leafs')." In supplying the vector of words that best fits this calculation, in supplying an answer to the analogy, the model demonstrates some predictive capabilities for identifying both semantic and syntactic relations between words. Like any other computational model, the object of analysis is the input or training dataset, not language itself. While initially presented as a toy, the analogical reasoning task and other related methods or those built on this type of task might have the most value for digital humanists—especially when applied to textual sources that share some cultural or historical context.

Although designed to be used on very large document collections, the word2vec model can produce some interesting results from smaller datasets. If, for example, a model trained on the North American Slave Narrative archive is queried with the name of the abolitionist Wendell Phillips, it will return a vector with the names of other prominent nineteenth-century abolitionists such as William Lloyd Garrison, Henry Ward Beecher, George Thompson, Theodore Parker, and Edmund Quincy. From such a list, it can identify figures with the greatest distance in vector or semantic space from the others; in this case, it produces George Thompson as least like the others. This model also contains enough data to produce analogical pairings from these positive and negative relations. The results displayed in figure 5.1 shows the query "insurrection" is to "nat turner" as "woman_suffrage" is to *x*. The returned vector with the nearest value is "lucretia_mott," a reasonable response. The second word, *gage*, has lost its contextual clues and has been "stemmed" from its most common appearance as "Mrs. Gage" or Frances D. Gage, another prominent nineteenth-century activist working for women's suffrage. "Miss Susan B.," of course, is a partially tokenized version of the full name "Miss Susan B. Anthony." John G. Whittier, however, appears in contexts similar to those of the other names, but within the texts found within the North American Slave Narrative archive it is not connected to the question of woman's suffrage:

on the same <u>platform</u> with **Garrison**, **Phillips**, and **Lucretia Mott**

I have sat on the <u>platform</u> with **John G. Whittier**.

Phillips and **Lucretia Mott** were also on the <u>platform</u>

The word2vec algorithm has calculated the vectors from the close-context windows surrounding the phrase "woman_suffrage." These vectors are close to the vectors from context windows surrounding several of the other names. This simple query demonstrates the possible relations of word embeddings in three separate texts when combined into a single larger input dataset for the word2vec algorithm.

But an important question for mining applications like these remains: How can one make tools like the word2vec model useful for a historically contingent or at least a contextually limited humanistic mode of inquiry? Are such limited scopes in tension with the model of meaning presupposed by such tools? How much data, in other words, is needed to produce useful results? Mikolov writes in the sample analogical reasoning demonstration application that comes bundled with word2vec, "Note that for the word analogy to perform well, the model should be trained on much larger data set."[7] Larger datasets provide more examples of word embeddings—the larger the number of words and windows around word embeddings available, the greater the statistical power of the algorithm. But if given too large of a dataset from too many sources, the algorithm will produce generalizable results that might not be interpretable—at least within a humanities frame. We might, in other words, learn something of value for linguistics or about contemporary language use, but what can these results tell us about culture? As demonstrated

```
In [13]:  src_model.most_similar(positive=['nat_turner', 'woman_suffrage'], negative=['insurrection'])

Out[13]:  [('lucretia_mott', 0.6808589696884155),
          ('gage', 0.6047872900096283),
          ('miss_susan_b', 0.6004625558853149),
          ('john_g_whittier', 0.598328888416290l3),
          ('broadway_tabernacle', 0.5822384357452393),
          ('folsom', 0.5798661708831787),
          ('boston_post', 0.5795968770980835),
          ('garrison_phillips', 0.5787340402603149),
          ('h_garnet', 0.5783672332763672),
          ('alcott', 0.5724521875381147)]
```

FIGURE 5.1   Word2Vec analogical reasoning task

```
In [14]:  src_model.most_similar("frederick_douglass",topn=20)

Out[14]:  [('mr_douglass', 0.6789201498031616),
          ('wendell_phillips', 0.6422789692878723),
          ('william_lloyd_garrison', 0.6040972471237183),
          ('autobiographies', 0.5962321162223816),
          ('douglass', 0.589881420135498),
          ('decoration_day', 0.5729281306266785),
          ('mr_garrison', 0.5727505683898926),
          ("douglass's", 0.5660401582717896),
          ('anti_slavery_convention', 0.563313364982605),
          ("mr_douglass's", 0.5495040416717529),
          ('anti_slavery_movement', 0.5458614826202393),
          ('agitator', 0.5411466360092163),
          ('various_phases', 0.5406709909439087),
          ('patrick_henry', 0.5403376817703247),
          ('harriet_beecher_stowe', 0.5360968708992004),
          ('gerritt_smith', 0.5353233814239502),
          ('henry_wilson', 0.534428596496582),
          ('charles_l_remond', 0.5323055386543274),
          ('journalistic', 0.5313712954521179),
          ('autographs', 0.5309398174285889)]
```

FIGURE 5.2   Vector similarity in DocSouth North American Slave Narrative Archive for term "frederick_douglass"

throughout this book, the constructed computational model determines the object of analysis. If one wants to analyze culture with quantitative approaches, then careful attention to the way in which the selected input data shape the contours of what counts as a valid cultural contribution is needed alongside critical inquiry into the models of the world embedded within the algorithms manipulating these data.

Restricted semantic spaces are required for any form of cultural analysis that is not entirely ahistorical and presentist. The model produced by Mikolov and his colleagues uses a roughly contemporary dataset of textual sources and, while it has the potential for some use by humanists, the relations extracted from their model are not suitable for text mining of historical texts (see figure 5.3). The semantic space modeled by the word2vec using (what are assumed mostly to be) contemporary sources has limited use for understanding either (a) semantic shift or (b) historical relations. A method of measuring the differences between multiple semantic spaces is needed in order to extract potentially more meaningful relations between a text, a set of texts, and the larger historical semantic context in which the texts were constructed and circulated. Such an operation involves combining or rather aligning various models of semantic space trained on distinct textual

```
In [15]:  google_model.most_similar("Frederick_Douglass",topn=20)

Out[15]:  [('Fredrick_Douglass', 0.6643674969673157),
           ('Harriet_Tubman', 0.6538548469543457),
           ('Langston_Hughes', 0.6378294825553894),
           ('WEB_Dubois', 0.6361298561096191),
           ('abolitionist_Frederick_Douglass', 0.6212432384490967),
           ('WEB_DuBois', 0.6167810559272766),
           ('Sojourner_Truth', 0.6166481971740723),
           ('Booker_T._Washington', 0.5926769971847534),
           ('Phillis_Wheatley', 0.5811346769332886),
           ('Thurgood_Marshall', 0.5717906355857849),
           ('G._Woodson', 0.568604588508606),
           ('WEB_Du_Bois', 0.5670568943023682),
           ('Ralph_Bunche', 0.5626702904701233),
           ('Phyllis_Wheatley', 0.5608549118041992),
           ('Mary_McLeod_Bethune', 0.5546070337295532),
           ('Fannie_Lou_Hamer', 0.5512949228286743),
           ('Tubman', 0.5479763746261597),
           ('Benjamin_Banneker', 0.5479563474655151),
           ('Eleanor_Roosevelt', 0.5426533222198486),
           ('Malcolm_X', 0.5422308444976807)]
```

FIGURE 5.3 Vector similarity in Google News dataset for term "Frederick_Douglass"

archives. The term *alignment* is useful in this context because it names the need for producing a deformation of one vector space to another. While individual texts (at the codex or volume level) typically do not provide enough textual data for extracting semantic relations with the word2vec model, collections of texts can be modeled and compared.[8] These collections could be based on author, gender, race, genre, period, and so on. These collections of texts can then be modeled via word2vec and aligned to the semantic space generated by iterations of word2vec on other collections using a variety of methods, including linear regression. Aligning the semantic space of one of collection of texts to another enables a greater granularity of control over the composition of the collective semantic space. Aligning literary to nonliterary spaces might present opportunities for examining the degree to which texts participate in or are outliers of the more general semantic space of their historical moment. Historical relations can be transformed from one moment to another (see figure 5.4). Such a mode of semantic alignment might also make it possible to identify creative variations on commonplace relations, in other words, literary use of language, by identifying unexpected semantic shifts.

The mapping and aligning of semantic space demonstrates some of the promise and limitations of computational models for humanities scholars,

```
In [16]: combined_most_similar_neighbors("frederick_douglass",topn=20)

Out[16]: [('mr_douglass', 0.32107986263292665),
          ('wendell_phillips', 0.35772104992424181),
          ('william_lloyd_garrison', 0.39590273197090209),
          ('BookExpo', 0.39807692986095866),
          ('Andrei_Sakharov', 0.40841162322395386),
          ('douglass', 0.41011861214084999),
          ('feminist_icon', 0.41086614525319021),
          ('Julian_Bond', 0.42012511674663988),
          ('Paul_Robeson', 0.42399577753377249),
          ('Steinem', 0.42421127121989977),
          ('decoration_day', 0.42707189705680892),
          ('mr_garrison', 0.42724955171080203),
          ('Louise_Mirrer', 0.42754550148413384),
          ('historian_Doris_Kearns', 0.42768691113746837),
          ('Wally_Serote', 0.43090307555114549),
          ('Mahashweta_Devi', 0.43156523792348467),
          ('Tony_Judt', 0.43233772692871941),
          ("douglass's", 0.43395979808404406),
          ('Harriet_Tubman', 0.43432488585549678),
          ('Eugene_V._Debs', 0.43469860966633733)]
```

FIGURE 5.4   Vector similarity in aligned dataset for term "frederick_douglass"

especially those working with historical texts and data. It may be the case that
such alignment methods are the best materialization of the notion of deformation as computational humanists willfully warp imagined, constructed, and
measured semantic space to other constructed spaces and the ever-receding
horizon of futurity.

Notes

Preface

1. The phrase "distant reading" was coined by Franco Moretti. "Quantitative formalism" is primarily used by the members of the Stanford Literary Lab, which included Lab founder Moretti at the time of publication of *Canon/Archive: Studies in Quantitative Formalism from the Stanford Literary Lab* (New York: N+1 Books, 2017). Jockers uses the term *microanalysis*, while "algorithmic criticism" originates with Stephen Ramsay. Matthew L. Jockers, *Macroanalysis: Digital Methods and Literary History* (Urbana: University of Illinois Press, 2013); Ramsay, *Reading Machines: Toward an Algorithmic Criticism* (Urbana: University of Illinois Press, 2011).

2. The goal of automated analysis is not a valid goal within the humanities, as it suggests the unreflective application of method to object. My understanding of methodology in the humanities is opposed to the notion of humanities computing as defined by Robert A. Busa, one of the field's founding figures: "Humanities computing is precisely the automation of every possible analysis of human expression (therefore, it is exquisitely a "humanistic" activity), in the widest sense of the word, from music to the theater, from design and painting to phonetics, but whose nucleus remains the discourse of written texts." "Foreword: Perspectives on the Digital Humanities," in *A Companion to Digital Humanities*, edited by Susan Schreibman, Ray Siemens, and John Unsworth (Oxford: Blackwell, 2004), xvi.

3. See, for example, Richard J. Lane's claim that "the shift to lab-based hybrid humanities/scientific research practices, and the accompanying self-reflexivity and theoretical engagement, does have the potential to not only 'rebuild' the otherwise declining arts and humanities (declining in terms of funding and student numbers,

as well as the decreasing public respect for an apparently obscurant humanistic discourse), but also produce 'the best work.'" *The Big Humanities: Digital Humanities/ Digital Laboratories* (New York: Routledge, 2016), 2.

4. Wayne C. Booth discusses the differences between telling and showing in *The Rhetoric of Fiction* (Chicago: University of Chicago Press, 2010), 19. Frederic Jameson's account of the novel, and especially the romance, as an imaginative resolution to cultural contradictions can be found in *The Political Unconscious* (Ithaca, NY: Cornell University Press, 1981), 245.

5. This phrase belongs to Matthew Wilkens, but this understanding of digital texts as sources for the extraction of "information" about the larger "culture" (variously defined) is widely shared. "Canons, Close Reading, and the Evolution of Method," in *Debates in the Digital Humanities*, edited by Matthew K. Gold and Lauren Klein (Minneapolis: University of Minnesota Press, 2012), 249–58, quote on 251.

6. There are a few exceptions to this abstracted approach, particularly in those instances in which we need to reconstruct, as well as possible, another scholar's published description of his or her methodology in order to critique the methods and procedures.

7. At present, the complete North American Slave Narrative archive can be accessed through a Web interface and downloaded as a single zipped archive: http://docsouth .unc.edu/neh/.

8. William L. Andrews, "An Introduction to the Slave Narrative," http://docsouth .unc.edu/neh/intro.html.

Chapter 1. Protocols, Methods, and Workflows

1. For a sampling of these various definitional projects, see the essays collected in *Defining Digital Humanities: A Reader,* ed. Melissa Terras, Julianne Nyhan, and Edward Vanhoutte (Burlington, VT: Ashgate, 2013). Matthew Kirschenbaum's essay in this collection locates the origin of the phrase "digital humanities" in John Unsworth's naming, in 2001 and 2002, of a book project and an organization: the Blackwell collection *Companion to Digital Humanities* (2005) and the Alliance of Digital Humanities Organizations.

2. This understanding of the digital humanities is shared by a number of scholars (see, for one example, Jockers, *Macroanalysis*, 15), especially those with an investment in literary studies, but it has also been widely contested. Laura Mandell observes that the split between archival work and the computational methods examined by this book (arguably the two major subfields) has been gendered in problematic ways that reproduce the feminization and denigration of "service" oriented editorial work and perpetuate the canonical preferences already existing within (book) print culture. "Gendering Digital Literary History," in *A New Companion to Digital Humanities*, ed. Susan Schreibman, Ray Siemens, and John Unsworth (New York: Wiley, 2016), 521.

3. There are other approaches that might be more suitable to particular types of texts and certain disciplinary needs. It is likely that methods from computer vision,

for example, might produce more interesting results than text mining for those invested in the history of the book.

4. David M. Berry, "The Computational Turn: Thinking about the Digital Humanities," *Culture Machine* 12 (2011): 1–21, quote on 16.

5. Tarleton Gillespie provides an abbreviated history of the term algorithm and the critical possibilities for the cultural analysis of the various ways in which algorithms are used and discussed in "Algorithm," in *Digital Keywords*, ed. Benjamin Peters (Princeton, NJ: Princeton University Press, 2016), 18–30.

6. Anne Burdick, Johanna Drucker, Peter Lunenfeld, Todd Presner, and Jeffrey Schnapp, *Digital_Humanities* (Cambridge, MA: MIT Press, 2012), 3.

7. N. Katherine Hayles, *How We Think: Digital Media and Contemporary Technogenesis* (Chicago: University of Chicago Press, 2012), 46.

8. See Bethany Nowviskie's "On the Origin of 'Hack' and 'Yack'" in *Debates in the Digital Humanities*, ed. Lauren F. Klein and Matthew Gold, 66–70. (Minneapolis: University of Minnesota Press, 2016), for a cogent summary and analysis of the debate between these positions.

9. Hans-Georg Gadamer, *Truth and Method*, trans. Joel Weinsheimer and Donald Marshall (New York: Crossroad, 1989), xxii.

10. The approach for a critical digital humanities articulated within this book depends on an understanding of critique as central to the project of the humanities. This critique, however, is more capacious than just those modes of inquiry associated with any "hermeneutics of suspicion."

11. See, for example, Martha Nell Smith's recollection of those working in humanities computing who imagined it as a space free from critical inquiry, as practiced by much of the rest of the humanities: "It was as if these matters of objective and hard science provided an oasis for folks who did not want to clutter sharp, disciplined, methodical philosophy with considerations of the gender-, race-, class-determined facts of life. . . . Humanities computing seemed to offer a space free from all this messiness and a return to objective questions of representation." "The Human Touch Software of the Highest Order: Revisiting Editing as Interpretation," *Textual Cultures* 2, no. 1 (2007): 1–15.

12. See, for just one example of this dialogue, the special issue of *English Language Notes*, ed. David Glimp and Russ Castronovo. In the wake of Bruno Latour's "Why Has Critique Run Out of Steam? From Matters of Fact to Matters of Concern" (*Critical Inquiry* 30, no. 2 [2004]: 225–48), the editors survey postcritical projects: "To name only a few of the research agendas that implicitly or explicitly reject or rethink critique, we include: modes of reparative reading (Sedgwick); speculative realism and object oriented ontologies (Latour, Serres, Meillassoux, Harman); vitalist materialism (Bennet); reflexive sociologies of justification and critique (Thévenot and Boltanski); a rethought phenomenology and affect studies (Ahmed, Stewart, among many others); as well as the emergence of new objects of inquiry, such as digital humanities, or the revitalization of older types of scholarship, such as book history, that do not necessarily or inherently organize their work around critique."

("After Critique," special issue, *English Language Notes* 51, no. 2 [2013]). See also Elizabeth S. Anker and Rita Felski, eds. *Critique and Postcritique* (Durham, NC: Duke University Press, 2017).

13. Rita Felski, *The Limits of Critique* (Chicago: University of Chicago Press, 2015), 52.

14. For a historical account of the emergence and transformation of literary studies, see Gerald Graff, *Professing Literature: An Institutional History* (Chicago: University of Chicago Press, 1987).

15. Stanley Edgar Hyman, *The Armed Vision: A Study in the Methods of Modern Literary Criticism* (New York: Knopf, 1948).

16. Alexander R. Galloway, "The Cybernetic Hypothesis," *differences* 25, no. 1 (2014): 107–31.

17. I. A. Richards, *Practical Criticism: A Study of Literary Judgment* (New York: Harcourt and Brace, 1929), 3.

18. This is Murray Krieger's critique of Richards: "I. A. Richards: Neurological and Poetic Organization," in Krieger, *The New Apologists for Poetry* (Minneapolis: University of Minnesota Press, 1956), 57–63.

19. For the origins of information theory, see Claude E. Shannon, "A Mathematical Theory of Communication," *Bell System Technical Journal* 27, no. 3 (1948): 379–423. The classic reference for Alan Turing's theory of computation can be found in "On Computable Numbers, with an Application to the *Entscheidungsproblem*," *Proceedings of the London Mathematical Society* 42, no. 2 (1937): 230–65.

20. David Golumbia has written provocatively on the use of *traditional* within the discourse of the digital humanities to rhetorically assign noncomputational work in the humanities to the past. The critical digital humanities offered by this book is very much a part of the important legacy of the critical tradition in the humanities and thus I try to avoid, wherever possible, use of the traditional–digital binary, http://www.uncomputing.org/?p=1868.

21. Daniel Allington, Sarah Brouillette, and David Golumbia, "Neoliberal Tools (and Archives): A Political History of Digital Humanities," *Los Angeles Review of Books* (May 2016), https://lareviewofbooks.org/article/neoliberal-tools-archives-political -history-digital-humanities/.

22. For a sample of the response to this critical essay, see Matthew Kirschenbaum, "Am I a Digital Humanist? Confessions of a Neoliberal Tool," https://medium .com/@mkirschenbaum/am-i-a-digital-humanist-confessions-of-a-neoliberal-tool -1bc64caaa984#.pw2y3ej9g, and Roopika Risam, "Digital Humanities in Other Contexts," http://roopikarisam.com/uncategorized/digital-humanities-in-other -contexts.

23. Hayles uses the term "regime of computation" to characterize the present moment as operating within, or at least making available, a worldview that, for her, "offers new answers to metaphysical questions." I share her enthusiasm for new methods of thinking and new approaches to addressing complex digital systems, but I have reservations about our ability to bracket hermeneutical questions as either

irrelevant to computation or superseded by empirical methodologies. *My Mother Was a Computer: Digital Subjects and Literary Texts* (Chicago: University of Chicago Press, 2005), 17.

24. Sara Ahmed, "Interview with Judith Butler," *Sexualities* 19, no. 4 (2016): 482–92.

25. Viktor Mayer-Schönberger and Kenneth Cukier, *Big Data: A Revolution That Will Transform How We Live, Work, and Think* (Boston: Houghton Mifflin Harcourt, 2013).

26. David Lazer, Ryan Kennedy, Gary King, and Alessandro Vespignani, "The Parable of Google Flu: Traps in Big Data Analysis," *Science* 343, no. 6176 (2014): 1203–5.

27. For an important critique of big data as a socio-technical phenomenon, see danah boyd and Kate Crawford, "Critical Questions for Big Data: Provocations for a Cultural, Technological, and Scholarly Phenomenon," *Information, Communication and Society* 15, no. 5 (June 2012): 662–79.

28. Stephen Marche makes an argument in favor of separating text and data in "Literature Is Not Data: Against Digital Humanities," *Los Angeles Review of Books*, October 2012, https://lareviewofbooks.org/article/literature-is-not-data-against -digital-humanities/.

29. Lev Manovich, "The Science of Culture? Social Computing, Digital Humanities and Cultural Analytics," *CA: Journal of Cultural Analytics* (2016), http://culturalanalytics .org/2016/05/the-science-of-culture-social-computing-digital-humanities-and -cultural-analytics/.

30. Richard Rogers, *Digital Methods* (Cambridge, MA: MIT Press, 2013), 19.

31. N. Katherine Hayles, "Print Is Flat, Code Is Deep: The Importance of Media-Specific Analysis," *Poetics Today* 25, no. 1 (2004): 67–90.

32. David Golumbia, "Cultural Studies and the Discourse of New Media" in *The Renewal of Cultural Studies*, ed. Paul Smith (Philadelphia: Temple University Press, 2011), 83–92.

33. Paul Ricoeur, following Nietzsche, Freud, and Marx, names the critical tradition the "hermeneutics of suspicion" in *Freud and Philosophy: An Essay on Interpretation*, trans. Denis Savage (New Haven, CT: Yale University Press, 1970).

34. Gabriele Griffin and Matt Hayler, Introduction to *Research Methods for Reading Digital Data in the Digital Humanities*, ed. Gabriele Griffin and Matt Hayler (Edinburgh: Edinburgh University Press, 2016), 1.

35. Dawn Archer, "Data Mining and Word Frequency Analysis," in *Research Methods for Reading Digital Data in the Digital Humanities*, ed. Gabriele Griffin and Matt Hayler, 72–92; quote on 72.

36. John Rupert Firth, *Papers in Linguistics 1934–1951* (London: Oxford University Press, 1957), 11. For greater detail on the theory and implementation of collocation algorithms, see Christopher Manning and Hinrich Schütze, *Foundations of Statistical Natural Language Processing* (Cambridge, MA: MIT Press, 1999).

37. This is the output produced by executing "help(nltk.Text)" after importing the NLTK version 3.2.2 library with the Python interpreter.

38. Jockers, *Macroanalysis*, 10.

39. Matthew L. Jockers, *Text Analysis with R for Students of Literature* (New York: Springer, 2014), 59. Emphasis in original.

40. Geoffrey Rockwell and Stéfan Sinclair, *Hermeneutica: Computer-Assisted Interpretation in the Humanities* (Cambridge, MA: MIT Press, 2016).

41. See Lisa Gitelman and Virginia Jackson, Introduction to *"Raw Data" Is an Oxymoron* (Cambridge, MA: MIT Press, 2012), and Johanna Drucker, "Humanities Approaches to Graphical Display," *Digital Humanities Quarterly* 5, no. 1 (2011).

42. Barbara Herrnstein Smith, "What Was 'Close Reading'? A Century of Method in Literary Studies," *Minnesota Review 2016*, no. 87 (2016): 57–75; quote on 69.

43. For an argument explicitly in favor of information science and social science approaches to computational analysis of text, see Tanya E. Clement, "Where Is Methodology in Digital Humanities?" in *Debates in the Digital Humanities,* ed. Lauren F. Klein and Matthew Gold, 153–175 (Minneapolis: University of Minnesota Press, 2016). Also available at http://dhdebates.gc.cuny.edu/debates/text/65.

44. See, for example, LaCapra's *Soundings in Critical Theory* (Ithaca, NY: Cornell University Press, 1989).

45. Jacques Derrida, *Limited Inc.* (Evanston, IL: Northwestern University Press, 1988), 143.

46. Jacques Derrida, *Of Grammatology*, corr. ed., trans. Gayatri Chakravorty Spivak (Baltimore, MD: Johns Hopkins University Press, 1997), 161.

47. Scholes defines his Derridean-influenced conception of a "nihilistic hermeneutics" in his chapter "Interpretation: The Question of Protocols," in Scholes, *Protocols of Reading* (New Haven, CT: Yale University Press, 1989), 50–88.

Chapter 2. Can an Algorithm Be Disturbed?

1. As I primarily work within American literary studies, many of my references will be the local application of what I describe as larger movements within the humanities. On description as method, see Heather Love, "Close but Not Deep: Literary Ethics and the Descriptive Turn," *New Literary History* 41, no. 2 (2010): 371–91. An example of the renewed interest in literary aesthetics can be found in Christopher Looby and Cindy Weinstein, Introduction to *American Literature's Aesthetic Dimensions* (New York: Columbia University Press, 2012). For an example of the new formalism, see Samuel Otter, "Aesthetics in All Things," *Representations* 104, no. 1 (2008): 116–25.

2. Paul Ricoeur's exact phrase is "the school of suspicion," which he uses to name the common intention he finds in Freud, Marx, and Nietzsche. *Freud and Philosophy: An Essay on Interpretation*, trans. Denis Savage (New Haven, CT: Yale University Press, 1970), 32. Rita Felski has made this argument many times. She offers some suggestions of what might come after suspicion, after critique: "Critique needs to be supplemented by generosity, pessimism by hope, negative aesthetics by a sustained reckoning with the communicative, expressive, and world-disclosing aspects of art." "After Suspicion," *Profession* 35 (2009): 33.

3. Jockers, *Macroanalysis*.

4. Stephen Best and Sharon Marcus, "Surface Reading: An Introduction," *Representations* 108 (2009): 1–21; quote on 17.

5. Love, "Close but Not Deep."

6. Jockers, *Macroanalysis*, 15.

7. Stephen Ramsay, "The Hermeneutics of Screwing Around; or What You Do with a Million Books," in *Pastplay: Teaching and Learning History with Technology*, ed. Kevin Kee (Ann Arbor: University of Michigan Press, 2014), 111–20. My critique of "screwing around" as a form of play within an unacknowledged constrained space is indebted to D. W. Winnicott's account of play and his notion of potential space. *Playing and Reality* (New York: Routledge, 2005).

8. Katherine Bode, "The Equivalence of 'Close' and 'Distant' Reading; or, Toward a New Object for Data-Rich Literary History," *Modern Language Quarterly* 78, no. 1 (2017): 77–106; quote on 91.

9. In many fields moving toward shared workflows and open-access data, the move toward open data standards has taken several decades. This work requires considerable coordination with software developers, data archival sites, and research centers. On the Text Encoding Initiative standard, see "P5: Guidelines for Electronic Text Encoding and Interchange." Version 3.2.0. Last updated on July 10, 2017, revision ofcf651, http://www.tei-c.org/release/doc/tei-p5-doc/en/html/.

10. Phillip R. Polefrone, John Simpson, and Dennis Yi Tenen, "Critical Computing in the Humanities," in *Doing Digital Humanities: Practice, Training, Research,* ed. Constance Crompton, Richard J. Lane, and Ray Siemens, 85–103 (New York: Routledge, 2016).

11. Writing code might be a form of what Matt Ratto calls "critical making," yet the use of computational methods, as this book argues, requires theoretical engagement to examine the entire stack of assumptions and ideologies incorporated or bundled into data, tools, algorithms, and computation itself. "Critical Making: Conceptual and Material Studies in Technology and Social Life," *The Information Society* 27, no. 4 (2011): 252–60.

12. The "Quantitative Formalism: An Experiment" pamphlet from the Stanford Literary Lab, the introductory essay in *Canon/Archive*, explains that, in order to understand the nuances and complications of their computational answer to the question of whether one can develop a genre classifier, "it is necessary to look at the entire process of our study," yet they do not expose the code or even offer an account of the specific libraries and methods used in their workflow. Sarah Allison, Ryan Heuser, Matthew Jockers, Franco Moretti, and Michael Witmore, *Canon/Archive: Studies in Quantitative Formalism from the Stanford Literary Lab,* ed. Franco Moretti (New York: N+1 Books, 2017), 1.

13. Ramsay, *Reading Machines*, xi.

14. Bruno Latour, "Why Has Critique Run Out of Steam? From Matters of Fact to Matters of Concern," *Critical Inquiry* 30, no. 2 (2004): 225–48 (see esp. 225–30); Eve Kosofsky Sedgwick, *Touching Feeling: Affect, Pedagogy, Performativity* (Durham, NC: Duke University Press, 2003), 138–43; Felski, "After Suspicion," 31.

15. Franco Moretti, "Conjectures on World Literature," *New Left Review* 1 (2000): 54–68.

16. Franco Moretti, *Graphs, Maps, Trees: Abstract Models for a Literary Theory* (New York: Verso, 2005), 9.

17. Berry, *Philosophy of Software*, 51–52.

18. Gitelman and Jackson, *Raw Data*.

19. For the canonical definition of machine learning as used in computer science, see Bishop, *Pattern Recognition*.

20. The problem of discovering and sharing data provenance has become a pressing issue for many computational fields. The following has been offered as a vision of an ideal world: "reproduce their results by replaying previous computations, understand why two seemingly identical runs with the same inputs produce different results, and find out which data sets, algorithms, or services were involved in the derivation of their results." Moreau et al., "The Provenance of Electronic Data," *Communications of the ACM* 51, no. 4 (2008), 54.

21. There has been very little attention drawn to the distinction between supervised and so-called unsupervised methods and the appropriateness of either for humanities research. For one exploration of what is referred to as the semisupervised method of topic modeling in relation to historical "domain expert knowledge," see Federico Nanni, Hiram Kümper, and Simone Paolo Ponzetto, "Semi-supervised Textual Analysis and Historical Research Helping Each Other: Some Thoughts and Observations," *International Journal of Humanities and Arts Computing* 10, no. 1 (March 2016): 63–77.

22. This essay appears in a "Theories and Methodologies" cluster of *PMLA* titled "On Franco Moretti's Distant Reading." Richard Jean So, "All Models Are Wrong," *PMLA* 132, no. 3 (2017): 668–73.

23. See also Andrew Piper's account of modeling in the humanities "as the construction of a hypothetical structure that mediates our relationship to texts." "Novel Devotions: Conversional Reading, Computational Modeling, and the Modern Novel," *New Literary History* 46, no. 1 (2015): 63–98; quote on 67.

24. Chris Anderson, "The End of Theory: The Data Deluge Makes the Scientific Method Obsolete," *Wired*, June 23, 2008.

25. Bernard Stiegler has produced some of the best commentary on the "end of theory" claims in Anderson. *Automatic Society*, vol. 1, *The Future of Work*, trans. Daniel Ross (Malden, MA: Polity, 2016), 48–55; quote on 51.

26. The extended version of Box's maxim on the correction of minor errors appears in an article subsection titled "Worrying Selectively," in which he writes, "Since all models are wrong the scientist must be alert to what is importantly wrong. It is inappropriate to be concerned about mice when there are tigers abroad." George E. P. Box, "Science and Statistics," *Journal of the American Statistical Association* 71, no. 356 (1976): 791–99; quote on 792.

27. There has been much discussion of bias in the use of modeling and machine learning in the legal process. For an excellent analysis of several black-box methods

used in sentencing and policing, including the "COMPAS Recidivism Algorithm," see Julia Angwin, Jeff Larson, Surya Mattu, and Lauren Kirchner, "Machine Bias," *ProPublica*, May 23, 2016, https://www.propublica.org/article/machine-bias-risk -assessments-in-criminal-sentencing.

28. From a Marxist perspective, some uses of modeling within the social sciences and the humanities could be framed as a form of false consciousness, in that they provide a false representation of a social reality. At the same time, to point to the gap between any social reality and a false representation of that reality can only reassert the status of some presupposed reality—itself an ideological move. See Slavoj Žižek, *The Sublime Object of Ideology* (New York: Verso, 1989), 28–35.

29. Scholars have been interested in the automatic extraction of topics or themes and even the plotting of these themes using Fourier analysis through the length of a text since the appearance of a foundational essay on this topic in 1978. See John B. Smith, "Computer Criticism," *Style* 12 (1978): 262–73.

30. For a general discussion of topic models in the humanities and the Latent Dirichlet Allocation algorithm, see the article by algorithm's creator, David M. Blei: "Topic Modeling and Digital Humanities," *Journal of the Digital Humanities* 2, no. 1 (2012), http://journalofdigitalhumanities.org/2-1/topic-modeling-and-digital -humanities-by-david-m-blei/.

31. Descriptions, examples, and documentation for both the LDA and NMF algorithms can be found at the Scikit-learn website, http://scikit-learn.org/stable/ auto_examples/applications/plot_topics_extraction_with_nmf_lda.html.

32. These frequently appearing words, as Johanna Drucker reminds, are never simply words: "Even the use of a definite or indefinite article changes a noun's value. Meaning is what language *does*, and any sense that a word simply *is* goes against a century of linguistic theory, at the least. So the technique that counts a word as a matched letter string has nothing to do with meaning or reading as an interpretive act. Text analysis conflates reading with sorting, counting, and matching." I would only modify her argument by continuing to insist that while text mining might not be reading, it should be regarded as an interpretive act. "Why Distant Reading Isn't," *PMLA* 132, no. 3 (2017): 628–35.

33. One of the most popular stemming algorithms is the Porter Stemming algorithm. This is incorporated within the workflows as a preprocessing step by many software packages. See M. F. Porter, "An Algorithm for Suffix Stripping," *Program* 14, no. 3 (1980): 130–37.

34. See Andrew Kachites McCallum, *MALLET: Machine Learning for Language Toolkit*, 2002, http://mallet.cs.umass.edu.

35. The Stanford Named Entity Recognition algorithm is described in Jenny Rose Finkel, Trond Grenager, and Christopher Manning, "Incorporating Non-local Information into Information Extraction Systems by Gibbs Sampling," *Proceedings of the 43rd Annual Meeting of the Association for Computational Linguistics* (2005): 363–70.

36. See, for example, Alan Liu, "The Meaning of the Digital Humanities," *PMLA* 128, no. 2 (2013): 409–23.

37. Jacques Derrida, *Dissemination*, trans. Barbara Johnson (Chicago: University of Chicago Press, 1981), 3–22.

38. Another Derridean concept, *"parergon"* a frame that we take to exist outside the space of the work of art, might be useful for understanding the stakes of suggesting the existence of nonsignifying elements of a text. Jacques Derrida, *The Truth in Painting,* trans. Geoffrey Bennington and Ian McLeod (Chicago: University of Chicago Press, 1987), 97–98.

39. Andrew Goldstone and Ted Underwood, "The Quiet Transformations of Literary Studies: What Thirteen Thousand Scholars Could Teach Us," *New Literary History* 45, no. 3 (2014): 359–84.

40. On the methods of the Literary Lab, see Franco Moretti, "Literature, Measured," in *Canon/Archive: Studies in Quantitative Formalism from the Stanford Literary Lab*, ed. Allison et al., ix–xvii. Underwood's account of distant reading connects 1980s cultural criticism to his social-science-inspired methods. Ted Underwood, "A Genealogy of Distant Reading" *Digital Humanities Quarterly* 11, no. 2 (2017), http://www.digitalhumanities.org/dhq/vol/11/2/000317/000317.html.

41. Northrop Frye, *Anatomy of Criticism: Four Essays* (Princeton, NJ: Princeton University Press, 1957), 14.

42. Geoffrey Hartman, *Beyond Formalism: Literary Essays, 1958–1970* (New Haven, CT: Yale University Press, 1971), 33.

43. Northrop Frye, "Literary and Mechanical Models," in *Research in Humanities Computing 1: Selected Papers from the ALLC/ACH Conference, Toronto, June 1989,* ed. Ian Lancashire (New York: Oxford University Press, 1991), 6.

44. Roland Barthes, *The Rustle of Language*, trans. Richard Howard (Berkeley: University of California Press, 1989), 6.

45. For a general theoretical and historical background on structuralism, its main currents of thought, and adoption within the American academy, see Robert Scholes, *Structuralism in Literature: An Introduction* (New Haven, CT: Yale University Press, 1974). Scholes describes the assumption of an a priori order of the world: "The perception of order or structure where only undifferentiated phenomena had seemed to exist before is the distinguishing characteristic of structuralist thought" (41). See also Jonathan Culler, *Structuralist Poetics* (Ithaca, NY: Cornell University Press, 1975), 37–63.

46. Geoffrey Hartman destabilizes Frye's spatialization of literature by introducing the problem of temporality to Frye's understanding of literature as unfolding "quasi-simultaneously in space" (*Beyond Formalism: Literary Essays, 1958–1970* [New Haven, CT: Yale University Press, 1971], 32–33). The classic deconstructive critique of structuralism based on a "decentering" of the structure is Jacques Derrida's "Structure, Sign and Play in the Discourse of the Human Sciences," in *Writing and Difference*, trans. Alan Bass (Chicago: University of Chicago Press, 1978), 278–93.

47. Sigurd Burckhardt, "Notes on the Theory of Intrinsic Interpretation," in Burckhardt, *Shakespearean Meanings* (Princeton, NJ: Princeton University Press, 1968), 298.

48. Hans-Georg Gadamer, *Truth and Method*, trans. Joel Weinsheimer and Donald Marshall (New York: Crossroad, 1989), 262.

49. On the long history of classification, including computer-assisted classification, see Geoffrey C. Bowker and Susan Leigh Star, *Sorting Things Out: Classification and Its Consequences* (Cambridge, MA: MIT Press, 1999).

50. Roland Barthes, *Camera Lucida: Reflections on Photography*, trans. Richard Howard (New York: Hill and Wang, 1981), 26–27.

51. I am connecting the notion of correct execution of an algorithm to Burckhardt's notion of the hermeneutical "stumblingblock" by calling into question our reliance on the separation between methodology and interpretation, and the way in which algorithmic thinking denies the possibility of being disturbed, and the situated or idiosyncratic reading. In his introductory text on algorithms, Thomas Cormen defines an algorithm as "a set of steps to accomplish a task that is described precisely enough that a computer can run it." He continues to refine this concept through the addition of iterability: "Computer algorithms solve computational problems. We want two things from a computer algorithm: given an input to a problem, it should always produce a correct solution to the problem, and it should use computational resources efficiently while doing so" (Thomas H. Cormen, *Algorithms Unlocked* [Cambridge, MA: MIT Press, 2013], 1–2). See also the explanation of error-handling algorithms in Cormen's co-authored *Introduction to Algorithms*: "An algorithm is said to be *correct* if, for every input instance, it halts with the correct output. We say that a correct algorithm *solves* the given computational problem. An incorrect algorithm might not halt at all on some input instances, or it might halt with an incorrect answer. Contrary to what you might expect, incorrect algorithms can sometimes be useful, if we can control their error rate" (Cormen, Charles E. Leiserson, Ronald L. Rivest, and Clifford Stein, *Introduction to Algorithms* [Cambridge, MA: MIT Press, 2009], 6).

52. Felski, "After Suspicion," 28–30.

Chapter 3. Digital Historicism and the Historicity of Digital Texts

1. Stephen Robertson, "The Differences between Digital Humanities and Digital History," *Debates in the Digital Humanities*, ed. Matthew K. Gold and Lauren Klein (Minneapolis: University of Minnesota Press, 2016), 289–307.

2. William G. Thomas III, "Computing and the Historical Imagination," in *A Companion to Digital Humanities*, ed. Susan Schreibman, Ray Siemens, and John Unsworth (New York: Blackwell, 2004), 56–68; quote on 66.

3. Tom Scheinfeldt, "Sunset for Ideology, Sunrise for Methodology?" in *Debates in the Digital Humanities*, ed. Matthew K. Gold (Minneapolis: University of Minnesota Press, 2012), 124, 125.

4. Daniel J. Cohen, Michael Frisch, Patrick Gallagher, Steven Mintz, Kirsten Sword, Amy Murrell Taylor, William G. Thomas III, and William J. Turkel, "Interchange: The Promise of Digital History," *Journal of American History* 95, no. 2 (2008): 452–91; quote on 481.

5. Daniel J. Cohen and Roy Rozenzweig's co-authored volume, *Digital History: A Guide to Gathering, Preserving, and Presenting the Past on the Web* (Philadelphia: University of Pennsylvania Press, 2006), is dedicated to the understanding of the subfield of digital history as the construction of archival websites.

6. D. Sculley and Bradley M. Pasanek point out in the theory of machine learning there is an assumption that "the distribution's probabilistic behavior does not change over time, and that it will continue to produce as many examples as requested" while humanities researchers "almost always work with historical data and attend to some important moment of change: an author's formation of a 'late style,' the establishment of vernacular literature in the shadow of a classical inheritance, the refinement and reinvention of the sonnet cycle in the early modern period, or the rise or elevation of the novel in the eighteenth century to name a few" (411). "Meaning and Mining: The Impact of Implicit Assumptions in Data Mining for the Humanities," *Literary and Linguistic Computing* 23, no. 4 (2008): 409–24.

7. Laura C. Mandell, "Gendering Digital Literary History: What Counts for Digital Humanities," in *A New Companion to Digital Humanities,* ed. Susan Schreibman, Ray Siemens, and John Unsworth (New York: John Wiley, 2016): 511–23; quote on 520.

8. Saidiya V. Hartman, *Scenes of Subjection: Terror, Slavery, and Self-Making in Nineteenth-Century America* (New York: Oxford University Press, 1997), 11.

9. Lauren F. Klein, "The Image of Absence: Archival Silence, Data Visualization, and James Hemings," *American Literature* 85, no. 1 (2013): 661–88; quote on 665.

10. On the history of the academic study of literature, with a marked emphasis on American institutions, see Graff, *Professing Literature.*

11. Jameson, *Political Unconscious.*

12. Stephen Greenblatt, *Shakespearean Negotiations: The Circulation of Social Energy in Renaissance England* (Berkeley: University of California Press, 1988), 1.

13. H. Aram Veeser, Introduction to *The New Historicism,* ed. H. Aram Veeser (New York: Routledge, 1989), xi.

14. Joel Fineman, "The History of the Anecdote: Fiction and Fiction," in *The New Historicism*, ed. H. Aram Veeser (New York: Routledge, 1989), 56–57.

15. On the various uses of *posthistoricism,* see Walter Benn Michaels, "Posthistoricism," *Transition*, no. 70 (1996): 4–19; Jeffrey Inkso, "The Prehistory of Posthistoricism" in *The Limits of Literary Historicism,* ed. Allen Dunn and Thomas F. Haddox (Knoxville: University of Tennessee Press, 2011): 105–23; Rita Felski, *The Limits of Critique* (Chicago: University of Chicago Press, 2015), 155.

16. Felski, *Limits of Critique*, 154.

17. In a special section of *Victorian Studies* dedicated to the topic "V21 Forum on Strategic Presentism," David Sweeney Coombs and Danielle Coriale gloss the import of presentism: "While the strategies for deploying presentism in each of these projects will differ, what they share is the effort to reimagine presentism as a mode of posthistoricist critique. V21's call for strategic presentism, then, asks us to think critically about the past in the present in order to change the present.

Far from fostering complacency, presentism might offer us new ways to engage in the urgent task of asking how the Victorian era might help us imagine alternative futures to the various mass extinctions that loom just over the horizon of the present" (David Sweeney Coombs and Danielle Coriale, "Introduction," *Victorian Studies* 59, no. 1 [2016]: 87–89; quote on 88).

18. Bode, "Equivalence of 'Close' and 'Distant' Reading, 92.

19. Amy Earhart, *Traces of the Old; Uses of the New: The Emergence of Digital Literary Studies* (Ann Arbor: University of Michigan Press, 2015).

20. Jerome McGann, *Radiant Textuality: Literature after the World Wide Web* (New York: Palgrave, 2001).

21. On the possibilities of a cultural analysis of an object like the Sony Walkman, see Keith Negus, Paul Du Gay, Stuart Hall, Linda Janes, and Hugh Mackay, *Doing Cultural Studies: The Story of the Sony Walkman* (London: Sage, 1997).

22. Andrew Kopec, "The Digital Humanities, Inc.: Literary Criticism and the Fate of a Profession," *PMLA* 131, no. 2 (2016): 324–39; quote on 330.

23. On the Text Encoding Initiative and the electronic edition as a form of textual editing practice, see Susan Schreibman, "Computer-Mediated Texts and Textuality: Theory and Practice," *Computers and the Humanities* 36, no. 3 (2002): 283–93.

24. Matthew Wilkens's extraction and projection of dictionary-defined place names from thirty-seven works of nineteenth-century American fiction ("Canons, Close Reading, and the Evolution of Method") is particularly odd. He claims to present a counternarrative to "the stories we currently tell about Romanticism and the American Renaissance, which are centered firmly in New England during the early 1850s" (253) through his discovery of places across the world and clusters in the American South. Wilkens's periodizing term, the American Renaissance, comes from F. O. Matthiessen's reading (*The American Renaissance: Art and Expression in the Age of Emerson and Whitman* [New York: Oxford University Press, 1941]) of five major authors publishing from 1850 to 1855 in fiction (Hawthorne and Melville), in autobiographical prose (Thoreau), in poetry (Whitman), and in the essay form (Emerson). The presence of words matching places listed in a dictionary does not indicate a concern with these places, nor are the major works previously mentioned concerned only with New England.

25. Todd Presner, David Shepard, Yoh Kawano, *HyperCities: Thick Mapping in the Digital Humanities* (Cambridge, MA: Harvard University Press, 2014), 18.

26. Alan Liu, *Local Transcendence: Essays on Postmodern Historicism and the Database* (Chicago: University of Chicago Press, 2008), 258–61.

27. Maurice S. Lee, "Searching the Archives with Dickens and Hawthorne: Databases and Aesthetic Judgment after the New Historicism," *ELH* 79, no. 3 (2012): 747–71; quote on 755.

28. http://www.computerworld.com/article/3048497/personal-technology/lifelogging-is-dead-for-now.html.

29. Brook Thomas, *The New Historicism and Other Old-Fashioned Topics* (Princeton, NJ: Princeton University Press, 1991), 183.

30. Ramsay, *Reading Machines*, 32. See also Jerome K. McGann and Lisa Samuels, "Deformance and Interpretation," in McGann, *Radiant Textuality: Literature after the World Wide Web*, 105–36 (New York: Palgrave, 2001).

31. For another example of a type of secondary database used in humanities-oriented text mining, see Alison Booth's discussion of the "biographical elements and structure schema" in "Mid-Range Reading: Not a Manifesto," *PMLA* 132, no. 3 (2017): 620–27. See also http://cbw.iath.virginia.edu/exist/cbw/BESSdoc.

32. George A. Miller, Richard Beckwith, Christiane Fellbaum, Derek Gross, and Katherine Miller, "WordNet: An Online Lexical Database," *International Journal of Lexicography* 3, no. 4 (1990): 235–44.

33. Nancy Ide, "Preparation and Analysis of Linguistic Corpora," in *A Companion to Digital Humanities*, ed. Susan Schreibman, Ray Siemens, and John Unsworth (New York: Blackwell, 2004): 289–305; quote on 292.

34. Jennifer L. Fleissner, "Historicism Blues," *American Literary History* 25, no. 4 (2013): 699–717; quote on 700.

35. Stanley Fish, *Is There a Text in This Class?: The Authority of Interpretive Communities* (Cambridge, MA: Harvard University, 1980), 320.

36. Bing Liu, "Sentiment Analysis and Subjectivity," in *Handbook of Natural Language Processing*, 2nd ed., ed. Nitin Indurkhya and Fred J. Damerau (Boca Raton, FL: CRC Press, 2010), 629.

37. See the documentation provided at http://provalisresearch.com/products/content-analysis-software/wordstat-dictionary/sentiment-dictionaries/.

38. Colin Martindale, *Romantic Progression: The Psychology of Literary History* (Washington, DC: Hemisphere, 1975). The digitized version of Martindale's dictionary can be found at the following URL: http://provalisresearch.com/products/content-analysis-software/wordstat-dictionary/regressive-imagery-dictionary-by-colin-martindale-free/.

39. The Syuzhet package also contains a subset of the National Resource Council Word-Emotion Association lexicon. This external dataset provides word lists sorted into a broader set of ten sentiment categories: positive, negative, anger, anticipation, disgust, fear, joy, sadness, surprise, and trust (Saif Mohammad and Peter Turney, "Crowdsourcing a Word-Emotion Association Lexicon," *Computational Intelligence* 29, no. 3 [2013]: 436–65).

40. Syuzhet.R, source code line 49. The code is available at https://github.com/mjockers/syuzhet.

41. Andrew J. Reagan, Lewis Mitchell, Dilan Kiley, Christopher M. Danforth, and Peter Sheridan Dodds, "The Emotional Arcs of Stories Are Dominated by Six Basic Shapes," *EJP Data Science* 5, no. 31 (2016).

42. Jianbo Gao, Matthew L. Jockers, John Laudun, and Timothy Tangherlini, "A Multiscale Theory for the Dynamical Evolution of Sentiment in Novels," *Behavioral, Economic and Socio-Cultural Computing* (November 2016), http://ieeexplore.ieee.org/abstract/document/7804470/.

43. Jodie Archer and Matthew Jockers, *The Bestseller Code: Anatomy of the Block-buster Novel* (New York: St. Martin's Press, 2016), 3.

44. This advertisement for their manuscript review service as computational text analysis appears on the website promoting Jodie Archer and Matthew Jockers's *The Bestseller Code*: http://www.archerjockers.com/.

45. William K. Wimsatt and Monroe C. Beardsley, "The Affective Fallacy," *The Sewanee Review* 57, no. 1 (1949): 31–55; quote on 32.

46. Barbara Herrnstein Smith, "Contingencies of Value," *Critical Inquiry* 10, no. 1 (1983): 1–35; quote on 4.

47. Jane F. Thrailkill, *Affecting Fictions: Mind, Body, and Emotion in American Liter-ary Realism* (Cambridge, MA: Harvard University Press, 2007), 15.

48. Jean-Baptiste Michel, Yuan Kui Shen, Aviva Presser Aiden, Adrian Veres, Mat-thew K. Gray, The Google Books Team, Joseph P. Pickett, Dale Hoiberg, Dan Clancy, Peter Norvig, Jon Orwant, Steven Pinker, Martin A. Nowak, and Erez Lieberman Aiden, "Quantitative Analysis of Culture Using Millions of Digitized Books," *Science* 331, no. 6014 (2011): 176–82.

49. James M. Hughes, Nichols J. Foti, David C. Krakauer, and Daniel N. Rockmore, "Quantitative Patterns of Stylistic Influence in the Evolution of Literature," *Proceed-ings of the National Academy of Sciences* 109, no. 20 (2012): 7682–86.

50. LaCapra, *Soundings in Critical Theory*.

Chapter 4. The Cultural Significance of *k*-NN

1. The concept of algorithmic culture was introduced by Alexander R. Galloway, *Gaming: Essays on Algorithmic Culture* (Minneapolis: University of Minnesota Press, 2006), and extended by Ted Striphas, "Algorithmic Culture," *European Journal of Cul-tural Studies* 18, nos. 4–5 (2015): 395–412. The concept of algorithmic governmentality is associated with the work of Antoinette Rouvroy.

2. See, for example, Safiya Umoja Noble's analysis of the Google Image Search results in *Algorithms of Oppression: How Search Engines Reinforce Racism* (New York: New York University Press, 2018), 22–23, and Alexander Monea's reading of Google's Knowledge Graph, "Graph Force: Rhetorical Machines and the N-Arization of Knowl-edge," *Computational Culture: A Journal of Software Studies*, no. 5 (2016), http://computationalculture.net/article/graph-force-rhetorical-machines-and-the-n-arization-of-knowledge.

3. Several recent articles purport to detail business and personal connections between Cambridge Analytica and these two political campaigns: Jamie Doward and Alice Gibbs, "Did Cambridge Analytica Influence the Brexit Vote and the US Elec-tion?" *The Guardian*, March 4, 2017, https://www.theguardian.com/politics/2017/mar/04/nigel-oakes-cambridge-analytica-what-role-brexit-trump; Carole Cadwal-ladr, "The Great British Brexit Robbery: How Our Democracy Was Hijacked," *The Guardian*, March 7, 2017, https://www.theguardian.com/technology/2017/may/07/the-great-british-brexit-robbery-hijacked-democracy; Sue Halpern, "How He Used

Facebook to Win," *New York Review of Books*, June 8, 2017, http://www.nybooks.com/articles/2017/06/08/how-trump-used-facebook-to-win/.

4. Ian Kerr, "Prediction, Pre-Emption, Presumption: The Path of Law after the Computational Turn," in *Privacy, Due Process and the Computational Turn: The Philosophy of Law Meets the Philosophy of Technology,* ed. Mireille Hildebrandt and Katja de Vries (New York: Routledge, 2013). See also Vincanne Adams, Michelle Murphy, and Adele E. Clarke, "Anticipation: Technoscience, Life, Affect, Temporality," *Subjectivity* 28 (2009): 246–65.

5. Mark Andrejevic, Alison Hearn, and Helen Kennedy, "Cultural Studies of Data Mining: Introduction," *European Journal of Cultural Studies* 18, nos. 4–5 (2015): 379–94; quote on 379.

6. Alison Hearn, "Critical Digital Humanities," lecture at Dartmouth College, April 22, 2017.

7. Gillespie, "Algorithm," 19.

8. David Golumbia, *The Cultural Logic of Computation* (Cambridge, MA: Harvard University Press, 2009), 3.

9. I agree with Benjamin M. Schmidt's argument that "the first job of digital humanists should be to understand the goals and agendas of the transformations and systems that algorithms serve so that we can be creative users of new ideas, rather than users of the tools the purposes of which we decline to know," but I would suggest that critical digital humanists need also to insist on inquiry into the methods themselves instead of just the "best way to implement the underlying algorithms" (553). "Do Digital Humanists Need to Understand Algorithms," in *Debates in the Digital Humanities,* ed. by Matthew K. Gold and Lauren F. Klein (Minneapolis: University of Minnesota Press, 2016), 546–55.

10. Adrian Mackenzie, *Cutting Code: Software and Sociality* (New York: Peter Lang, 2006), 64.

11. The conception of the algorithm as "thing" is connected to both the material turn in the humanities and cultural studies and the movement toward "making" and building within the digital humanities. See Stephen Ramsay and Geoffrey Rockwell, "Developing Things: Notes toward an Epistemology of Building in the Digital Humanities," in *Debates in the Digital Humanities,* ed. Matthew K. Gold (Minneapolis: University of Minnesota Press, 2012), 3–7.

12. Bruno Latour and Steve Woolgar, *Laboratory Life: The Construction of Scientific Facts* (Princeton, NJ: Princeton University Press, 1979).

13. Ian Bogost, *Unit Operations: An Approach to Videogame Criticism* (Cambridge, MA: MIT Press, 2006), xii.

14. Ian Bogost, *Alien Phenomenology* (Minneapolis: University of Minnesota Press, 2012), 29.

15. Graham Harman, "On Vicarious Causation," in *Collapse II: Speculative Realism,* ed. Robin Mackay (London: Urbanomic, 2007), 171–206.

16. The interdisciplinary approach known as the social construction of technology raised a number of crucial questions about ideology, political economy, and history

that the present interest in a renewed formalism or phenomenology of technology occludes (Wiebe E. Bijker, Thomas P. Hughes, and Trevor Pinch, eds., *The Social Construction of Technological Systems: New Directions in the Sociology and History of Technology*, anniversary ed. [Cambridge, MA: MIT Press, 2012]).

17. Researchers have proposed various methods of studying and evaluating algorithms. John N. Hooker, for example, argues for a hypothesis-driven analysis of algorithms in "Needed: An Empirical Science of Algorithms," *Operations Research* 42, no. 2 (1994): 201–12.

18. Ed Finn, *What Algorithms Want: Imagination in the Age of the Computer* (Cambridge, MA: MIT Press, 2017), 54, 65.

19. Frank Pasquale schematizes the range of closed algorithmic black boxes into three categories: real secrecy, legal secrecy, and obfuscation. All serve to obscure data and process while producing a cloak of opacity over complex informational systems (*The Black Box Society: The Secret Algorithms That Control Money and Information* [Cambridge, MA: Harvard University Press, 2015]).

20. Alexander Galloway, *Protocol: How Control Exists after Decentralization* (Cambridge, MA: MIT Press, 2004), 27.

21. Michel Foucault, *The History of Sexuality*, vol. 1, trans. Robert Hurley (New York: Vintage, 1978). Gilles Deleuze, "Postscript on Control Societies," in *Negotiations, 1972–1990*, trans. Martin Joughin (New York: Columbia University Press, 1990), 177–82.

22. Antoinette Rouvroy, "The End(s) of Critique: Data Behaviourism versus Due Process," in *Privacy, Due Process and the Computational Turn: The Philosophy of Law Meets the Philosophy of Technology*, ed. Mireille Hildebrandt and Katja de Vries (New York: Routledge, 2012), 149.

23. David M. Berry and Anders Fagerjord, "Towards a Critical Digital Humanities," *Knowledge and Critique in a Digital Age* (Malden, MA: Polity, 2017), 136–50.

24. Aden Evens, *Logic of the Digital* (New York: Bloomsbury, 2015); Jonathan Sterne, *MP3: The Meaning of a Format* (Durham, NC: Duke University Press, 2012); Wendy Hui Kyong Chun, *Programmed Visions: Software and Memory* (Cambridge, MA: MIT Press, 2011); Matthew G. Kirschenbaum, *Mechanisms: New Media and the Forensic Imagination* (Cambridge, MA: MIT Press, 2008).

25. "'A White Mask Worked Better': Why Algorithms Are Not Colour Blind," https://www.theguardian.com/technology/2017/may/28/joy-buolamwini-when-algorithms-are-racist-facial-recognition-bias.

26. Cathy O'Neil, *Weapons of Math Destruction: How Big Data Increases Inequality and Threatens Democracy* (New York: Crown Random House, 2016), 21.

27. Donna Haraway, "A Manifesto for Cyborgs: Science, Technology, and Socialist Feminism in the 1980s," in *Feminism/Postmodernism*, ed. Linda J. Nicholson (New York: Routledge, 1990), 190–233.

28. Ian Hacking, *The Emergence of Probability: A Philosophical Study of Early Ideas of Probability, Induction and Statistical Thinking* (London: Cambridge University Press, 1975), 9.

29. Paul N. Edwards gives the best account of the discourse of computing in relation to its origins and development in *The Closed World: Computers and the Politics of Discourse in Cold War America* (Cambridge, MA: MIT Press, 1996).

30. One of the best accounts of Bayes's rule can be found in Andrew I. Dale's *History of Inverse Probability: From Thomas Bayes to Karl Pearson*, 2nd ed. (New York: Springer, 1999), 44–45. See also Brian Christian and Tom Griffiths, *Algorithms to Live By: The Computer Science of Human Decisions* (New York: Henry Holt, 2016): 128–48.

31. Sharon Bertsch McGrayne, *The Theory That Would Not Die: How Bayes' Rule Cracked the Enigma Code, Hunted Down Russian Submarines, and Emerged Triumphant from Two Centuries of Controversy* (New Haven, CT: Yale University Press, 2011), 11.

32. Thomas Bayes and Richard Price, "An Essay towards Solving a Problem in the Doctrine of Chances. By the Late Rev. Mr. Bayes, F. R. S. Communicated by Mr. Price, in a Letter to John Canton, A. M. F. R. S.," *Philosophical Transactions* 53 (1763): 370–418; quote on 376.

33. On the authorship and editing of Bayes's essay, see Andrew I. Dale, *A History of Inverse Probability: From Thomas Bayes to Karl Pearson* (New York: Springer, 1999), 34–35.

34. Alain Desrosières, *The Politics of Large Numbers: A History of Statistical Reasoning*, trans. Camille Naish (Cambridge, MA: Harvard University Press, 1998), 57.

35. Robert Mitchell, "Response," *Genre* 50, no. 1 (2017): 139–52; quote on 144.

36. Vittorio Castelli, a student of Thomas M. Cover, writes in a lecture on *k*-NN that "the classifier has historical importance: it gives rise to the first rule to be proven universally consistent" (http://www.ee.columbia.edu/~vittorio/lecture8.pdf).

37. Raymond Williams, *Marxism and Literature* (New York: Oxford University Press, 2009), 121–27.

38. Ronald A. Fisher, "The Use of Multiple Measurements in Taxonomic Problems," *Annals of Eugenics* 7 (1936): 179–88.

39. Hannah M. Dee, Lorna M. Hughes, Lloyd Roderick, and Alexander D. Brown, "Visual Digital Humanities: Using Image Data to Derive Approximate Metadata," in *Managing Digital Cultural Objects: Analysis, Discovery and Retrieval,* ed. Allen Foster and Pauline Rafferty (London: Facet, 2016), 89.

40. Matthew L. Jockers and Daniela M. Witten, "A Comparative Study of Machine Learning Methods for Authorship Attribution," *Literary and Linguistic Computing* 25, no. 2 (June 1, 2010).

41. For a historical and theoretical account of PCA, see Ian T. Jolliffe, *Principal Component Analysis* (New York: Springer, 1986).

42. Archer and Jockers, *Bestseller Code,* 234–40.

43. Erich L. Lehmann, *Reminiscences of a Statistician: The Company I Kept* (New York: Springer, 2008), vii.

44. Erich L. Lehmann, *Selected Works of E. L. Lehman,* ed. Javier Rojo (New York: Springer, 2012), 875–76.

45. A biographical note written by Evelyn Fix's colleagues claims that "the needed results [from her work] could be transmitted on time, usually to New York but occa-

sionally directly to England" (*University of California: In Memoriam, June 1967*, http://content.cdlib.org/view?docId=hb629oo6vt&doc.view=frames&chunk.id=div00009).

46. Thomas M. Cover and Peter Hart, "Nearest Neighbor Pattern Classification," *IEEE Transactions on Information Theory* 13, no. 1 (1967): 21–27, 27.

47. Wendy Chun, "We're All Living in Virtually Gated Communities and Our Real-Life Relationships Are Suffering," *Wired*, April 13, 2017.

48. Satosi Watanabe, *Pattern Recognition: Human and Mechanical* (New York: Wiley, 1985), 347.

49. John MacCormick, *Nine Algorithms That Changed the Future: The Ingenious Ideas That Drive Today's Computers* (Princeton, NJ: Princeton University Press, 2012), 85.

50. OpenCV, "Understanding *k*-Nearest Neighbor," http://docs.opencv.org/trunk/d5/d26/tutorial_py_knn_understanding.html.

51. Nils J. Nilsson and Richard O. Duda, "Proposal for Research: SRI No. ESU 68-111." September 4, 1968. Menlo Park, CA: SRI International. https://www.sri.com/sites/default/files/uploads/publications/pdf/1291.pdf.

52. On the prospects of developing a hermeneutics of both textual and computational patterns, see Mireille Hildebrandt, "The Meaning and the Mining of Legal Texts," in *Understanding the Digital Humanities*, ed. David M. Berry (New York: Palgrave, 2012), 145–60.

53. Watanabe, *Pattern Recognition*, 452–53. See also the Watanabe discussion of the "Ugly Duckling" theorem in *Knowing and Guessing: A Quantitative Study of Inference and Information* (New York: Wiley, 1969), 376–79.

Conclusion

1. Christopher M. Bishop writes that the term "neural network" "has been used very broadly to cover a wide range of different models, many of which have been the subject of exaggerated claims regarding their biological plausibility" (*Pattern Recognition and Machine Learning*, 226).

2. Mikhail Moiseevich Bongard discusses the use and limitations of Frank Rosenblatt's "Perceptron," an early neural network model developed in 1957, in *Pattern Recognition* (New York: Spartan, 1970).

3. This description is used most prominently by Andrew Ng, a computer scientist and cofounder of Coursera. In 2011, Ng's online version of his Stanford "CS229a" course on machine learning attracted more than one hundred thousand students. His course is responsible for the dissemination of his account of machine learning and for the enthusiasm for Massive Open Online Courses (MOOCs) that directly led to the founding of Coursera and other MOOC platforms and providers.

4. David M. Skapura, *Building Neural Networks* (New York: Addison-Wesley, 1996), 2.

5. For an application of this type of neural network to several problems in computer vision, including a fascinating cat detector, see Quoc V. Le, Marc'Aurelio Ranzato, Rajat Monga, Matthieu Devin, Kai Chen, Greg S. Corrado, Jeff Dean, and Andrew

Y. Ng, "Building High-Level Features Using Large Scale Unsupervised Learning," *ICASSP* (2013): 8595–98.

6. Tomas Mikolov, Illya Sutskever, Kai Chen, Greg S. Corrado, and Jeff Dean, "Distributed Representations of Words and Phrases and Their Compositionality," *Advances in Neural Information Processing Systems* (2013): 3111–19.

7. This comment is found in the "demo-analogy.sh" file distributed with the word-2vec package.

8. Only a few attempts have been made thus far to examine relations between various semantic models. One notable approach examines semantic drift, or changes over time. See William L. Hamilton, Jure Leskovec, and Daniel Jurafsky, "Diachronic Word Embeddings Reveal Statistical Laws of Semantic Change," in *ACL 2016—Proceedings of the 54th Annual Meeting of the Association for Computational Linguistics*, 2 vols., ed. Antal van den Bosch, Katrin Erk, and Noah A. Smith (Stroudsburg, PA: Association for Computational Linguistics, 2016), 1: 1489–1501.

Works Cited

Adams, Vincanne, Michelle Murphy, and Adele E. Clarke. "Anticipation: Technoscience, Life, Affect, Temporality." *Subjectivity* 28 (2009): 246–65.

Ahmed, Sara. "Interview with Judith Butler." *Sexualities* 19, no. 4 (2016): 482–92.

Allington, Daniel, Sarah Brouillette, and David Golumbia. "Neoliberal Tools (and Archives): A Political History of Digital Humanities." *Los Angeles Review of Books*, May 2016.

Allison, Sarah, Ryan Heuser, Matthew Jockers, Franco Moretti, and Michael Witmore. *Canon/Archive: Studies in Quantitative Formalism from the Stanford Literary Lab*. Edited by Franco Moretti. New York: N+1 Books, 2017.

Anderson, Chris. "The End of Theory: The Data Deluge Makes the Scientific Method Obsolete." *Wired*, June 23, 2008.

Andrejevic, Mark, Alison Hearn, and Helen Kennedy. "Cultural Studies of Data Mining: Introduction." *European Journal of Cultural Studies* 18, nos. 4–5 (2015): 379–94.

Anker, Elizabeth S., and Rita Felski, eds. *Critique and Postcritique* (Durham, NC: Duke University Press, 2017).

Archer, Dawn. "Data Mining and Word Frequency Analysis." In *Research Methods for Reading Digital Data in the Digital Humanities*, edited by Gabriele Griffin and Matt Hayler, 72–92. Edinburgh: Edinburgh University Press, 2016.

Archer, Jodie, and Matthew Jockers. *The Bestseller Code: Anatomy of the Blockbuster Novel*. New York: St. Martin's Press, 2016.

Barthes, Roland. *Camera Lucida: Reflections on Photography*. Translated by Richard Howard. New York: Hill and Wang, 1981.

———. *The Rustle of Language*. Translated by Richard Howard. Berkeley: University of California Press, 1989.

Bayes, Thomas, and Richard Price. "An Essay towards Solving a Problem in the Doctrine of Chances. By the Late Rev. Mr. Bayes, F. R. S. Communicated by Mr. Price, in a Letter to John Canton, A. M. F. R. S." *Philosophical Transactions* 53 (1763): 370–418.

Berry, David M. "The Computational Turn: Thinking about the Digital Humanities." *Culture Machine* 12 (2011): 1–21.

———. *The Philosophy of Software: Code and Mediation in the Digital Age*. New York: Palgrave, 2011.

Berry, David M., and Anders Fagerjord, "Towards a Critical Digital Humanities." In *Knowledge and Critique in a Digital Age*, edited by David M. Berry and Anders Fagerjord, 136–50. Malden, MA: Polity, 2017.

Best, Stephen, and Sharon Marcus. "Surface Reading: An Introduction." *Representations* 108 (2009): 1–21.

Bijker, Wiebe E., Thomas P. Hughes, and Trevor Pinch, eds. *The Social Construction of Technological Systems: New Directions in the Sociology and History of Technology*. Anniversary edition. Cambridge, MA: MIT Press, 2012.

Bishop, Christopher M. *Pattern Recognition and Machine Learning*. New York: Springer, 2006.

Blei, David M. "Topic Modeling and Digital Humanities." *Journal of the Digital Humanities* 2, no. 1 (2012). http://journalofdigitalhumanities.org/2-1/topic-modeling-and-digital-humanities-by-david-m-blei/.

Bode, Katherine. "The Equivalence of 'Close' and 'Distant' Reading; or, Toward a New Object for Data-Rich Literary History." *Modern Language Quarterly* 78, no. 1 (2017): 77–106.

Bogost, Ian. *Alien Phenomenology*. Minneapolis: University of Minnesota Press, 2012.

———. *Unit Operations: An Approach to Videogame Criticism*. Cambridge, MA: MIT Press, 2006.

Bongard, Mikhail Moiseevich. *Pattern Recognition*. New York: Spartan, 1970.

Booth, Alison. "Mid-Range Reading: Not a Manifesto." *PMLA* 132, no. 3 (2017): 620–27.

Booth, Wayne C. *The Rhetoric of Fiction*. Chicago: University of Chicago Press, 2010.

Bowker, Geoffrey C., and Susan Leigh Star. *Sorting Things Out: Classification and Its Consequences* (Cambridge, MA: MIT Press, 1999).

Box, George E. P. "Science and Statistics." *Journal of the American Statistical Association* 71, no. 356 (1976): 791–99.

boyd, danah, and Kate Crawford. "Critical Questions for Big Data: Provocations for a Cultural, Technological, and Scholarly Phenomenon." *Information, Communication and Society* 15, no. 5 (June 2012): 662–79.

Burckhardt, Sigurd. *Shakespearean Meanings*. Princeton, NJ: Princeton University Press, 1968.

Burdick, Ann, Johanna Drucker, Peter Lunenfeld, Todd Presner, and Jeffrey Schnapp. *Digital_Humanities*. Cambridge, MA: MIT Press, 2012.

Christian, Brian, and Tom Griffiths. *Algorithms to Live By: The Computer Science of Human Decisions*. New York: Henry Holt, 2016.

Chun, Wendy Hui Kyong. *Programmed Visions: Software and Memory.* Cambridge, MA: MIT Press, 2011.

———. "We're All Living in Virtually Gated Communities and Our Real-Life Relationships Are Suffering." *Wired*, April 13, 2017.

Clement, Tanya E. "Where Is Methodology in Digital Humanities?" In *Debates in the Digital Humanities*, edited by Matthew K. Gold and Lauren F. Klein, 153–75. Minneapolis: University of Minnesota Press, 2016.

Cohen, Daniel J., Michael Frisch, Patrick Gallagher, Steven Mintz, Kirsten Sword, Amy Murrell Taylor, William G. Thomas III, and William J. Turkel. "Interchange: The Promise of Digital History." *Journal of American History* 95, no. 2 (2008): 452–91.

Cohen, Daniel J., and Roy Rozenzweig. *Digital History: A Guide to Gathering, Preserving, and Presenting the Past on the Web.* Philadelphia: University of Pennsylvania Press, 2006.

Coombs, David Sweeney, and Danielle Coriale. "Introduction." *Victorian Studies* 59, no. 1 (2016): 87–89.

Cormen, Thomas H. *Algorithms Unlocked.* Cambridge, MA: MIT Press, 2013.

Cormen, Thomas H., Charles E. Leiserson, Ronald L. Rivest, and Clifford Stein. *Introduction to Algorithms.* Cambridge, MA: MIT Press, 2009.

Cover, Thomas, and Peter Hart. "Nearest Neighbor Pattern Classification." *IEEE Transactions on Information Theory* 13, no. 1 (1967): 21–27.

Culler, Jonathan. *Structuralist Poetics.* Ithaca, NY: Cornell University Press, 1975.

Dale, Andrew I. *A History of Inverse Probability: From Thomas Bayes to Karl Pearson.* 2nd ed. New York: Springer, 1999.

Dee, Hannah M., Lorna M. Hughes, Lloyd Roderick, and Alexander D. Brown. "Visual Digital Humanities: Using Image Data to Derive Approximate Metadata." In *Managing Digital Cultural Objects: Analysis, Discovery and Retrieval*, edited by Allen Foster and Pauline Rafferty, 89–110. London: Facet, 2016.

Deleuze, Gilles. "Postscript on Control Societies." In *Negotiations, 1972–1990*, 177–18. Translated by Martin Joughin. New York: Columbia University Press, 1990.

Derrida, Jacques. *Dissemination.* Translated by Barbara Johnson. Chicago: University of Chicago Press, 1981.

———. *Limited Inc.* Evanston, IL: Northwestern University Press, 1988.

———. *Of Grammatology.* Corr. ed. Translated by Gayatri Chakravorty Spivak. Baltimore, MD: Johns Hopkins University Press, 1997.

———. *The Truth in Painting.* Translated by Geoffrey Bennington and Ian McLeod. Chicago: University of Chicago Press, 1987.

———. *Writing and Difference.* Translated by Alan Bass. Chicago: University of Chicago Press, 1978.

Desrosières, Alain. *The Politics of Large Numbers: A History of Statistical Reasoning.* Translated by Camille Naish. Cambridge, MA: Harvard University Press, 1998.

Drucker, Johanna. "Humanities Approaches to Graphical Display." *Digital Humanities Quarterly* 5, no. 1 (2011).

———. "Why Distant Reading Isn't." *PMLA* 132, no. 3 (2017): 628–35.

Earhart, Amy. *Traces of the Old; Uses of the New: The Emergence of Digital Literary Studies*. Ann Arbor: University of Michigan Press, 2015.

Edwards, Paul N. *The Closed World: Computers and the Politics of Discourse in Cold War America*. Cambridge, MA: MIT Press, 1996.

Evens, Aden. *Logic of the Digital*. New York: Bloomsbury, 2015.

Felski, Rita. "After Suspicion." *Profession* 35 (2009): 28–35.

———. *The Limits of Critique*. Chicago: University of Chicago Press, 2015.

Fineman, Joel. "The History of the Anecdote: Fiction and Fiction." In *The New Historicism*, edited by H. Aram Veeser, 49–76. New York: Routledge, 1989.

Finkel, Jenny Rose, Trond Grenager, and Christopher Manning. "Incorporating Non-local Information into Information Extraction Systems by Gibbs Sampling." *Proceedings of the 43rd Annual Meeting of the Association for Computational Linguistics* (2005): 363–70.

Finn, Ed. *What Algorithms Want: Imagination in the Age of the Computer*. Cambridge, MA: MIT Press, 2017.

Firth, John Rupert. *Papers in Linguistics 1934–1951*. London: Oxford University Press, 1957.

Fish, Stanley. *Is There a Text in This Class? The Authority of Interpretive Communities*. Cambridge, MA: Harvard University, 1980.

Fisher, Ronald A. "The Use of Multiple Measurements in Taxonomic Problems." *Annals of Eugenics* 7 (1936): 179–88.

Fleissner, Jennifer L. "Historicism Blues." *American Literary History* 25, no. 4 (2013): 699–717.

Foucault, Michel. *The History of Sexuality*, vol. 1. Translated by Robert Hurley. New York: Vintage, 1978.

Frye, Northrop. *Anatomy of Criticism: Four Essays*. Princeton, NJ: Princeton University Press, 1971.

———. "Literary and Mechanical Models." In *Research in Humanities Computing 1: Selected Papers from the ALLC/ACH Conference, Toronto, June 1989*, edited by Ian Lancashire, 3–12. New York: Oxford University Press, 1991.

Gadamer, Hans-Georg. *Truth and Method*. Translated by Joel Weinsheimer and Donald Marshall. New York: Crossroad, 1989.

Galloway, Alexander, R. "The Cybernetic Hypothesis." *differences* 25, no. 1 (2014): 107–31.

———. *Gaming: Essays on Algorithmic Culture*. Minneapolis: University of Minnesota Press, 2006.

———. *Protocol: How Control Exists after Decentralization*. Cambridge, MA: MIT Press, 2004.

Gao, Jianbo, Matthew L. Jockers, John Laudun, and Timothy Tangherlini. "A Multiscale Theory for the Dynamical Evolution of Sentiment in Novels." Paper presented at the 2016 International Conference on Behavioral, Economic and Socio-Cultural Computing (BESC), Durham, NC, November 11–13, 2016. https://doi.org/10.1109/BESC.2016.7804470.

Gillespie, Tarleton. "Algorithm." In *Digital Keywords: A Vocabulary of Information Society and Culture*, edited by Benjamin Peters, 18–30. Princeton, NJ: Princeton University Press, 2016.

Gitelman, Lisa, and Virginia Jackson. *"Raw Data" Is an Oxymoron*. Cambridge, MA: MIT Press, 2012.

Glimp, David, and Russ Castronovo, eds. "After Critique." Special issue, *English Language Notes* 51, no. 2 (2013).

Goldstone, Andrew, and Ted Underwood. "The Quiet Transformations of Literary Studies: What Thirteen Thousand Scholars Could Teach Us." *New Literary History* 45, no. 3 (2014): 359–84.

Golumbia, David. "Cultural Studies and the Discourse of New Media." In *The Renewal of Cultural Studies*, edited by Paul Smith, 83–92. Philadelphia: Temple University Press, 2011.

———. *The Cultural Logic of Computation*. Cambridge, MA: Harvard University Press, 2009.

Graff, Gerald. *Professing Literature: An Institutional History*. Chicago: University of Chicago Press, 1987.

Greenblatt, Stephen. *Shakespearean Negotiations: The Circulation of Social Energy in Renaissance England*. Berkeley: University of California Press, 1988.

Griffin, Gabriele, and Matt Hayler. Introduction to *Research Methods for Reading Digital Data in the Digital Humanities*, edited by Gabriele Griffin and Matt Hayler, 1–13. Edinburgh: Edinburgh University Press, 2016.

Hacking, Ian. *The Emergence of Probability: A Philosophical Study of Early Ideas of Probability, Induction and Statistical Thinking*. London: Cambridge University Press, 1975.

Hamilton, William L., Jure Leskovec, and Daniel Jurafsky. "Diachronic Word Embeddings Reveal Statistical Laws of Semantic Change." In *ACL 2016—Proceedings of the 54th Annual Meeting of the Association for Computational Linguistics*, 2 vols., ed. Antal van den Bosch, Katrin Erk, and Noah A. Smith (Stroudsburg, PA: Association for Computational Linguistics, 2016), 1: 1489–1501.

Haraway, Donna. "A Manifesto for Cyborgs: Science, Technology, and Socialist Feminism in the 1980s." In *Feminism/Postmodernism*, edited by Linda J. Nicholson, 190–233. New York: Routledge, 1990.

Harman, Graham. "On Vicarious Causation." In *Collapse II: Speculative Realism*, edited by Robin Mackay, 171–206. London: Urbanomic, 2007.

Hartman, Geoffrey. *Beyond Formalism: Literary Essays, 1958–1970*. New Haven, CT: Yale University Press, 1971.

Hartman, Saidiya V. *Scenes of Subjection: Terror, Slavery, and Self-Making in Nineteenth-Century America*. New York: Oxford University Press, 1997.

Hayles, N. Katherine. *How We Think: Digital Media and Contemporary Technogenesis*. Chicago: University of Chicago Press, 2012.

———. *My Mother Was a Computer: Digital Subjects and Literary Texts*. Chicago: University of Chicago Press, 2005.

————. "Print Is Flat, Code Is Deep: The Importance of Media-Specific Analysis." *Poetics Today* 25, no. 1 (2004): 67–90.

Hildebrandt, Mireille. "The Meaning and the Mining of Legal Texts." In *Understanding the Digital Humanities*. Edited by David M. Berry, 145–60. New York: Palgrave, 2012.

Hooker, John N. "Needed: An Empirical Science of Algorithms." *Operations Research* 42, no. 2 (1994): 201–12.

Hughes, James M., Nichols J. Foti, David C. Krakauer, and Daniel N. Rockmore. "Quantitative Patterns of Stylistic Influence in the Evolution of Literature." *Proceedings of the National Academy of Sciences* 109, no. 20 (2012): 7682–86.

Hyman, Stanley Edgar. *The Armed Vision: A Study in the Methods of Modern Literary Criticism*. New York: Knopf, 1948.

Ide, Nancy. "Preparation and Analysis of Linguistic Corpora." In *A Companion to Digital Humanities*, edited by Susan Schreibman, Ray Siemens, and John Unsworth, 289–305. New York: Blackwell, 2004.

Inkso, Jeffrey. "The Prehistory of Posthistoricism." In *The Limits of Literary Historicism*, edited by Allen Dunn and Thomas F. Haddox, 105–23. Knoxville: University of Tennessee Press, 2011.

Jameson, Frederic. *The Political Unconscious*. Ithaca, NY: Cornell University Press, 1981.

Jockers, Matthew L. *Macroanalysis: Digital Methods and Literary History*. Urbana: University of Illinois Press, 2013.

————. *Text Analysis with R for Students of Literature*. New York: Springer, 2014.

Jockers, Matthew L., and Daniela M. Witten. "A Comparative Study of Machine Learning Methods for Authorship Attribution." *Literary and Linguistic Computing* 25, no. 2 (2010): 215–23.

Jolliffe, Ian T. *Principal Component Analysis*. New York: Springer, 1986.

Kerr, Ian. "Prediction, Pre-Emption, Presumption: The Path of Law after the Computational Turn." In *Privacy, Due Process and the Computational Turn: The Philosophy of Law Meets the Philosophy of Technology*, edited by Mireille Hildebrandt and Katja de Vries, 91–120. New York: Routledge, 2013.

Kirschenbaum, Matthew G. *Mechanisms: New Media and the Forensic Imagination*. Cambridge, MA: MIT Press, 2008.

————. "What Is Digital Humanities and What's It Doing in English Departments?" In *Defining Digital Humanities: A Reader*, edited by Melissa Terras, Julianne Nyhan, and Edward Vanhoutte, 195–204. Burlington, VT: Ashgate, 2013.

Klein, Lauren F. "The Image of Absence: Archival Silence, Data Visualization, and James Hemings." *American Literature* 85, no. 1 (2013): 661–88.

Kopec, Andrew. "The Digital Humanities, Inc.: Literary Criticism and the Fate of a Profession." *PMLA* 131, no. 2 (2016): 324–39.

Krieger, Murray. *The New Apologists for Poetry*. Minneapolis: University of Minnesota Press, 1956.

Kristeva, Julia. *Desire in Language: A Semiotic Approach to Literature and Art*. Edited by Leon S. Roudiez. Translated by Thomas Gora and Alice A. Jardine. New York: Columbia University Press, 1982.

LaCapra, Dominick. *Soundings in Critical Theory*. Ithaca, NY: Cornell University Press, 1989.

Lane, Richard J. *The Big Humanities: Digital Humanities/Digital Laboratories*. New York: Routledge, 2016.

Latour, Bruno. "Why Has Critique Run Out of Steam? From Matters of Fact to Matters of Concern." *Critical Inquiry* 30, no. 2 (2004): 225–48.

Latour, Bruno, and Steve Woolgar. *Laboratory Life: The Construction of Scientific Facts*. Princeton, NJ: Princeton University Press, 1979.

Lazer, David, Ryan Kennedy, Gary King, and Alessandro Vespignani. "The Parable of Google Flu: Traps in Big Data Analysis." *Science* 343, no. 6176 (2014): 1203–5.

Le, Quoc V., Marc'Aurelio Ranzato, Rajat Monga, Matthieu Devin, Kai Chen, Greg S. Corrado, Jeff Dean, and Andrew Y. Ng. "Building High-Level Features Using Large Scale Unsupervised Learning." ICASSP (2013): 8595–98.

Lee, Maurice S. "Searching the Archives with Dickens and Hawthorne: Databases and Aesthetic Judgment after the New Historicism." *ELH* 79, no. 3 (2012): 747–71.

Lehmann, Erich L. *Reminiscences of a Statistician: The Company I Kept*. New York: Springer, 2008.

———. *Selected Works of E. L. Lehman*. Edited by Javier Rojo. New York: Springer, 2012.

Liu, Alan. *Local Transcendence: Essays on Postmodern Historicism and the Database*. Chicago: University of Chicago Press, 2008.

———. "The Meaning of the Digital Humanities." *PMLA* 128, no. 2 (2013): 409–23.

Liu, Bing. "Sentiment Analysis and Subjectivity." *Handbook of Natural Language Processing*. 2nd ed, edited by Nitin Indurkhya and Fred J. Damerau, 627–66. Boca Raton, FL: CRC Press, 2010.

Looby, Christopher, and Cindy Weinstein. Introduction to *American Literature's Aesthetic Dimensions*. New York: Columbia University Press, 2012.

Love, Heather. "Close but Not Deep: Literary Ethics and the Descriptive Turn." *New Literary History* 41, no. 2 (2010): 371–91.

MacCormick, John. *Nine Algorithms That Changed the Future: The Ingenious Ideas That Drive Today's Computers*. Princeton, NJ: Princeton University Press, 2012.

Mackenzie, Adrian. *Cutting Code: Software and Sociality*. New York: Peter Lang, 2006.

Mandell, Laura C. "Gendering Digital Literary History: What Counts for Digital Humanities." In *A New Companion to Digital Humanities*, edited by Susan Schreibman, Ray Siemens, and John Unsworth, 511–23. New York: John Wiley, 2016.

Manning, Christopher, and Hinrich Schütze. *Foundations of Statistical Natural Language Processing*. Cambridge, MA: MIT Press, 1999.

Manovich, Lev. "The Science of Culture? Social Computing, Digital Humanities and Cultural Analytics." *CA: Journal of Cultural Analytics* 1 (2016). http://cultural analytics.org/2016/05/the-science-of-culture-social-computing-digital-humanities-and-cultural-analytics/.

Martindale, Colin. *Romantic Progression: The Psychology of Literary History*. Washington, DC: Hemisphere, 1975.

Matthiessen, F. O. *The American Renaissance: Art and Expression in the Age of Emerson and Whitman*. New York: Oxford University Press, 1941.

Mayer-Schönberger,Viktor, and Kenneth Cukier. *Big Data: A Revolution That Will Transform How We Live, Work, and Think*. Boston: Houghton Mifflin Harcourt, 2013.

McCallum, Andrew Kachites. *MALLET: Machine Learning for Language Toolkit*. 2002. http://mallet.cs.umass.edu.

McGann, Jerome K. *Radiant Textuality: Literature after the World Wide Web*. New York: Palgrave, 2001.

McGrayne, Sharon Bertsch. *The Theory That Would Not Die: How Bayes' Rule Cracked the Enigma Code, Hunted Down Russian Submarines, and Emerged Triumphant from Two Centuries of Controversy*. New Haven, CT: Yale University Press, 2011.

Michaels, Walter Benn. "Posthistoricism." *Transition* no. 70 (1996): 4–19.

Michel, Jean-Baptiste, Yuan Kui Shen, Aviva Presser Aiden, Adrian Veres, Matthew K. Gray, Google Books Team, Joseph P. Pickett, Dale Hoiberg, Dan Clancy, Peter Norvig, Jon Orwant, Steven Pinker, Martin A. Nowak, and Erez Lieberman Aiden. "Quantitative Analysis of Culture Using Millions of Digitized Books." *Science* 331, no. 6014 (2011): 176–82.

Mikolov, Tomas, Illya Sutskever, Kai Chen, Greg S. Corrado, and Jeff Dean. "Distributed Representations of Words and Phrases and Their Compositionality." *Advances in Neural Information Processing Systems* (2013): 3111–19.

Miller, George A., Richard Beckwith, Christiane Fellbaum, Derek Gross, and Katherine Miller. "WordNet: An Online Lexical Database." *International Journal of Lexicography* 3, no. 4 (1990): 235–44.

Mitchell, Robert. "Response." *Genre* 50, no. 1 (2017): 139–52.

Mohammad, Saif, and Peter Turney. "Crowdsourcing a Word-Emotion Association Lexicon." *Computational Intelligence* 29, no. 3 (2013): 436–65.

Monea, Alexander. "Graph Force: Rhetorical Machines and the N-Arization of Knowledge." *Computational Culture*, no. 5 (2016). http://computationalculture.net/article/graph-force-rhetorical-machines-and-the-n-arization-of-knowledge.

Moreau, Luc, Paul Groth, Simon Miles, Javier Vazquez-Salceda, John Ibbotson, Sheng Jiang, Steve Munroe, Omer Rana, Andreas Schreiber, Victor Tan, and Laszlo Varga. "The Provenance of Electronic Data." *Communications of the ACM* 51, no. 4 (2008): 52–58.

Moretti, Franco. "Conjectures on World Literature," *New Left Review* 1 (2000): 54–68.

———. *Graphs, Maps, Trees: Abstract Models for a Literary Theory*. New York: Verso, 2005.

Nanni, Federico, Hiram Kümper, and Simone Paolo Ponzetto. "Semi-supervised Textual Analysis and Historical Research Helping Each Other: Some Thoughts and Observations." *International Journal of Humanities and Arts Computing* 10, no. 1 (March 2016): 63–77.

Negus, Keith, Paul Du Gay, Stuart Hall, Linda Janes, and Hugh Mackay. *Doing Cultural Studies: The Story of the Sony Walkman*. London: Sage, 1997.

Nilsson, Nils J., and Richard O. Duda. "Proposal for Research: SRI No. ESU 68-111." September 4, 1968. Menlo Park, CA: SRI International. https://www.sri.com/sites/default/files/uploads/publications/pdf/1291.pdf.

Noble, Safiya Umoja. *Algorithms of Oppression: How Search Engines Reinforce Racism*. New York: New York University Press, 2018.

Nowviskie, Bethany. "On the Origin of 'Hack' and 'Yack.'" In *Debates in the Digital Humanities*, edited by Matthew K. Gold and Lauren F. Klein, 66–70. Minneapolis: University of Minnesota Press, 2016.

O'Neil, Cathy. *Weapons of Math Destruction: How Big Data Increases Inequality and Threatens Democracy*. New York: Crown Random House, 2016.

Otter, Samuel. "Aesthetics in All Things." *Representations* 104, no. 1 (2008): 116–25.

Pasquale, Frank, *The Black Box Society: The Secret Algorithms That Control Money and Information*. Cambridge, MA: Harvard University Press, 2015.

Piper, Andrew. "Novel Devotions: Conversional Reading, Computational Modeling, and the Modern Novel." *New Literary History* 46, no. 1 (2015): 63–98.

Polefrone, Phillip R., John Simpson, and Dennis Yi Tenen. "Critical Computing in the Humanities." In *Doing Digital Humanities: Practice, Training, Research*, edited by Constance Crompton, Richard J. Lane, and Ray Siemens, 85–103. New York: Routledge, 2016.

Porter, M. F. "An Algorithm for Suffix Stripping." *Program* 14, no. 3 (1980): 130–37.

Presner, Todd, David Shepard, Yoh Kawano. *HyperCities: Thick Mapping in the Digital Humanities*. Cambridge, MA: Harvard University Press, 2014.

Ramsay, Stephen. "The Hermeneutics of Screwing Around; or, What You Do with a Million Books." In *Pastplay: Teaching and Learning History with Technology*, edited by Kevin Kee, 111–20. Ann Arbor: University of Michigan Press, 2014.

———. *Reading Machines: Toward an Algorithmic Criticism*. Urbana: University of Illinois Press, 2011.

Ramsay, Stephen, and Geoffrey Rockwell. "Developing Things: Notes toward an Epistemology of Building in the Digital Humanities." In *Debates in the Digital Humanities*, edited by Matthew K. Gold, 3–7. Minneapolis: University of Minnesota Press, 2012.

Ratto, Matt. "Critical Making: Conceptual and Material Studies in Technology and Social Life." *The Information Society* 27, no. 4 (2011): 252–60.

Reagan, Andrew J., Lewis Mitchell, Dilan Kiley, Christopher M. Danforth, and Peter Sheridan Dodds. "The Emotional Arcs of Stories Are Dominated by Six Basic Shapes." *EJP Data Science* 5, no. 31 (2016). doi:10.1140/epjds/s13688-016-0093-1.

Richards, I. A. *Practical Criticism: A Study of Literary Judgment*. New York: Harcourt and Brace, 1929.

Ricoeur, Paul. *Freud and Philosophy: An Essay on Interpretation*. Translated by Denis Savage. New Haven, CT: Yale University Press, 1970.

Robertson, Stephen. "The Differences between Digital Humanities and Digital History." In *Debates in the Digital Humanities*, edited by Matthew K. Gold and Lauren F. Klein, 289–307. Minneapolis: University of Minnesota Press, 2016.

Rockwell, Geoffrey, and Stéfan Sinclair. *Hermeneutica: Computer-Assisted Interpretation in the Humanities*. Cambridge, MA: MIT Press, 2016.

Rogers, Richard. *Digital Methods*. Cambridge, MA: MIT Press, 2013.

Rouvroy, Antoinette. "The End(s) of Critique: Data Behaviourism versus Due Process." In *Privacy, Due Process and the Computational Turn: The Philosophy of Law Meets the Philosophy of Technology*, edited by Mireille Hildebrandt and Katja de Vries, 143–67. New York: Routledge, 2012.

Scheinfeldt, Tom. "Sunset for Ideology, Sunrise for Methodology?" In *Debates in the Digital Humanities*, edited by Matthew K. Gold, 124–26. Minneapolis: University of Minnesota Press, 2012.

Schmidt, Benjamin M. "Do Digital Humanists Need to Understand Algorithms?" In *Debates in the Digital Humanities*, edited by Matthew K. Gold and Lauren F. Klein, 546–55. Minneapolis: University of Minnesota Press, 2016.

Scholes, Robert. *Protocols of Reading*. New Haven, CT: Yale University Press, 1989.

———. *Structuralism in Literature: An Introduction*. New Haven, CT: Yale University Press, 1974.

Schreibman, Susan. "Computer-Mediated Texts and Textuality: Theory and Practice." *Computers and the Humanities* 36, no. 3 (2002): 283–93.

Schreibman, Susan, Ray Siemens, and John Unsworth, eds. *A Companion to Digital Humanities*. Oxford: Blackwell, 2004.

Sculley, D., and Bradley M. Pasanek. "Meaning and Mining: The Impact of Implicit Assumptions in Data Mining for the Humanities." *Literary and Linguistic Computing* 23, no. 4 (2008): 409–24.

Sedgwick, Eve Kosofsky. *Touching Feeling: Affect, Pedagogy, Performativity*. Durham, NC: Duke University Press, 2003.

Shannon, Claude E. "A Mathematical Theory of Communication." *Bell System Technical Journal* 27, no. 3 (1948): 379–423.

Skapura, David M. *Building Neural Networks*. New York: Addison-Wesley, 1996.

Smith, Barbara Herrnstein. "Contingencies of Value," *Critical Inquiry* 10, no. 1 (1983): 1–35.

———. "What Was 'Close Reading'? A Century of Method in Literary Studies." *Minnesota Review* 2016, no. 87 (2016): 57–75.

Smith, John B. "Computer Criticism." *Style* 12 (1978): 262–73.

Smith, Martha Nell. "The Human Touch Software of the Highest Order: Revisiting Editing as Interpretation." *Textual Cultures* 2, no. 1 (2007): 1–15.

So, Richard Jean. "All Models Are Wrong." *PMLA* 132, no. 3 (2017): 668–73.

Stearne, Jonathan. *MP3: The Meaning of a Format*. Durham, NC: Duke University Press, 2012.

Stiegler, Bernard. *Automatic Society*. Vol. 1, *The Future of Work*. Translated by Daniel Ross. Malden, MA: Polity, 2016.

Striphas, Ted. "Algorithmic Culture." *European Journal of Cultural Studies* 18, nos. 4–5 (2015): 395–412.

Terras, Melissa, Julianne Nyhan, and Edward Vanhoutte. *Defining Digital Humanities: A Reader*. Burlington, VT: Ashgate, 2013.

Thomas, Brook. *The New Historicism and Other Old-Fashioned Topics*. Princeton, NJ: Princeton University Press, 1991.

Thomas, William G. III. "Computing and the Historical Imagination." In *A Companion to Digital Humanities*, edited by Susan Schreibman, Ray Siemens, and John Unsworth, 56–68. New York: Blackwell, 2004.

Thrailkill, Jane F. *Affecting Fictions: Mind, Body, and Emotion in American Literary Realism*. Cambridge, MA: Harvard University Press, 2007.

Turing, Alan. "On Computable Numbers, with an Application to the *Entscheidungsproblem*." *Proceedings of the London Mathematical Society* 42, no. 2 (1937): 230–65.

Underwood, Ted. "A Genealogy of Distant Reading." *Digital Humanities Quarterly* 11, no. 2 (2017). http://www.digitalhumanities.org/dhq/vol/11/2/000317/000317 .html.

Veeser, H. Aram. Introduction to *The New Historicism*, edited by H. Aram Veeser. New York: Routledge, 1989.

Watanabe, Satosi. *Knowing and Guessing: A Quantitative Study of Inference and Information*. New York: Wiley, 1969.

———. *Pattern Recognition: Human and Mechanical*. New York: Wiley, 1985.

Wilkens, Matthew. "Canons, Close Reading, and the Evolution of Method." In *Debates in the Digital Humanities*, edited by Matthew K. Gold, 249–58. Minneapolis: University of Minnesota Press, 2012.

Williams, Raymond. *Marxism and Literature*. New York: Oxford University Press, 2009.

Wimsatt, William K., and Monroe C. Beardsley. "The Affective Fallacy." *Sewanee Review* 57, no. 1 (1949): 31–55.

Winnicott, D. W. *Playing and Reality*. New York: Routledge, 2005.

Žižek, Slavoj. *The Sublime Object of Ideology*. New York: Verso, 1989.

Index

affective fallacy, 97–99
Ahmed, Sara, 16, 143n12
Air Force, 123–25
algorithmic governmentality, 102, 108–9, 129
algorithms: anticipatory, 103, 108–9; bias and, 2, 110–11, 130, 148n27; definition, 103–4, 110; failure of, 64; as mode of thought, 151n51; study of, 106–8
analogical reasoning, 135–37
An Autobiography: The Story of the Lord's Dealings with Mrs. Amanda Smith the Colored Evangelist, 23
Anderson, Chris, 47–48
Andrews, William L., x–xi
anecdote, 73–73, 81–82
area bombing, 123–24
Autobiography of a Female Slave, 49–50
auto-critique, 39–40

bag of words, 50, 78, 95
Barthes, Roland, 61, 64, 78
Bayes, Thomas, 111–15
Berry, David M., 3, 43, 109–10
black box, 8, 22, 37, 40, 96–97
Bode, Katherine, 36–38, 75–76, 79

Bogost, Ian, 105–6
Buolamwini, Joy, 110
Burckhardt, Sigurd, 62–63
Butler, Judith, 16

Cambridge Analytica, 102
capta, 28
Chun, Wendy, 110, 126
close reading, 15, 24, 28–29, 33–34, 42
collocation, 22–24
computationality, 3
confusion matrix, 63–64, 121
Cormen, Thomas, 151n51
correlationism, 17, 47
Cover, Thomas M., 125–27
critical digital humanities, 5, 27–31, 41, 108, 111
critique, x, 3–4, 6–7, 16, 22
cultural analytics, 2, 18
cultural studies, ix, 4, 32, 78
culturomics, 18–19, 99–100
curse of dimensionality, 116–17

data: big, 16–17, 24, 29, 47–48; raw, 28, 43–44; training, 44–45, 79, 110, 133–35
datafication, 3, 17–18, 67

deconstruction, 34, 56, 61–62
deformance/deformation, 41, 139–40;
    defined, 82–83
Deleuze, Gilles, 108
Derrida, Jacques, 30–31, 56
Desrosières, Alain, 114
digital: history, 68–70; humanities, 1–3;
    literary history, 36, 75
distant reading, 29, 32–36, 41–43, 78–79,
    141n1
documentary realism, 100
Douglass, Frederick, 139–40
Drucker, Johanna, 28, 149n32

Earhart, Amy, 76–77
Evens, Aden, 110

feature selection, 2, 16–17, 119–21, 129,
    133–34
Felski, Rita, 11, 42, 65, 74–75, 146n2
fiction, ix, 77–78, 90
Finn, Ed, 107
Fish, Stanley, 27, 86
Fisher, Ronald, 117–19
Fix, Evelyn, 125–26
Fleissner, Jennifer L., 85–86
Foucault, Michel, 78, 108, 128–29
frequency: lexical, 25–26; word, 22–23, 28,
    49–51
Frye, Northrop, 57–60

Gadamer, Hans-Georg, 6, 63
Gallop, Jane, 71–72
Galloway, Alexander, 12–13, 107–8
Golumbia, David, 14, 19–20, 104, 144n20
Google: Books, 3, 60, 99; Maps, 80, 82;
    News, 134, 139; Ngram Viewer, 15, 60,
    99; PageRank (algorithm), 22; Search,
    102; translation tools, 47–48
Greimas square, 135
Gitelman, Lisa, 28, 43, 45

Haraway, Donna, 111
Hartman, Geoffrey, 58–64, 150n46
Hartman, Saidiya, 70
Hayles, N. Katherine, 5, 18–19, 27–28
hermeneutics: hermeneutical circle and,
    63; interpretive, 15, 34; of suspicion,
    20, 29, 32–33, 74, 143n10

Hildebrandt, Mireille, 159n52
historicism: digital, 76, 79, 82, 99–100;
    new historicism, 61, 72–74, 77–78
Hodges, Joseph, 123–25
homophily, 126
hubris, big data, 16–18
Husserl, Edmund, x
Hyman, Stanley, 11–12, 15

Incidents in the Life of a Slave Girl, 92

Jacobs, Harriet, 92–93
Jockers, Matthew, 24–29, 33–36, 54–56,
    89–92, 119–20
Jupyter notebook, 39–41

Kirschenbaum, Matthew, 110, 142n1,
    144n22
Klein, Lauren, 70–71
k-Nearest Neighbor: development
    of, 115–28; example use of, 120–22;
    homophily and, 126; illusion of
    democracy and, 126–28
Kristeva, Julia, viii

LaCapra, Dominick, 29, 100
Latent Dirichlet Allocation (LDA), 50–51,
    54
Latour, Bruno, 41, 74, 105–6, 143n12
Lehmann, Erich L., 121–25
literary studies, 28–29, 35, 56–57; digital,
    43–44, 67, 77
Liu, Alan, 81, 149n36
Liu, Bing, 87–89, 92–93, 95
Los Angeles Review of Books, 14–16
Love, Heather, 33–34, 57–59

machine learning, 114–17, 120, 127–28;
    supervised, 45; unsupervised, 41–44,
    148n21
Machine Learning for Language Toolkit
    (MALLET), 54–56
Mandell, Laura, 69, 71, 142n2
Manovich, Lev, 18
mapping, digital, 80–82
Martindale, Colin, 89
McGrayne, Sharon Bertsch, 113–14
Mechanical Turk, 93–94
minimal computing, 38–39

Moby-Dick, 25–26
models and modeling, viii, 22, 34–35, 43–45, 46–49
Moretti, Franco, 29–30, 34–36, 41–42, 141n1
MyLifeBits, 81

Named Entity Recognition (NER), 54–55
Natural Language Processing (NLP), 77, 86, 134
Natural Language Toolkit (NLTK), 23–25, 40, 54
neural networks, 47, 102, 131–40, 159n1
New Criticism, 12, 34, 61–62, 75, 98
new media, 3, 19–20
Noble, Safiya Umoja, 155n2
Non-negative Matrix Factorization (NMF), 50–52, 149n31
North American Slave Narratives, x–xiii, 120–21, 135
Nowviskie, Bethany, 143n8

Of Grammatology, 29–30
O'Neil, Cathy, 110
OpenCV, 127–28
open source, 22, 37–38, 41

pattern recognition, 111, 126–28, 130
periodization, 120–22
posthistoricism, 66, 71–75, 152n15
preprocessing, 9, 23–25, 54–56, 92, 134
presentism, strategic, 75, 152n17
principal components analysis (PCA), 119–20, 158n41
probability, 111–14, 126
project gutenberg, 99–100, 119
protocols of reading, 6, 10–13, 146n47
psychoanalysis, 15, 89–90
Python, 21, 23, 39–40, 51, 119

Ramsay, Stephen, 35–36, 41, 57, 82–83
Richards, I. A., 13, 97–99
Rouvroy, Antoinette, 108–9, 128–29

Scholes, Robert, 30, 146n47, 150n45
Schreibman, Susan, 153n23

science and technology studies (STS), 104–5
scientific criticism, 12, 57–58, 60
semantic space, 88, 131–34, 139
sentiment analysis, 86–93
Smith, Barbara Herrnstein, 28–29, 97–98
So, Richard Jean, 46–49
social science: critique of, 28–29; experimental, 18–19, 77, 99; text mining as, 10, 18, 22, 65
Stiegler, Bernard, 47, 148n25
stopwords: defined, 23; selection of, 52–54, 56, 83, 92
structuralism, 35, 57–62, 150n45
stylistics, computational, 24, 99–100, 119
subjectivity: critical, 33, 45–46; intrusion of, 8, 20, 43, 133; Judith Butler's account of, 109
support vector machine (SVM), 44, 120
surface reading, 11, 33–34, 62, 96

Text Encoding Initiative (TEI), 37, 79
text-external referential systems, 38, 79–86, 88, 91, 97
text mining, ix–x, 10–12, 22–24, 34–45, 49–50
Thrailkill, Jane, 98–99
topic modeling: definition, 50, 149n30; tf-idf, 50; use of, 21, 49–57, 134, 148n21
transparency, 36–41, 106–7

Underwood, Ted, 56–57, 59, 63, 150n40

vector space, 120, 138–40
Veeser, H. Aram, 72–73
voronoi tessellation, 116–17
V21: Victorian Studies for the Twenty-First Century, 75, 152n17

Washington, Booker T., xi
Watanabe, Satosi, 126, 130, 159n48, n53
word2vec, 134–39
workflow, 8–10, 15, 25–27, 39–41
WordNet, 85
WordStat, 89

JAMES E. DOBSON is a lecturer in the Department of English and Creative Writing at Dartmouth College. He is the author of *Modernity and Autobiography in Nineteenth-Century America: Literary Representations of Communication and Transportation Technologies.*

TOPICS IN THE DIGITAL HUMANITIES

From Papyrus to Hypertext: Toward the Universal Digital Library
    Christian Vandendorpe, translated from the French by Phyllis Aronoff and Howard Scott
Reading Machines: Toward an Algorithmic Criticism   *Stephen Ramsay*
Macroanalysis: Digital Methods and Literary History   *Matthew L. Jockers*
Digital Critical Editions   *Edited by Daniel Apollon, Claire Bélisle, and Philippe Régnier*
Teaching with Digital Humanities: Tools and Methods for Nineteenth-Century
    American Literature   *Edited by Jennifer Travis and Jessica DeSpain*
Critical Digital Humanities: The Search for a Methodology   *James E. Dobson*

The University of Illinois Press
is a founding member of the
Association of American University Presses.

Composed in 10.25/14 Chaparral Pro
with Lucida Sans display
by Kirsten Dennison
at the University of Illinois Press
Cover designed by Megan McCausland
Cover images: Aerial photograph, Tokyo, March 11, 1945
(National Archives, photo no. 342-FH-3A3851-56542ac);
background image ©iStock.com/A. Zabnina.

University of Illinois Press
1325 South Oak Street
Champaign, IL 61820-6903
www.press.uillinois.edu